Feminism, Postfeminism and Legal Theory

There is much debate about postfeminism, what it is, and its role in feminist politics. While postfeminism has become increasingly influential in the study of literature, popular culture, and philosophy, it has so far received comparatively little attention in law. This book aims to remedy this situation. The book brings together feminist legal scholars working in different contexts to examine the idea of postfeminism and assess its contemporary relevance. It explores a range of questions including the following: Does postfeminism describe an age that follows modernism, an age where identity politics has realised its goals and feminism is no longer needed? Or does postfeminism describe the feminism of a postmodernist age where identity can mean anything at all? Or, differently again, does the term capture a 'new feminism' that discredits feminism and attempts to reshape its political consciousness? And what might the answers to these questions mean for law and legal theory, and a feminist politics of law reform?

Dr. Dorota Gozdecka is a senior lecturer at the ANU College of Law and an Adjunct Professor (Docent) at the University of Helsinki.

Dr. Anne Macduff is a senior lecturer at the ANU College of Law.

Feminism, Postfeminism, and Legal Theory

Beyond the Gendered Subject

Edited by
Dorota Gozdecka and
Anne Macduff

Routledge
Taylor & Francis Group
LONDON AND NEW YORK

First published 2019
by Routledge
2 Park Square, Milton Park, Abingdon, Oxon OX14 4RN

and by Routledge
52 Vanderbilt Avenue, New York, NY 10017

First issued in paperback 2020

Routledge is an imprint of the Taylor & Francis Group, an informa business

British Library Cataloguing-in-Publication Data
A catalogue record for this book is available from the British Library

Library of Congress Cataloging-in-Publication Data
Names: Gozdecka, Dorota Anna, editor. | Macduff, Anne, editor.
Title: Feminism, postfeminism and legal theory: beyond the gendered subject / edited by Dorota Gozdecka and Anne Macduff.
Description: Abingdon, Oxon; New York, NY: Routledge, 2018. | Includes index.
Identifiers: LCCN 2018042747 | ISBN 9781138488342 (hbk)
Subjects: LCSH: Feminist jurisprudence.
Classification: LCC K349 .F4533 2019 | DDC 340/.1082—dc23
LC record available at https://lccn.loc.gov/2018042747

ISBN 13: 978-0-367-66307-0 (pbk)
ISBN 13: 978-1-138-48834-2 (hbk)

Typeset in Galliard
by codeMantra

This book is dedicated to the memory of Eun Ju Kim Baker, our student, friend, and co-conspirator for change. May their passion and commitment to diversity, law and identity politics inspire others in the future, as it has in the past.

Contents

List of contributors

Mariana Prandini Assis holds an LL.B. and an M.A. in Political Science from the Federal University of Minas Gerais (Brazil). She is now a Ph.D. Candidate in Politics at the New School for Social Research, from where she also received an M.Phil. in Politics. As an attorney and activist, Mariana is involved in a range of social struggles in Brazil, such as the movement for the right to housing and to the city, and feminist movements. Her research interests are related to feminist legal and political theory, social movements and legal mobilization, human rights, and transnationalism.

Joyce Das holds a PhD in gender studies from ANU's Crawford School of Public Policy. Her doctoral research looked into the complex area of gender and law among religious minority women in South Asia. As a career-path student, Joyce took the Master of Applied Anthropology and Participatory Development, with specialisation in Gender and Development at ANU. Joyce brings a decade-long experience of working in the development sector in Bangladesh.

Margaret Davies is a Matthew Flinders Distinguished Professor of Law at Flinders University, South Australia. She completed undergraduate degrees in literature and law at Adelaide University in the 1980s, followed by an MA in critical theory and a PhD at Sussex University in the early 1990s. Margaret is the author of several books on legal theory, including *Asking the Law Question* (4th edition, 2017), *Law Unlimited* (2017), *Property: Meanings, Histories, Theories* (2006), *Are Persons Property?* (2001, with Ngaire Naffine), and *Delimiting the Law* (1996). She has been an academic visitor at a number of universities, in Canada, New Zealand, Sweden, Finland, and the United Kingdom.

Dorota Anna Gozdecka is a Senior Lecturer at ANU College of Law at the Australian University and an Adjunct Professor (Docent) at the University of Helsinki. She is the Associate Director of the Centre for Law, Arts and Humanities. Her primary research area focuses on legal theoretical aspects related to the accommodation of cultural diversity and the intersections between law and the humanities. Her publications such as the special issue on *Identity, Subjectivity and the Access to the Community of Rights* (*Social*

Identities, Issue 4, 2015), the monograph *Rights, Religious Pluralism and the Recognition of Difference: Off the Scales of Justice* (Routledge, 2015), and the edited volume *Europe at the Edge of Pluralism* explore questions of otherness created by contemporary legal regimes. She has also been appointed an expert for the Council of Europe's Drafting Group on Human Rights in Culturally Diverse Societies in preparation of the new Guidelines on Human Rights in Culturally Diverse Societies adopted by the Council of Europe in 2016.

Anne Macduff holds a PhD (law) from the ANU. She also completed her LLB and her BA (Hons) at the ANU. Her research interests are in the areas of critical race and feminist legal theory. In particular, she uses postmodern theories of identity to critique the law and legal categories. Her PhD focuses on how legal discourses of Australian citizenship construct a racialised national imaginary. She now works as a Senior Lecturer at the ANU College of Law and teaches feminist legal theory and family law.

Sanna Mustasaari holds a PhD (law) from the University of Helsinki. Her research focuses on the regulation and recognition of transnational families at the intersections of family law, private international law and migration law as well as unofficial laws. Her research interests include socio-legal studies on transnational families, legal pluralism, migration studies, feminist theory, and studies on citizenship and belonging. Currently she works as a postdoctoral researcher and teaches family law.

Jennifer M. Nielsen completed her Science/Law Degree with Honours at Monash University and holds a Doctor of Philosophy from the University of Melbourne. Her research applies critical race and whiteness theory to reveal the normative standards inherent in mainstream Australian law that privilege 'white' interests in preference to those of First Nations' peoples and other 'non-white' groups. Since 2013, she has been part of a four-person team that delivers staff training on race and racism – *Courageous Conversations About Race* – to the Southern Cross University community.

Kati Nieminen holds a PhD (law) from the University of Helsinki (UH). She also has a master's degree on comparative religion and gender studies. Her research interests are in the areas of legal and feminist theory, and her methodological interests are particularly in legal argumentation and discourse analysis. She now works at the Institute of Criminology and Legal Policy (UH) as a postdoctoral researcher, where her research covers areas such as access to justice and legal policy.

Margaret Thornton is Professor of Law and ANU Public Policy Fellow at the Australian National University. She has degrees from Sydney, New South Wales and Yale Universities. Her research interests are in the areas of feminist legal theory, discrimination law, legal education, the legal profession, and the corporatisation of universities. She is a former Australian Research Council Professorial Fellow and is presently engaged in a project entitled

'Balancing Law and Life'. She has an extensive publication record addressing the intersection between law and feminism. She is a Fellow of the Academy of Social Sciences in Australia and a Foundation Fellow of the Australian Academy of Law.

Maliha Zia is a lawyer and women's rights activist, researcher, and trainer in Pakistan. Maliha Zia holds an LLM in International Human Rights Law from School of Oriental and African Studies, London. Her work focuses on the use of law and the justice sector in enforcing and protecting human rights and in eliminating violence against women. She currently holds the position of Associate Director at the Legal Aid Society, Pakistan.

Introduction

The provocation of the 'post' in postfeminist legal theory

In the 1990s, feminist legal theory burst into university law schools and onto the pages of law journals (Graycar & Morgan 1990; Thornton 1990, 1995; Naffine & Owens 1997). Yet almost as quickly as feminist legal theory appeared on the scene, it virtually disappeared (Thornton 2010, 92). There are many different explanations given for this dramatic retreat. Thornton suggests that the retreat was due to the rise of neoliberalism and the massification of higher education (Thornton 2010). Others suggest that feminist legal theory was unable to respond to the postmodern destabilisation of identity politics and the subsequent challenge to the very idea of a 'feminist project' (Conaghan 2004). The retreat might also be a paralysis produced within feminism, caused by an acknowledgement of its complicity with the exclusion of differently situated women (Armstrong 2004). Alternatively, the retreat might be linked to a popular rejection of the contemporary relevance of feminism (Faludi 2006), a desire 'to take a break from feminism' (Halley 2006), or a combination of any, or all, of these reasons.

Many, although not all, of these explanations for the retreat of legal feminism have been associated with 'postfeminism'. However, the term 'postfeminism' is itself unclear (McRobbie 2004). Some understand the term to signal a phase where feminism has realised its goals and moved on (Baumgardner & Richards 2005; McNeilly 2011). Others understand it to be an anti-feminist movement, a movement that discredits 'old' feminism and attempts to create new possibilities for political consciousness free from a gendered past (Brooks 1997). Yet others argue that it means that identity can, and should, mean anything (Scott 1988; Butler 1990; Snyder 2008).

Despite the apparent retreat from feminist legal theory in law schools, politics, and society, it continues to be an important perspective for critically engaging with the law. Feminist legal theory informs a diverse range of feminist projects. For example, they recover (in the sense of the archive) the operation of gender in law (Auchmuty 2011; Trailblazing Women and the Law Project 2013; Auchmuty & Rackley 2016), or they make visible (in the sense of rendering intelligible) feminist analyses of the law (Majury 2006; Rackley 2012; Douglas, Bartlett, Luker & Hunter 2014). Feminist projects increasingly use diverse methods to identify the ways that law and its practices disadvantage women, from wide-ranging structural issues in the law (Thornton 1995), to an examination of the localised ways that laws govern everyday interactions and relationships (Cooper 2013). Feminist jurisprudence continues to be written, drawing upon an increasingly diverse range of theories and perspectives (Davies 2008).

The idea for this book emerged as an attempt to respond to this contradiction; the apparent postfeminist retreat on the one hand and the flourishing of feminist legal scholarship on the other. As editors, we wished to explore the provocation of the 'post' in postfeminism to generate debate amongst and between feminists, lawyers, activists, and scholars.[1] While the prefix 'post' has experienced an exponential growth of interest in literature (Harzewski 2011), popular culture (McRobbie 2004; Negra 2009), and philosophy and politics (Whelehan 1995), postfeminism has thus far been given comparatively little attention in legal studies (Thornton 2010; McNeilly 2012). In 2015, we organised a workshop that used the notion of postfeminism to engage with the range of issues pertinent to contemporary legal feminism. We found that the provocation of the 'post' in postfeminism created an opportunity to generate new questions about the ways in which the gendered subject is currently activated in, through, and beyond the law.

This book does not seek to argue for any particular meaning of postfeminism. Instead, the authors were invited to consider what questions the term postfeminism provoked for them, in their different contexts. Some of the questions addressed by the authors include the following: How have feminist theoretical engagements with the law become institutionalised, accepted, and historicised through postfeminism, in what ways and why? In a postfeminist age, is there a schism between feminist legal theorists and the political activist? Is postfeminism a phenomenon present only in Western contexts or does it have any relevance in other contexts? What notions of identity, community, and agency arise from postfeminist encounters with diverse political and historical specificities? What are the questions that postfeminism asks of law and what new imaginings might it enable?

In asking these questions, the book does not seek to resuscitate a lost feminist legal theory (Thornton 2004, 7), nor to find a new, unified one. Rather, the book seeks to articulate ways in which feminist and legal theory 'might speak to us, in our times' (Genovese 2013, 42). The chapters respond to Thornton's call, made almost a decade ago in the *Australian Feminist Law Journal*, to 'discursively constitute a new episteme of feminist legal theory that is linked to the political' (Thornton 2004, 22). Engaging with the tensions of postfeminism, this book articulates both the richness of theoretical debate and the depth of political action in legal feminism today.

The book demonstrates that in the age of 'postfeminism', the conversation within and about legal feminism is at least as diverse and vigorous as it was in the 1990s. This book uses the term 'postfeminism' to explore three key themes: legal feminism, politics, and law. Each part of the book focuses on a different theme. Part I 'Legal Feminism' interrogates the conditions under which legal feminism might be understood. Part II 'The Politics of Law Reform' brings together chapters which focus on what 'postfeminism' offers for collective action and a politics of feminist law reform. Part III 'Law', explores what postfeminism might offer feminists theorising the law, the legal system, and its institutions. While the chapters in the book address overlapping concerns, and indeed many chapters address all three themes, the grouping of the chapters highlights contrasting approaches and conclusions. The diversity in positions and arguments in all three parts affirms that legal feminists should resist easy, simple conclusions about what postfeminism might mean.

Part I examines how legal feminism is understood, including the present challenges to legal feminism. It has three chapters and begins with a chapter by Margaret Thornton, who places postfeminism in a historical context of feminist movements. She argues that the fortunes of feminism in the Australian legal academy are closely intertwined with the prevailing political ideology. The author insists that social liberalism, with its commitment to egalitarianism, a robust civil society, and a modicum of tolerance for the Other, coincided with the flourishing of second-wave feminism. This led to the appointment of feminist academics in law schools and the incorporation of feminist perspectives into their teaching. By contrast, what came after second-wave feminism was a feminism linked with aggressive neoliberalism, enmeshed in active entrepreneurialism and promotion of the self. According to Thornton, this new focus encouraged the sloughing off a commitment to feminist values and a turn away from collective action. Mirroring the values of neoliberalism, this incarnation of postfeminism, which one might term 'neoliberal feminism', encouraged entrepreneurialism and productivity, particularly on the part of upwardly mobile, individual women. Neoliberal feminism also resonated with the neoliberal law school where students were anxious to secure a position on the corporate track in light of mounting tuition debts and increased competition. All this leads Thornton to be cautious about the usefulness of postfeminism for legal feminism today, as its emphasis on individualism and choice can be co-opted by aggressive neoliberalism.

This part continues with a more optimistic exploration of how postfeminism might be beneficial for feminist legal theory today. In Chapter 2, Dorota Gozdecka analyses postfeminism through a postmodern lens and argues that rather than facilitating a retreat from feminism, postfeminism enables legal feminists to think more widely and embrace diverse narratives of emancipation. Gozdecka analyses different feminist understandings of emancipation through the example of the legal regulation of female clothing. She examines several cases concerning veiling, bearing breasts, and neo-burlesque performance to ask whether legal feminism today needs to limit emancipation to certain acts, or whether it can allow diverse practices of emancipation depending on the context. The author insists that axes of emancipation in contemporary societies are diverse and can coexist. Therefore, she attempts to construct a dynamic way to navigate diverse emancipatory discourses which ensure that the notion of emancipation, as well as its subject, remains fluid, dynamic, and able to be imagined in endless combinations and variations. Assuming that different emancipations coexist alongside each other, she insists that postfeminism is a theory that does not abandon the revolutionary ideals of feminism, but rather allows us to see multiple and diverse emancipatory acts as feminist.

This part concludes with Chapter 3 by Kati Nieminen and Sanna Mustasaari. This chapter examines the narratives of belonging that produce imagined communities of 'us' and 'them'. It contends that a postfeminist approach to legal analysis can be useful for making visible the ways in which law reifies a particular notion of 'us'. This is because the authors understand postfeminism as recognising its own existence within and as part of narrative reality. The authors suggest that postfeminism prompts feminists to critically question how a homogenous subject 'us' is constructed through narratives of 'authenticity' and 'autonomy', narratives which are understood in relation to religious identity, gender, and corporeality. The chapter explores the operation and interplay of these narratives by focusing on two examples. First, the chapter considers the turmoil following a Swedish politician's refusal to shake hands with a female journalist. Then, it examines a recent case in the European Court of Human Rights of *Osmanoğlu and Kocabaş v. Switzerland*, where Muslim parents sought to rely on their right to freedom of religion to have their daughters exempted from mixed gender swimming lessons. Postfeminism enables a reading of the (legal) narratives of authenticity and autonomy, which enables a critical assessment of the underlying, seemingly self-evident conceptions that uphold ethnification and exclusion. The examples discussed in this chapter invite us to stay self-reflective to the ways in which power relations are reproduced in feminist discourses, and to the ways in which autonomy and authenticity are constructed in them. The challenge is to stay alert to the appropriation of feminism, for example, for Islamophobic purposes.

The three chapters in Part II explore whether postfeminism undermines the conditions of collective political action, including whether it can generate feminist law reform. The contributors in this part draw on a range of legal reform contexts, and reach diverse conclusions about the usefulness of postfeminism.

Part II begins with Chapter 4 by Maliha Zia. She argues that in Pakistan postfeminism is not useful as it undermines the strong sense of unity needed to achieve important law reform for gender equality. Zia traces the diversity of engagements of women with the law and argues that Pakistani feminism needs to be understood in its specific social, cultural, and political context. The author argues that contemporary feminism in Pakistan must work within an Islamic framework. As a result of multiple challenges, Zia observes that the notion of feminism has largely been de-politicised, and legal jurisprudence relating to women has lacked the interaction with feminist legal theory. The author suggests that postfeminism is now used as a tool by apologists and opponents of feminist ideologies. This undermines the potential of feminism in Pakistan to challenge legal and social norms in relation to women.

This part continues with a chapter by Mariana Prandini Assis. She argues that the unified political notion of 'woman' has tended to limit the reach of international women's rights discourses. It begins with Assis analysing the history of essentialism in feminist thought, the question of who constitutes a woman, and how postfeminism is a useful tool for conceptualising who belongs to the feminist movement. Assis then examines the construction of the gendered subject at the centre of 'women's human rights' and its evolving meaning in the field of international human rights law. The chapter insists that 'women's human rights' is a problematic concept that challenges exclusions based on sexual difference, but at the same time, reinstates that difference and creates new exclusions of its own. She suggests that postfeminism ensures that we continue to question who speaks as a 'woman', and continually revisit who is included and who is excluded.

The part concludes with Chapter 6 by Anne Macduff. This chapter looks at the postfeminist possibilities of a feminist politics of law reform. She begins by examining how postmodern feminism has challenged the identity category 'woman' and the concerns that this challenge has raised for legal feminists. The concern is that without a shared identity underpinning law reform, there can be no effective politics, and it could demoralise activists. Macduff then draws on critical race theory to provide new insights into these concerns. She argues that Bell's theory of interest convergence suggests that a shared identity is neither necessary nor sufficient to enact law reform. While this argument might provide further cause for feminists to lose hope, she draws upon Bell again to find a new grounding for feminist political and legal action. Macduff uses Bell to argue for a politics that is not driven by the likelihood of success, but rather an ethical commitment. She then draws upon the Mouffe's theory of agonism to provide the basis for a robust politics that goes beyond the need for a shared, essentialised gender identity, without collapsing into a fragmented, neoliberal individualism. The chapter explores how new possibilities for a post-essentialist politics of law reform might take shape.

Part III turns to look at what postfeminism might offer feminists in terms of reimagining the law. Again, there is a wide range of understandings of postfeminism and views about its usefulness in helping us to critically understand law, its institutions, and practices.

Chapter 7 by Jennifer M. Nielson argues that the diversity of subject positions in postfeminism enables us to see how legal research might be understood differently, enhancing the possibility of developing clearer understandings of diverse perspectives on the self and law. Her chapter begins by asking how feminist researchers can best respond to the concerns of the First Nations' feminism. While Nielsen acknowledges that legal scholarship does not pursue a uniform agenda or use a single analytical lens, she also observes that it often fails to be sufficiently 'context specific'. She argues that postfeminism is relevant for decentring white women's Western feminism and suggests that it can be a helpful platform for non-Indigenous researchers to engage with local, Indigenous, and postcolonial voices. Nielsen reflects on her own engagements with the legal research process and analyses the opportunities that postfeminist methods might open to make non-Indigenous researchers' approaches more meaningful, respectful, and open to dialogues with plural, local, and Indigenous voices and knowledges about the law.

Part III continues with Chapter 8 by Joyce Das, who asks whether feminism has sufficiently engaged with the question of women's experience of law. The author argues that while mainstream legal feminism has contributed significantly to the scholarship of gender and law, it has also primarily focused on the legal centralist paradigm of public law. Drawing on her ethnographic research on a religious minority community in a postcolonial context, she asks whether this focus fully represents women's experience of law. With a focus on Christians in Bangladesh, she argues that women's full experiences of law cannot be captured by only engaging with the state's legal system. Das argues that postfeminism might provide the break from feminism that is needed to enable feminists to see law in all its forms. In the context of religious minorities in Bangladesh, she argues that postfeminism would enable legal feminists to look beyond state-issued law and critically evaluate the impact of cultural and religious context.

Part III concludes with Chapter 9 by Margaret Davies. Davies examines the popularity of the prefix 'post', its significations, and mobilisations. In this chapter, Davies outlines the terrain of some key 'post' theories in order to situate the ideas of postfeminism and posthumanism in the theoretical contexts of recent decades. In doing this, the author's intention is not to examine forensically the specific meanings and connections of all of these 'post' ideas, but to ask whether it is time to work towards a new attitude or ethos in theory that is essentially transitional, but temporally and normatively complex. The chapter doubts whether postfeminism is a helpful concept for this task and asks whether it is more conducive for the future of feminist thought to focus on posthuman feminism instead. In general, posthumanism leads us towards notions of identity, subjectivity, and agency that exist beyond the human. Engagements beyond the human focus upon our connectedness with technology and 'nature' rather than our individual separateness. Posthumanism therefore brings forth our contingency, connectedness, and vulnerability. She argues that the concept of post for consistency I think human feminism provides a helpful theoretical focal point for reimagining some of the constructs that feminists have grappled with for many years, such as the distinctions between nature and culture, and the central place of the rational (European) man as the benchmark of humanity. Posthuman feminism has the potential to displace the human from the position of the subject, the centre of being, and instead emphasises the nature of the human as an 'object, dependent upon the world'. In addition to critique, posthuman feminism promises changed foundations for both theory and action and demands that attention be turned to a non-binary world, past gendered divisions of mind and body, culture and nature, and subject and object.

Overall, this book invites the reader to acknowledge that in the postfeminist worlds there are no ultimate common goals or permanent indicators of feminist legal justice and equality. By juxtaposing the different approaches of each chapter within each part, the book illustrates how the provocation of the 'post' generates diverse ways in which legal feminism (or feminisms) can be understood and enacted. This book, however, illustrates that despite the uncertainty, contradictions, and contestations about what postfeminism might mean, the multiple and diverse opportunities that the provocation of the 'post' offers can render legal feminism visible and articulate. This contradicts the claim that the emergence of postfeminism signals the retreat of legal feminism.

Note

1 The authors are grateful to the ANU Gender Institute and the ANU Law School for funding the workshop 'Post feminism. Post Theory. Post Critique?', which was held at the ANU College of Law in May 2015.

References

Armstrong, Susan. 2004. "Is Feminist Law Reform Flawed?" *Australian Feminist Law Journal* 20: 43–63.

Auchmuty, Rosemary. 2011. "Whatever Happened to Miss Bebb? *Bebb v The Law Society* and Women's Legal History." *Legal Studies* 31, no. 2: 199–230.

Auchmuty, Rosemary and Erika Rackley. 2016. "The Women's Legal Landmarks Project: Celebrating 100 Years of Women in the Law in the UK and Ireland." *Legal Information Management* 16, no. 1: 30–34.

Baumgardner, Jennifer and Amy Richards. 2005. *Grassroots: A Field Guide for Feminist Activism.* New York: Macmillan.

Brooks, Ann. 1997. *Postfeminisms: Feminism, Cultural Theory, and Cultural Forms.* London and New York: Routledge.

Butler, Judith. 1990. *Gender Trouble.* New York and London: Routledge.

Cooper, Davina. 2013. *Everyday Utopias: The Conceptual Life of Promising Spaces.* Durham, NC: Duke University Press.

Davies, Margaret. 2008. "Feminism and the Flat Law Theory." *Feminist Legal Studies* 16, no. 3: 281–304.

Douglas, Heather, Fracesca Bartlett, Trish Luker and Rosemary Hunter. 2014. *Australian Feminist Judgments.* Oxford and Portland, OR: Hart Publishing.

Faludi, Susan. 2006. *Backlash: The Undeclared War against American Women.* New York: Broadway Books.

Genovese, Anne. 2013. "Inheriting and Inhabiting the Pleasures and Duties of Our Own Existence: The Second Sex and Feminist Jurisprudence." *Australian Feminist Law Journal* 38: 41–57.

Graycar, Regina, and Jenny Morgan. 1990. *The Hidden Gender of Law.* Sydney: Federation Press.

Halley, Janet. 2006. *Split Decisions: How and Why to Take a Break from Feminism.* Princeton, NJ: Princeton University Press.

Harzewski, Stephanie. 2011. *Chick Lit and Postfeminism.* Charlottesville: University of Virginia Press.

Majury, Diana. 2006. "Introducing the Women's Court of Canada." *Canadian Journal of Women and the Law* 18: 1–13.

McNeilly, K., 2012. "Illusions of Post-Feminism, Ghosts of Gender and the Discourses of Law." *feminists@ law* 1, no. 2: http://journals.kent.ac.uk/index.php/feministsatlaw/article/view/27/101.

McRobbie, Angela. 2004. "Post-feminism and Popular Culture." *Feminist Media Studies* 4, no. 3: 255–264.

Naffine, Ngaire, and Rosemary Owens. 1997. *Sexing the Subject of Law*. North Ryde, NSW: Law Book Company.
Negra, Diane. 2009. *What a Girl Wants?: Fantasizing the Reclamation of Self in Postfeminism*. London: Routledge.
Rackley, Erika. 2012. "Why Feminist Legal Scholars Should Write Judgments: Reflections on the Feminist Judgments Project in England and Wales." *Canadian Journal of Women and the Law* 24: 389–413.
Scott, Joan W. 1988. "Deconstructing Equality-versus-Difference: Or, the Uses of Post-Structuralist Theory for Feminism." *Feminist Studies*, 14, no. 1: 33–50.
Snyder, Claire. 2008. "What is Third-wave Feminism." *Signs: Journal of Women in Culture and Society* 34, no. 1: 175–196.
Thornton, Margaret. 1990. *The Liberal Promise*. Melbourne: Oxford University Press.
———. 1995. *Public and Private*. Melbourne: Oxford University Press.
———. 2004. "Neoliberal Melancholia: The Case of Feminist Legal Scholarship." *Australian Feminist Law Journal* 20, no. 1: 7–22.
———. 2010. "'Post-Feminism' in the Legal Academy?" *Feminist Review* 95, no. 1: 92–98.
Trailblazing Women and the Law Project. 2013. http://www.esrc.unimelb.edu.au/projects/trailblazing-women-and-the-law-project, accessed 4 August 2018.
Whelehan, Imelda. 1995. *Modern Feminist Thought: From the Second Wave to "Post-Feminism"*. New York: NYU Press.

Part I

Legal feminism

1 The feminist fandango with the legal academy[1]

Margaret Thornton

Introduction

This chapter argues that the fortunes of feminism in the Australian legal academy are closely intertwined with the prevailing political ideology. Social liberalism, with its commitment to egalitarianism, a robust civil society, and a modicum of tolerance for the Other, coincided with the flowering of second-wave feminism. This led to the appointment of feminist academics in law schools and the incorporation of feminist perspectives into their teaching. In contrast, neoliberalism, with its aggressive entrepreneurialism and promotion of the self, encouraged a sloughing off of a commitment to feminist values. Mirroring the values of neoliberalism and reacting against the second wave, postfeminism initially resulted in a depoliticisation and a turning away from collective action with neoliberalism moving in quickly to colonise it. This incarnation of postfeminism, which one might term 'neoliberal feminism', encouraged entrepreneurialism and productivity, particularly on the part of upwardly mobile individual women. It also resonated with the neoliberal law school where students were anxious to secure a position on the corporate track in light of mounting tuition debts and increased competition. More recently, there has been a reaction against neoliberalism, which has once again brought with it a revived incarnation of feminism and a progressive understanding of the 'post'.

Feminism possesses neither a precise denotation nor a manifesto, but an amorphous constellation of values. First- and second-wave feminisms were primarily political movements concerned with improving the quality of women's lives, but no comparable assertion can confidently be made about postfeminism, which is beset with ambiguities. Indeed, the only reason for holding onto the word 'feminist' by one strand of *post*feminism may be to accentuate a reactive anti-feminist standpoint. In contrast, third-wave feminism is a variation of the 'post', which recognises that feminism is both possible and necessary (Budgeon 2011). Nevertheless, these terms are not discrete, and to avoid a confusing proliferation of terms, I use 'postfeminism' to encompass its various iterations. The inference I seek to draw is that the fortunes of feminism are closely intertwined with the dominant political values of the day.

With particular reference to the Australian context, I consider the ramifications for the legal academy of the transition from the second wave to postfeminism and beyond but stress the contradictions that multiple feminisms pose for law, which prefers clear lines and neat categories.

The twin variables of liberalism – freedom and equality – have been key animating forces underpinning the trajectory of feminism. First-wave feminism of the 19th century was inspired by the struggles for freedom and equality that were central to both the anti-slavery and the universal suffrage movements (Phillips-Anderson 2012). White women sought to be 'let in' to the public sphere in order to exercise the same rights as men. The second wave of the late 20th century was influenced by contemporary currents of political radicalism, such as the struggle against apartheid and the sexual revolution, as well as the anti-conscription and anti-Vietnam War movements (Curthoys 1988). I stress the political radicalism that underpinned the women's liberation movement and the multifarious strands of the second wave. This is despite the revisionist accounts of feminism, which averred that all women were victims who lacked agency. Such accounts, however, appear to have been largely a product of the subsequent backlash.[2]

Second-wave feminism was primarily concerned with securing gender equality, social justice, and autonomy for women, graphically symbolised by the well-known aphorism 'the personal is the political',[3] where the aim was to shine a light on the dark recesses of private life so long hidden. Domestic violence, sexuality – consensual and non-consensual – as well as issues such as contraception, abortion, and child care became politicised and the subject of law reform. A major strand of concern for the second wave related to inequality and discrimination at work, including the sexual division of labour, maternity leave, and pay equity. Some aspects of the private sphere, such as wages for housework, were discussed but never resolved (Curthoys 1988, 16).

I wish to stress at the outset that I am not seeking to hark back to the 'good old days' in emphasising the conjunction between second-wave feminism and social liberalism, but to suggest that the feminist reform agenda of the second wave was cognisable to law in a way that has not been the case since.[4] While the politics of feminism have fragmented over the 40-year period, liberal legalism has remained highly resistant to change; we cannot talk meaningfully about post-legality in the way we talk about postfeminism, for example. Taking its cue from the political economy of neoliberalism, one dimension of postfeminism is preoccupied with individual choice and promotion of the self. Individual choice, as the pièce de résistance, induced Sarah Projansky (2001, 89) to define postfeminism as a 'self-defined particular historical moment', a subjectivity that can only bemuse legal positivism, which consistently remains the dominant legal theory of our times. I suggest that the ambiguities of postfeminism, particularly in its 'spent force' sense, in conjunction with the conservatism associated with neoliberalism has induced a turning away from institutionalised feminism in the legal academy. The major intellectual movements of postmodernism and poststructuralism have destabilised the feminist subject but barely touched liberal legalism, which remains a quintessentially modernist discourse. This is apparent when one looks at the reported decisions of any appellate court.

The political landscape has changed dramatically in 40 years. For example, more varied iterations of race have emerged in the 21st century fuelled by 9/11 and the war on terror, together with the refugee crisis and the struggle over constitutional recognition of Indigenous peoples in Australia. Most significantly for conceptualising the 'post', the simple binarisms of male/female and hetero-sexual/homosexual that were for so long central to law have been complicated by new iterations emerging from their intersectionality. In this respect, we see glimmers of the transformative understanding of the 'post' in postfeminism.

My focus is the changing nexus between feminism and the legal academy by elaborating, first, on the way social liberalism facilitated feminist reformism on the part of the state and, second, to show how, in conjunction with the neoliberal turn, 'the gains of the 1970s and 1980s have been relentlessly undermined' (McRobbie 2009, 11) leading to a turning away from feminism in the legal academy. More recently, however, a revival of overt misogyny, as evinced by prominent figures, such as President Donald Trump, has triggered a corresponding revival of feminism. It is too early to gauge what impact this most recent iteration of feminism will have, but it is clear that the short history of feminism in the legal academy cannot be represented by a linear trajectory.

Social liberalism

While necessarily constrained by capitalism, social liberalism includes an element of distributive justice effected by the state through welfare policies and a regime of progressive taxation. Programs include universal health care and education, as well as income support for the unemployed, senior citizens, people with disabilities, and single mothers. Although social liberalism is a market system committed to competition, the values of public good and distributive justice prevent the market from having free rein. The high point of social liberalism in Australia is associated with Labor Prime Minister Gough Whitlam (1972–1975) (Kelly and Bramston 2015) when a swag of social justice reforms were enacted that accorded with the feminist agenda. They included no-fault divorce, equal pay initiatives, removal of the sales tax on contraceptives, paid maternity leave for federal public servants, support for single mothers, universal health care, anti-discrimination initiatives, and the abolition of conscription.

The public service, which was expanded to administer these reforms, was regarded as a strategic destination for feminist activists and policymakers. Indeed, the Australian neologism, 'the femocrat', coined to encapsulate the idea of a feminist bureaucrat (Eisenstein 1996), was crucial in formulating election policies and preparing cabinet documents (Dowse 1982, 332 *et seq.*). The interrelationship between feminism and the state was further underscored by the appointment of women's advisory councils to government. The tenor of these reforms meant that engagement with the state was viewed positively by feminist activists. Indeed, the Women's Liberation Movement, which was generally sceptical about the institutionalisation of feminism, was supportive of refuges and rape crisis centres being funded by government for the first time (Curthoys 1988, 86). This nexus between second-wave feminism and the state paved the way for the relationship between feminism and the legal academy.

Feminism comes to law school

Lawyers were in demand to administer the new legislation and this factor, in conjunction with the optimism about reform, the growth in the economy, the circulation of a popular pro-feminist discourse, and the abolition of university fees in 1974, led to a rapid increase in the enrolment of women in law school – from around 10 per cent in the 1960s to approximately 25 per cent by the 1970s, with the tipping point being reached in the 1980s. Young women who chose to enrol in law were excited by the possibility of what a feminist lawyer might be able to achieve. Newly established law schools, such as the University of New South Wales, promised a commitment to social justice and, during the 1970s, it was associated with progressive causes such as the Prisoners' Action Group and the establishment of the Redfern Legal Centre (Genovese 2010, 55–58).

The feminist critique of the claimed universality of knowledge, which exposed its partiality, struck a particular chord with feminist legal scholars because of the dominance of doctrinal or 'black letter law' pedagogy, together with the pervasive myth that justice is blind (Thornton 1986; Naffine 1990, 24ff.). Feminist legal scholars were concerned with demonstrating how 'law's internal presumption created subjects of law that were inherently gendered' (Genovese 2015, 1). They were inspired to incorporate feminist perspectives into their teaching – cautiously at first and then with growing confidence. The overtly gendered nature of law within areas such as sexual assault, violence against women and family law lent itself more readily to the inclusion of feminist critiques than, say, constitutional or commercial law, which purported to be gender neutral. In time, optional subjects such as discrimination law and women and the law appeared, followed by law and gender and feminist legal theory, the teaching of which was aided by the first feminist textbooks (Graycar and Morgan 1990, 2002; Davies 1994, 2008). Such courses were contingent on the appointment of a critical mass of creative feminist scholars who were able to support one another (Naffine with Heath 2015, 24). However, the discipline of law was never subject to the full-scale epistemological assault similar to that experienced by the humanities and the social sciences. The various state and territory admitting authorities were able to constrain the deconstructive exercise by virtue of their role in certifying that law graduates are qualified to practise law. Their privileged role includes the specification of a raft of 11 compulsory subjects known as the 'Priestley Eleven'.[5] Critical approaches to law, including legal theory and social justice, have never featured in these requirements (Thornton 2017).

Feminism nevertheless exerted an impact on the core curriculum during the two decades in which it flourished, despite the assertion of Richard Johnstone and Sumitra Vignaendra in 2003 that the influence of feminism on the

Australian legal academy was almost zero (Johnstone and Vignaendra 2003, 130). This not only discounted the considerable body of innovative scholarship that was published (e.g. Graycar 1990; Naffine 1990; Thornton 1990; Petersen 1993; Howe 1994; Kirkby 1995; Thornton 1995; Chea, Fraser, and Grbich 1996; Thornton 1996; Naffine and Owens 1997; Easteal 1998; Berns 1999; Charlesworth and Chinkin 2000; Moreton-Robinson 2000; Occasions and Events 2015) but also measures such as the Australian government-supported initiative in 1993 designed to sensitise all law students to issues of gender bias. This initiative emerged after Justice Bollen, in the course of a South Australian Supreme Court judgement dealing with rape in marriage, stated that a little 'rougher than usual handling' was acceptable on the part of a husband towards a wife who was less than willing to engage in sexual intercourse (*R. v Johns* 1992, 12–13).

Following extensive adverse media publicity, the Commonwealth Attorney-General accepted a submission from feminist legal scholars that law students needed to familiarise themselves with gender issues and to understand that the stance of Justice Bollen could no longer be tolerated. Accordingly, gender-sensitive materials for the compulsory core – the 'Priestley Eleven' – were prepared by several prominent feminist legal academics on the themes of citizenship, work, and violence.[6] Copies of the materials were sent to all law schools and made available on the Internet. The fact that Justice Bollen's remarks featured in dozens of front-page stories in newspapers around the country is testament to the responsiveness of popular culture to second-wave feminism. The outcry meant that the crude sexism that had long pervaded the legal discourse of sexual assault in both courtrooms and law school classrooms began to recede, even if it did not disappear altogether.

The take-up of the gender-sensitive materials was nevertheless not believed to be very high and the materials eventually disappeared from sight, undoubtedly aided by the neoliberal turn. Ironically, they were completed in 1996, the very year that conservative Prime Minister, John Howard, assumed office, which signalled the retreat from social liberalism.

The neoliberal turn

The ostensible success of institutional feminism in the legal academy was short-lived. Indeed, the seeds of a more market-oriented incarnation of liberalism had been sown by Gough Whitlam himself in advocating trade liberalisation in the 1960s and cutting tariffs by 25 per cent in the 1973 budget (Cahill 2004, 89).[7] This initiative was built upon by Labor Prime Ministers Hawke and Keating in the 1980s and 1990s, although they both remained supportive of Labor's social liberal values. Neoliberalism did not become the dominant political ideology until John Howard's Prime Ministership (1996–2007).

While neoliberalism lacks a coherent ideology, its key elements include the erosion of the welfare state, the privatisation of public goods, profit maximisation, entrepreneurialism, regressive taxation, and individualism at the expense of the collective good, with the overall political aim of restoring the power of economic élites (Harvey 2007, 19; Dumenil and Lévy 2011, 329). The paradigmatic individual of neoliberalism can be described as self-motivating and autonomous, and is free to exercise choice and reinvent the self in order to maximise his or her life chances. Flexibility and choice are the key to managing the self, preferably in a competitive, marketised context. However, neoliberalism is not 'just a system of economic power relations but a political project of governing and persuasion intent on producing new forms of subjectivity and particular modes of conduct' (Giroux 2008; cf Brown 2006). This subjectivity is designed to strengthen the entrepreneurial capacities of individuals (Rose 1996, 150–168; cf Burchell 1996). If they are 'unsuccessful' or unhappy, they must bear responsibility themselves (Davies 2015).

The neoliberal focus on individualism creates a particular form of governmentality that has the effect of marginalising collective action. In this sense, neoliberalism resonates with the classical liberalism of an earlier age. Neoliberalism prefers to deflect attention away from systemic discrimination in the workplace, arising from the long-hours culture and the inadequacy of childcare, because productivity and profit maximisation are its primary concerns.[8] Women with dependent children were encouraged to blame feminism for their exhaustion and disillusionment; rhetoric that encouraged the idea that 'feminism was anti-family' (Whelehan 1995, 221–223). Women's departure from full-time work satisfied the neoconservative morality that went hand in hand with neoliberal rationality.

As neoliberalism began to seep into the social psyche, the media adopted an increasingly negative attitude towards feminism, depicting it as cumbrous and old-fashioned. Because women had been 'let in' to the public sphere, it was averred, equality had been achieved, and feminism had become irrelevant (Henderson 2008). Neoliberalism unleashed the anti-feminism that had largely been latent, particularly on the part of men who felt that women had trespassed on their territory and had 'gone too far' (Henderson 2008, 30; cf Faludi 1991). Under siege from both postmodernism and neoliberalism, the category 'woman' began to fracture so that [she] could not be put back together again (Thornton 2004). Young women internalised the negative depiction of feminism as a spent force and sought to distance themselves from it.

Neoliberal policies, in conjunction with a conservative morality, were pursued with a vengeance and the Howard government's rapid demolition of the social liberal agenda is notable (Summers 2003). It evinced a particular animus towards feminism. Prime Minister John Howard was himself quoted as having said that 'feminism is now passé' (Summers 2003, 21). Perhaps unsurprisingly, the word 'feminism' then began to disappear from official discourse (Thornton 2006).

Postfeminism

The 'post' in postfeminism is ambiguous, for it can mean either that feminism is a spent force or an epistemological break has occurred in feminism's encounter with difference (Lewis 2014, 1849). McRobbie (2006, 60) refers to postfeminism as a 'double entanglement' because of the way that feminism is both taken account of and repudiated. In the absence of a precise denotation, this understanding of postfeminism is defined by what the second wave is *not* (Coppock, Haydon, and Richter 1995, 4). It represents a constellation of discontents purporting to have arisen from the second wave – that it represented an obsession with an outdated notion of 'victim feminism', that feminists unrealistically expected working women to be superwomen and do everything, that feminism made men feel emasculated, that heterosexual sex was regarded as oppressive, and that insufficient attention had been paid to differences between women, especially in respect of race, class, and sexuality. In order to distinguish themselves from the second wave, the 'post' in the sense of the 'spent force' feminists tended to depict second wavers as unhappy, embittered, and man-hating (Coppock, Haydon, and Richter 1995, 4). Feminism was not just reviled, it represented abjection.

As a reaction against the caricature of the unattractive, strident, and humourless feminists of their mothers' generation, one incarnation of postfeminism is associated with conventional representations of the feminine in popular culture that privileges beauty, fun, sex, and girliness, all of which are subsumed within the rubric of lifestyle choice. Anthea Taylor (2012) suggests that the contradictions and tensions arising from the entanglement of feminist and anti-feminist ideas are embodied in the figure of the single woman in popular culture. This paradigmatic postfeminist subject is supposedly able to exercise choice in all facets of her life. However, I agree with Gwynne (2013, 15) that the postfeminist sensibilities of choice and empowerment disguise a social reality where little has in fact changed in terms of sexual politics. Indeed, postfeminism overlooks the fact that it is still women, not men, who are expected to regulate their conduct according to prevailing social norms under the rubric of choice, while continuing to assume the preponderance of responsibility for child and elder care. The private sphere accordingly remains an opaque realm of inequality, just as it always has. The hope that men would assume equal responsibility for housework and childcare has remained largely illusory, despite the media attention accorded to the occasional male paragon. Research has established that a flexibility stigma attaches to fathers who work irregular hours in order to care for children, which operates as a major disincentive for men to do so (Coltrane et al. 2013; Thornton 2016). Gender equality, the linchpin of second-wave feminism, is nevertheless regarded as tired and outdated; it is diversity and difference that are lauded.

The extent to which this strand of postfeminism has absorbed the neoliberal political message is striking, a symbiosis that is clearly signalled by the term 'neoliberal feminism', in which neoliberalism and feminism intersect (Vavrus 2007, 51; Rottenberg 2014). In this fusion, neoliberalism's anti-collective, anti-equality, and anti-social justice predilections can be seen to have been absorbed by the new incarnations of feminism. Inequality, after all, is the raison d'être of competition policy, albeit fetishised as individual choice. Once the market has become the measure of all things, a paradigm in which commodification, consumerism, and the self are privileged, spending money on luxury goods and designer clothes comports with the key neoliberal tropes of self-gratification and choice. In this regard, the postfeminist and third-wave iterations are often elided, occupying 'common ground between consumption and critique, and engaging with feminine/sexual and individual forms of agency' (Genz and Brabon 2009, 162).

Adriaens (2009) locates postfeminism at the crossroads with other 'posts', namely, *post*modernism, *post*structuralism, and *post*colonialism. These 'posts', she argues, all suggest both a rift with the past and the possibility of an ongoing process of transformation (Genz and Brabon 2009, 4), which emphasises the positive connotations of the 'post', as well as its contradictions. Mohanty (2013, 968) nevertheless suggests that none of these provocative 'posts' are helpful in making sense of the landscape of violence, oppression, or incarceration that constitutes everyday life for oppressed peoples. She confirms my thesis that it is neoliberalism that has 'transformed material and ideological conditions in ways that have profound implications for radical critique' (Mohanty 2013, 970). Mohanty argues that the convergence between neoliberal and postmodern theory has served to depoliticise radical theory, or what she calls 'insurgent knowledge'. The devaluation, dismissal, and misappropriation of race is similarly criticised by American black feminists (Alexander-Floyd 2010, 816). While the second-wave subject is attacked for its essentialism (predominantly white, middle class, and heterosexual), Genz and Brabon (2009, 8) note that, similarly, the 'ideal postfeminist subject is seen to be a white, middle-class heterosexual girl'.

Closely imbricated with the self, neoliberal feminism seeks to play down both gender and racial inequalities. Like justice, equality is rarely heard in neoliberal discourse as it conflicts with competitiveness and promotion of the self. Indeed, the creation of a permanent underclass is accepted as an inevitable cost of market rationality, which has even been referred to as 'the equal right to inequality' (Brown 2006, 695). The one domain where equality is in vogue is in respect of sexuality, although the discourse is largely restricted to marriage equality for same-sex couples.[9] Once again, however, it is notable that the focus is on choice, the key trope within the neoliberal lexicon.

As neoliberal governance operates through discourse, postfeminism in the workplace is a very clear manifestation of the phenomenon. Kati Kauppinen (2013, 134) illustrates the potential for an interconnection between neoliberalism and postfeminism by analysing advice given in the popular magazine, *Cosmopolitan*. The self-management of success, happiness, and well-being can be achieved by (female) readers if they follow the advice proffered, but the overall aim is to benefit the economy. Such examples show how the subversive power of feminism is transmuted into a productive force through the creation of entrepreneurial subjects (Kauppinen 2013, 147).

The deployment of feminist discourse by neoliberalism is compellingly analysed by Catherine Rottenberg (2014, 2017). Drawing on Sheryl Sandberg's text, *Lean In* (2013), Rottenberg (2014, 422) shows how successful middle-class women are encouraged to succeed by promoting themselves and optimising their own resources. Neoliberalism is very effectively deployed by individual women who make the 'right' choices to ensure gender equality in the boardroom. This manifestation of feminism disavows the existence of collective inequality, for '"true equality" is predicated upon individuals moving up the professional ladder, one woman at a time' (Rottenberg 2014, 426).

We therefore see how neoliberalism has set out to colonise all spheres of life with the aim of producing new forms of human capital (Rottenberg 2017, 332). While deploying the feminist language of choice, the focus of the *Lean In* version of postfeminism is on satisfying the political ends of neoliberalism. The emphasis on the success of individual women neutralises the critical propensities associated with the second wave, which threaten the neoliberal agenda. Upwardly mobile middle-class women concerned with promotion of the self and their success have given feminism a new lease of life while producing a new form of neoliberal governmentality. Foucault (1991, esp. 102–103) coined this term to refer to the way an entire field of thought and action is structured to secure political control without being dependent solely on government.

Despite the visible success of women such as Sheryl Sandberg, the substantive inequalities that neoliberalism produces are deemed unseeable and unsayable within postfeminist discourse. The individualised focus of postfeminism within a neoliberal context has therefore caused feminism to lose its emancipatory impetus (Rottenberg 2017, 340). This is despite the fact that Aboriginal women, Muslim women, elderly women, and women with disabilities continue to be marginalised and oppressed. The precarity that characterises the nature of work for many women is readily absorbed by the language of choice and flexibility in a way that suits the neoliberal agenda. A few hours of casual work here and there is believed to fit in with caring for children, whereas it ensures the ongoing subordination of women. If these women lose their jobs, they are dispensable, as their capital is deemed to be of relatively little worth. Thus, the once progressive ideal of equal rights at work has been effectively resignified by neoliberalism (Budgeon 2015, 312–313). Through its 'post' prefix, the teeth have been extracted from feminism in order that it might better serve capitalism. Feminism has been rebadged in a way that is anodyne and politically palatable.

Postfeminism in the legal academy?

Neoliberal government policies have exerted a dramatic impact upon higher education. Instead of being pursued as a public good in accordance with the social liberal ideal, higher education in Australia was commodified as a result of the Dawkins reforms of 1987 and has become a key source of income generation (Universities Australia 2017). The attractiveness of law as a source of income generation for universities has resulted in more than a tripling of the number of law schools in Australia – from 12 to 40 – and a sevenfold increase in the number of students in little more than 25 years, with 7,583 graduating in law at bachelor's level in 2015 (Council of Australian Law Deans 2016).[10] The rapid increase in the number of graduates has contributed to a highly competitive labour market and impacted significantly on the curriculum. It has induced a shift towards vocationalism and applied knowledge away from the social and the humanistic (Collier 2013, 456). Both law schools and students themselves privilege intellectual property, business, commerce, and international trade as this cluster of subjects befits a neoliberal paradigm dominated by global competition and profitability (Thornton 2012). Of course, subjects with a commercial orientation can be taught from a critical perspective, and sometimes they are, but by and large, critique does not suit the applied and instrumental orientation of neoliberalism. The contemporary focus on vocationalism, 'job readiness', and a user-pays mentality privileges functional knowledge, which signals a retreat from theory and critique. Neoliberalism in the academy therefore has not only had the effect of commodifying legal education by ensuring that what is taught has use value in terms of the new knowledge economy, but it has also contributed to the diminution if not the total erasure of legal feminism.

The neoliberalisation of the legal academy has resulted in ever-increasing tuition debts for students, which has encouraged an applied orientation to the curriculum. Vocationalism has become the primary end of the law degree underscored by greater competition as a result of so-called massification. This environment encourages law students to become neoliberal subjects concerned to promote themselves and vie with others for positions in the highly competitive corporate legal labour market. In the process, they tend to slough off the social liberal concern for justice and equality, despite the fact that they may have originally enrolled in law in the hope of making the world a better place.

While second-wave feminism raised both the legal and the social consciousness about sexual assault, domestic violence, and discrimination, postfeminism has neutralised the gender of the victim as well as the perpetrator in legal doctrine (McNeilly 2012). McNeilly argues that both postfeminist and 'post-equality' narratives do this by encouraging the invisibility of the material significance of gendered harms. To raise the issue of gender in the context of these harms inevitably accentuates postfeminism's asseveration of 'victim feminism'. The result is that postfeminism has generally preferred to abandon its fleeting but discomfiting liaison with law and turn elsewhere, such as to cultural studies (Brooks 1997; McRobbie 2006; Genz and Brabon 2009). Postfeminism then not only fails to grapple with gender inequality and a host of related issues cognisable to law reform, it also underscores the retreat from the theoretical, political, and methodological commitments of the second wave (Crawford 2011, 227). Postfeminism also prefers to use popular social media formats rather than scholarly articles to disseminate its message (Crawford 2007). While social media undoubtedly facilitates communication in unprecedented ways, this tends to be superficial (e.g. 140 characters on Twitter) that accords with the post-theoretical understanding of postfeminism.

I wrote in 2003 that '[m]ost prospective lawyers, men as well as women, are likely to have had some exposure to feminist legal theory during their law school experiences…' (Thornton 2003, 8). I could no longer make such a claim as feminist perspectives all but disappeared from mainstream law curricula with the millennial turn. Even optional feminist legal theory courses became rare. In a survey of law school websites that I conducted in 2013, only one instance of a feminist legal theory subject was found in an Australian law school, although there were a handful of cognate offerings, such as 'Women and the Law' and Women's Rights', together with a few subjects with 'Gender' or 'Sexuality' in the title (Thornton 2012–2013, 243). Students have internalised the postfeminist message, averring that they no longer want the word 'feminist' on their transcripts (Thornton 2011), for it suggests an idea whose time has passed. Would a course titled 'Postfeminism in the Legal Academy' attract more students? Probably not, and even if it were to be offered, what would it entail? Chick-lit, perhaps? Domestic violence, femicide, sexual assault, sexual harassment, and cyber-bullying are rife, but contemporary feminist discourses are generally loath to accord these issues the attention they deserve.

Many feminist scholars in the neoliberal legal academy are nevertheless familiar with postmodern and poststructural theory and do not feel obliged to defer to legal orthodoxy in their scholarship, even if they have to teach compulsory subjects from a doctrinal perspective. Some legal academics are taking postfeminism in creative new scholarly directions. Initiatives such as the feminist judgements projects, which involved the writing of imaginary judgements in decided cases from a feminist perspective, are notable examples (e.g. Douglas et al. 2014; Hunter, McGlynn, and Rackley 2010; Majury 2006). There are numerous other examples of creative scholarship, to which the pages of journals such as *Feminist Legal Studies* and the *Australian Feminist Law Journal* attest. The result, however, is a widening gap between teaching and academic research in the legal academy.

Entrepreneurialism in the neoliberal academy requires academics to enhance their performance by generating research income and increasing research 'outputs'. While research performativity and productivity are not supposed to compromise teaching, the competition associated with research rankings and league tables means that academics devote more time to research, compelling them to cut corners in their teaching by adopting an atheoretical or 'black letter' approach to comply with the Priestley Eleven. Law school rankings also encourage homogeneity in terms of what is taught (Sauder and Espeland 2009), which further discourages the teaching of feminist perspectives. In this way, the neoliberal legal academy, in accordance with the governmentality thesis (Foucault 1991), is complicit in sloughing off theory and critique, especially in compulsory subjects.

As Budgeon (2015, 314) points out, neoliberal feminism does not offer an immanent critique of neoliberal governmentality comparable to the reflexivity offered by liberal feminism. Thus, subjects such as discrimination law, which interrogate the causes of inequality, have also fallen out of favour. Following the drift away from feminism, courses such as law and literature, law and culture, and law and the humanities have appeared in the legal academy from time to time. They suggest the possibility of gratifying and pleasurable choices that are preferable to wrestling with the negativity of critique and the depressing reality of ongoing instances of femicide, violence against women, and sexual harassment.

Generally speaking, there is little attempt on the part of postfeminists to engage with law, other than as consumers. Bridget Crawford (2007, 158) postulates that one reason why they do not do so is that their writing is 'pre-legal'. By this she appears to be suggesting that there is a tendency to rely on first-person narratives in order to avoid the political and the theoretical, an approach that accords with that of Sandberg in *Lean In*. If feminists turn their backs on law, however, little changes for the majority, although a few individuals might succeed. Legal feminism provides a powerful political forum through which to ventilate issues and contribute to public discourse.

Depoliticisation is a noted characteristic of both postfeminism and neoliberalism. As Chandra Mohanty (2013, 972) notes, through depoliticisation 'the state is made postfeminist before feminists achieve gender justice'. The impact of neoliberalism on feminist legal academics themselves therefore cannot be gainsaid. Overcome by ennui, they may have to reinvent themselves to remain in the academy. Some migrate into what they see as 'more intellectually engaging pastures', such as postcolonialism, queer theory, law and culture, or law and emotion (Cossman 2015, 3 ff.). The response by legal scholars such as Janet Halley has been to 'take a break from feminism' (Halley 2006, 340), because it has lost its 'zing' and Halley has become tired of what she sees as the relentless objectification of women, which erases their agency (2006, 346). She is of the view that there are other potentially more devastating problems in the world that justify a 'brain drain' away from feminism for a while (2006, 340–341).

Nevertheless, the deleterious impact of neoliberalism on women's lives continues unabated. 'Taking a break' deflects attention away from this reality and allows the continued unravelling of the gains of second-wave feminism. Not only do women preponderate in casualised positions, their numbers in the precariat are increasing, a reality that is disguised by the numerical feminisation of the academy (Kniest 2017). Neoliberalism has effectively induced a remasculinisation of authoritative positions in the academy due to the hardening of the research–teaching binary. Hence, we see an increasing emphasis on entrepreneurialism and top-down managerialism, as well as the increasing emphasis on teaching, particularly casual teaching, which is overwhelmingly feminised (Thornton 2013; cf. Blackmore 2015).

Conclusion

The suggestion that there might be an intimate relationship between contemporary incarnations of feminism and the prevailing political ideology at first appears rather shocking, especially when feminism has prided itself on being an outsider movement committed to critiquing the status quo. Nevertheless, a cursory look at any strand of postfeminism reveals a rejection of the idea of collective good and its replacement with the neoliberal values of individual choice, entrepreneurialism, flexibility, and promotion of the self. Rather than equality and social justice, neoliberalism fosters *in*equality through competition and profit maximisation. In the workplace, the focus is not on equal employment opportunity (EEO) but an employer's ability to exact greater productivity from workers. This shift from worker well-being to the interests of capital parallels the marked shift from the second wave to postfeminism that occurred because of the neoliberal turn.

The symbiotic relationship between social liberalism and second-wave feminism is clearly discernible because of the common understanding of a commitment to the idea of collective good and social justice. The injustices that were of concern to the second wave were partially addressed by social liberalism through measures effected by law reform, such as no-fault divorce, apprehended violence orders, the revamping of sexual assault laws, equal opportunity legislation, and so on. Under neoliberalism, feminism has largely disappeared from legal education syllabi, as well as from public discourse more generally. The assumption is that equality has been achieved; the occasional allusion to numerical inequality in parliaments, in the sciences, or on corporate boards suggests that it is an anomaly that can be easily rectified.

In any case, the simplistic focus on numerosity ignores the fact that it is merely the first step. As Londa Schiebinger (2017) points out, 'fixing the numbers' must be followed by 'fixing the institutions' (structural change) and 'fixing the knowledge' (integrating gender-based analysis into research). We reached the second stage under social liberalism whereupon neoliberalism intervened and obstructed the path of liberal progressivism. Furthermore, the Trump administration in the United States is winding back pro-feminist initiatives regarding abortion, women's health, and EEO, sparking comparisons between the reality of a neoliberal world and Margaret Atwood's dystopian account of the Republic of Gilead in *The Handmaid's Tale* (2010).[11]

The ambiguity of the 'post' in postfeminism, however, is underscored by the fact that there is another quite different incarnation of an insurgent feminism that has emerged because of the conservative rollback. This has meant that a new generation of young feminists is reacting against the 'post-feminist masquerade' (McRobbie 2015). Indeed, there has been a marked revival of interest in feminism, as young women search for answers to the dilemmas of power, sexuality, and violence that remain as intractable as ever.

Postscript: the Harvey Weinstein moment

Since writing this chapter, there has been a remarkable surge of interest in sexual harassment, a phenomenon that was named only 40 years ago, albeit well known to working women (MacKinnon 1979). In 2017, the Australian university community was taken aback by a report of the Australian Human Rights Commission (2017), which showed that 51 per cent of university students had been sexually harassed in a university setting in 2016 and 6.9 per cent sexually assaulted. Coincidentally, sexual harassment was to receive worldwide attention soon afterwards with the revelation that Hollywood movie mogul, Harvey Weinstein, had sexually harassed a succession of women, including prominent movie stars (BBC News 2018). Not only did the women attest personally to years of predatory behaviour, but their speaking out led to the exposé of many other prominent male harassers around the world. In sharp contrast to the past, women's voices were heard and the allegations treated seriously, which led to the men being publicly reviled. 'Times Up' and '#MeToo' quickly became global movements in which women took to the streets en masse to protest against sexual harassment and gender inequality. What was striking was that the message of the second wave had clearly not gone away but had merely been quiescent.

While feminism has been accorded a new lease of life, I am unable to predict what impact the Harvey Weinstein moment is likely to exert on the legal academy. We can only look forward to the next movement of the fandango as the '#MeToo' generation of young women put pressure on their law schools to prioritise gender equality in the curriculum once more.

Notes

1 This chapter echoes an earlier feminist fandango (Dowse 1982) A preliminary version of this paper was presented as the keynote address at the 'Post feminism. Post theory. Post critique?' workshop at the ANU College of Law, The Australian National University, 15–16 May 2015. I thank Anne Macduff, Dorota Gozdecka, and Laura Sweeney for organising the workshop and inviting me to speak.
2 Faludi (1991, 70) provides a detailed account of the postfeminist backlash following the success of second-wave feminism. She points out that backlash was not peculiar to the second wave as illustrated by the 1920s media response to first-wave feminism.
3 There is a substantial literature on the significance of the public–private dichotomy for feminism, as well as its changing character (e.g. Pateman 1983; Thornton 1995; Armstrong and Squires 2002; Thompson 2011).
4 Dowse (1982, 328) refers to the uniqueness on the international stage of the convergence of 'new wave' feminism and the election of a social democratic government after a long period of conservative rule.
5 After Justice Priestley who chaired the committee that effected the uniform admission rules in 1992.
6 The citizenship materials were prepared by Professor Sandra Berns, Ms Paula Baron, and Professor Marcia Neave, and the work and violence materials by Professor Regina Graycar and Associate Professor Jenny Morgan (Graycar and Morgan 1996). The writer chaired the overseeing committee.
7 Davies (2014, 40) suggests that the genealogy of neoliberalism can be traced as far back as the 1890s when the first pieces of modern competition law were introduced in Germany, Austria, and the United States.
8 The Howard Government's Work Choices legislation was a notorious example. See *Workplace Relations Amendment (Work Choices) Act 2005* (Cth); *Workplace Relations Regulations 2006* (Cth).
9 A change to the definition of marriage in the *Marriage Act 1961* (Cth) in 2017 enabled same-sex couples to marry.
10 Since these figures were compiled, both Charles Sturt University and the first private for-profit law school in Australia, Sydney City School of Law, TOP Education Institute, began law degrees in 2016. In addition, there are miscellaneous courses, such as the part-time diploma course offered by the Legal Profession Admission Board of NSW.

11 *The Handmaid's Tale* was also made into a prominent television series by Daniel Wilson Productions, MGM Television, Hulu Originals, Beverley Hills, USA, 2017.

References

Adriaens, Fien. 2009. "Post Feminism in Popular Culture: A Potential for Critical Resistance?" *Politics and Culture* 4, http://politicsandculture.org.

Alexander-Floyd, Nikol G. 2010. "Critical Race Black Feminism: A 'Jurisprudence of Resistance' and the Transformation of the Academy." *Signs: Journal of Women in Culture and Society* 35, no. 4: 810–820.

Armstrong, Chris, and Judith Squires. 2002. "Beyond the Public/Private Dichotomy: Relational Space and Sexual Inequalities." *Contemporary Political Theory* 1: 261–283.

Atwood, Margaret. 2010. *The Handmaid's Tale*. London: Vintage Books.

Australian Human Rights Commission. 2017. *Change the Course: National Report on Sexual Assault and Sexual Harassment in Australian Universities*. Sydney: Australian Human Rights Commission.

BBC News (Entertainment and Arts). 2018. "Harvey Weinstein Timeline: How the Scandal Unfolded." January 24, 2018, http://www.bbc.com/news/entertainment-arts-41594672.

Berns, Sandra. 1999. *To Speak as a Judge: Difference, Voice and Power*. Aldershot: Ashgate.

Blackmore, Jill. 2015. "Disciplining Academic Women: Gender Restructuring and the Labour of Research in Entrepreneurial Universities." In *Through a Glass Darkly: The Social Sciences Look at the Neoliberal University*, edited by Margaret Thornton, 179–194. Canberra: ANU Press.

Brooks, Ann. 1997. *Postfemisms: Feminism, Cultural Theory and Cultural Forms*. London: Routledge.

Brown, Wendy. 2006. "American Nightmare: Neoliberalism, Neoconservatism, and De-Democratization." *Political Theory* 34, no. 6: 690–714.

Budgeon, Shelley. 2015. "Individualized Femininity and Feminist Politics of Choice." *European Journal of Women's Studies* 22, no. 3: 303–318.

———. 2011. "The Contradictions of Successful Femininity: Third-Wave Feminism, Postfeminism and 'New' Femininities." In *New Femininities: Postfeminism, Neoliberalism and Subjectivity*, edited by Rosalind Gill and Christina Scharff, 279–292. Houndsmills, Hants: Palgrave Macmillan.

Burchell, Graham. 1996. "Liberal Government and Techniques of the Self." In *Foucault and Political Reason: Liberalism, Neo-liberalism and Rationalities of Government*, edited by Andrew Barry, Thomas Osbourne and Nikolas Rose, 19–36. Chicago: University of Chicago Press.

Cahill, Damien. 2004. "New-Class Discourse and the Construction of Left-Wing Elites." In *Us and Them: Anti-Elitism in Australia*, edited by Marian Sawer and Barry Hindess, 77–95. Perth: API Network, Australian Research Institute, Curtin University.

Charlesworth, Hilary, and Christine Chinkin. 2000. *The Boundaries of International Law: A Feminist Analysis*. Manchester: Manchester University Press.

Chea, Pheng, David Fraser, and Judith Grbich, eds. 1996. *Thinking through the Body of Law*. Sydney: Allen & Unwin.

Collier, Richard. 2013. "Privatizing the University and the New Political Economy of Socio-Legal Studies: Remaking the (Legal) Academic Subject." *Journal of Law and Society* 40, no. 3: 450–467.

Coltrane, Scott, Elizabeth C. Miller, Tracey DeHaan, and Lauren Stewart. 2013. "Fathers and the Flexibility Stigma." *Journal of Social Issues* 69, no. 2: 279–302.
Coppock, Vicki, Deena Haydon, and Ingrid Richter. 1995. *The Illusions of "Post-Feminism": New Women, Old Myths*. London: Taylor & Francis.
Cossman, Brenda. 2015. "Feminism in Hard Times: From Criticism to Critique." In *Feminisms of Discontent: Global Contestations*, edited by Ashleigh Barnes, 3–21. New Delhi: Oxford University Press.
Council of Australian Law Deans. 2016. *Data Regarding Law School Graduate Numbers and Outcomes*. http://www.cald.asn.au/assets/lists/Education/Factsheet-Law_Students_in_Australia.pdf
Crawford, Bridget J. 2007. "Toward a Third-wave Feminist Legal Theory: Young Women, Pornography and the Praxis of Pleasure." *Michigan Journal of Gender & Law* 14: 99–168.
———. 2011. "Third-wave Feminism, Motherhood and the Future of Feminist Legal Theory." In *Gender, Sexualities and Law*, edited by Jackie Jones, Anna Grear, Rachel Anne Fenton, and Kim Stevenson, 227–240. Abingdon, Oxon: Routledge.
Curthoys, Ann. 1988. *For and Against Feminism: A Personal Journey into Feminist Theory and History*. Sydney: Allen & Unwin.
Davies, Margaret. 1994, 2008. *Asking the Law Question*. North Ryde: Law Book.
Davies, William. 2014. *The Limits of Neoliberalism: Authority, Sovereignty and the Logic of Competition*. London: Sage.
———. 2015. *The Happiness Industry: How the Government and Big Business Sold Us Well-Being*. London: Verso.
Douglas, Heather, Francesca Bartlett, Trish Luker, and Rosemary Hunter, eds. 2014. *Australian Feminist Judgments: Righting and Rewriting Law*. Oxford: Hart.
Dowse, Sara. 1982. "The Women's Movement's Fandango with the State: Some Thoughts on the Movement's Role in Public Policy since 1972." *The Australian Quarterly* 54, no. 4: 324–345.
Dumenil, Gérard, and Dominique Lévy, 2011. *The Crisis of Neoliberalism*. Cambridge, MA: Harvard University Press.
Easteal, Patricia, ed. 1998. *Balancing the Scales: Rape, Law Reform and Australian Culture*. Sydney: Federation Press.
Eisenstein, Hester. 1996. *Inside Agitators: Australian Femocrats and the State*. Philadelphia, PA: Temple University Press.
Faludi, Susan. 1991. *Backlash: The Undeclared War against Women*. London: Chatto & Windus.
Foucault, Michel. 1991. "Governmentality." In *The Foucault Effect: Studies in Governmentality, with Two Lectures by and an Interview with Michel Foucault*, edited by Graham Burchell, Colin Gordon and Peter Miller, 87–104. Chicago, IL: University of Chicago Press.
Genovese, Ann. 2015. "Occasions and Events: Australian Feminist Jurisprudence at 25." *Australian Feminist Law Journal* 41, no. 1: 1–2.
———. 2010. "A Radical Prequel: Historicising the Concept of Gendered Law in Australia." In *Sex Discrimination in Uncertain Times*, edited by Margaret Thornton, 47–73. Canberra: ANU E Press.
Genz, Stéphanie, and Benjamin A. Brabon. 2009. *Postfeminism: Cultural Texts and Theories*. Edinburgh: Edinburgh University Press.
Giroux, Henry. 2008. "Slouching towards Bethlehem: The New Gilded Age and Neoliberalism's Theatre of Cruelty." *Dissident Voice*, March 11, 2008. http://dissidentvoice.org/2008/03/slouching-towards-bethlehem/

Graycar, Regina, ed. 1990. *Dissenting Opinions: Feminist Explorations in Law and Society.* Sydney: Allen & Unwin.

Graycar, Regina, and Jenny Morgan. 1990, 2002. *The Hidden Gender of Law.* Sydney: Federation Press.

———. 1996. "Legal Categories, Women's Lives and the Law Curriculum – Or, Making Gender Examinable." *Sydney Law Review* 18: 431–450.

Gwynne, Joel. 2013. *Erotic Memoirs and Postfeminism: The Politics of Pleasure.* Houndmills, Hants: Palgrave Macmillan.

Halley, Janet. 2006. *Split Decisions: How and Why to Take a Break from Feminism.* Princeton, NJ: Princeton University Press.

Harvey, David. 2007. *A Brief History of Neoliberalism.* Oxford: Oxford University Press.

Henderson, Margaret. 2008. "Feminism in the Hearts and Minds and Words of Men: Revisiting Men's Cultural Remembrance of Australian Feminism in the New Millennium." *Dialogue: Academy of the Social Sciences in Australia* 27, no. 3: 29–46.

Howe, Adrian. 1994. *Punish and Critique: Towards a Feminist Critique of Penality.* London: Routledge.

Hunter, Rosemary, Clare McGlynn, and Erika Rackley, eds. 2010. *Feminist Judgments: From Theory to Practice.* Oxford: Hart.

Johnstone, Richard, and Sumitra Vignaendra. 2003. *Learning Outcomes and Curriculum Development in Law: A Report commissioned by the Australian Universities Teaching Committee (AUTC).* Canberra: Commonwealth of Australia.

Kauppinen, Kati. 2013. "'Full Power Despite Stress': A Discourse Analytical Examination of the Interconnectedness of Post-feminism and Neoliberalism in the Domain of Work in an International Women's Magazine." *Discourse & Communication* 7, no. 2: 133–151.

Kelly, Paul, and Tony Bramston. 2015. *The Dismissal: In the Queen's Name.* Melbourne: Penguin (Australia).

Kirkby, Diane, ed. 1995. *Sex, Power and Justice: Historical Perspectives of Law in Australia.* Melbourne: Oxford University Press.

Kniest, Paul. 2017. "Workforce Feminisation and Job Security in our Universities." *National Tertiary Education Union (NTEU) Advocate* 24, no. 2: 24–25.

Lewis, Patricia. 2014. "Postfeminism, Femininities and Organization Studies: Exploring a New Agenda." *Organization Studies* 35, no. 12: 1845–1866.

MacKinnon, Catharine. 1979. *Sexual Harassment of Working Women: A Case of Sex Discrimination.* New Haven, CT: Yale University Press.

Majury, Diana. 2006. "Introducing the Women's Court of Canada." *Canadian Journal of Women and the Law* 18: 1–12.

McNeilly, Kathryn. 2012. "The Illusions of Post-feminism, Ghosts of Gender and the Discourses of Law." *feminists @ law* 1, no. 2: http://journals.kent.ac.uk/index.php/feministsatlaw/article/view/27/101

McRobbie, Angela 2015. "Notes on the Perfect: Competitive Femininity in Neoliberal Times." *Australian Feminist Studies* 30, no. 83: 3–20.

——— 2009. *The Aftermath of Feminism: Gender, Culture and Social Change.* London: Sage.

——— 2006. "Postfeminism and Popular Culture: Bridget Jones and the New Gender Regime." In *Media and Cultural Theory,* edited by J. Curran and D. Morley, 59–70. New York: Routledge.

Mohanty, Chandra Talpade. 2013. "Transnational Feminist Crossings: On Neoliberalism and Radical Critique." *Signs: Journal of Women in Culture and Society* 38, no. 4: 967–991.

Moreton-Robinson, Aileen. 2000. *Talking Up to the White Woman: Indigenous Women and Feminism*. Brisbane: University of Queensland Press.
Naffine, Ngaire. 1990. *Law and the Sexes: Explorations in Feminist Jurisprudence*. Sydney: Allen & Unwin.
Naffine, Ngaire, with Mary Heath. 2015. "On *Law and the Sexes*: A Conversation." *Australian Feminist Law Journal* 41, no. 1: 19–27.
Naffine, Ngaire, and Rosemary Owens, eds. 1997. *Sexing the Subject of Law*. North Ryde, NSW: LBC Information Services/Sweet & Maxwell.
"Occasions and Events." 2015. *Australian Feminist Law Journal* 41, no. 1: 1.
Pateman, Carole. 1983. "Feminist Critiques of the Public/Private Dichotomy." In *Public and Private in Social Life*, edited by S. I. Benn, and G. F. Gaus, 281–303. London & Canberra: Croom Helm.
Petersen, Kerry. 1993. *Abortion Regimes*. Aldershot: Ashgate.
Phillips-Anderson, Michael. 2012. "Sojourner Truth, 'Address at the Woman's Rights Convention in Akron, Ohio." (29 May 1851) *Voices of Democracy* 7: 21–46.
Projansky, Sarah. 2001. *Watching Rape: Film and Television in Postfeminist Culture*. New York: New York University Press.
Rose, Nikolas. 1996. *Powers of Freedom: Reframing Political Thought*. Cambridge: Cambridge University Press.
Rottenberg, Catherine. 2017. "Neoliberal Feminism and the Future of Human Capital." *Signs: Journal of Women in Culture and Society* 42, no. 2: 329–348.
——— 2014. "The Rise of Neoliberal Feminism." *Cultural Studies* 28, no. 3: 418–437.
R. v. Johns 1992. Supreme Court of South Australia, Bollen J., August 26, 1992. (Unreported).
Sandberg, Sheryl. 2013. *Lean In: Women, Work, and the Will to Lead*. Croydon: W H Allen.
Sauder, Michael, and Wendy Nelson Espeland. 2009. "The Discipline of Rankings: Tight Coupling and Organizational Change." *American Social Review* 74: 63–82.
Schiebinger, Londa. 2017. "Interview." In *Gender in the Global Research Landscape: Analysis of Research Performance through a Gender Lens across 20 Years, 12 Geographies, and 27 Subject Areas*, 74–76. Amsterdam: Elsevier BV.
Summers, Anne. 2003. *The End of Equality*. Sydney: Random House Australia.
Taylor, Anthea. 2012. *Single Women in Popular Culture: The Limits of Postfeminism*. Houndmills, Hants: Palgrave Macmillan.
Thompson, John B. 2011. "Shifting Boundaries of Public and Private Life."' *Theory, Culture & Society* 28, no. 4: 49–70.
Thornton, Margaret. 2017. "Dreaming of Diversity in Legal Education." In *New Directions for Law in Australia: Essays in Contemporary Law Reform*, edited by Ron Levy, Molly O'Brien, Simon Rice, Pauline Ridge, and Margaret Thornton, 549–557. Canberra: ANU Press.
——— 2016. "Work/Life or Work/Work? Corporate Legal Practice in the Twenty-first Century." *International Journal of the Legal Profession* 23, no. 1: 13–39.
——— 2013. "The Mirage of Merit: Reconstituting the 'Ideal Academic.'" *Australian Feminist Studies* 28, no. 76: 127–143.
——— 2012–2013. "The Changing Gender Regime in the Neoliberal Legal Academy." *Zeitschrift für Rechtssoziologiei (The German Journal of Law and Society)* 33: 235–251.
——— 2012. *Privatising the Public University: The Case of Law*. Abingdon, Oxon: Routledge.

——— 2011. "An Inconstant Affair: Feminism and the Legal Academy." In *Transcending the Boundaries of Law: Generations of Feminism and Legal Theory*, edited by Martha Albertson Fineman, 25–39. New York: Cavendish-Routledge.

———. 2006. "Feminism and the Changing State: The Case of Sex Discrimination." *Australian Feminist Studies* 50, no. 21: 151–172.

———. 2004. "Neo-liberal Melancholia: The Case of Feminist Legal Scholarship." *Australian Feminist Law Journal* 20: 7–22.

———. 2003. "Feminist Legal Theory: An Introduction." *Reform* 83: 5–9.

———. 1996. *Dissonance and Distrust: Women and the Legal Profession*. Melbourne: Oxford University Press.

———. ed. 1995. *Public and Private: Feminist Legal Debates*. Melbourne: Oxford University Press.

———. 1990. *The Liberal Promise: Anti-Discrimination Legislation in Australia*. Melbourne: Oxford University Press.

———. 1986. "Feminist Jurisprudence: Illusion or Reality." *Australian Journal of Law & Society* 3: 5–29.

Universities Australia. 2017. "Media Release." February 3, 2017. https://www.universitiesaustralia.edu.au/Media-and-Events/media-releases/Australia-s-education-exports-at-record-high#.WWLUWmdLcY1

Vavrus, Mary Douglas. 2007. "Opting out Moms in the News: Selling New Traditionalism in the New Millennium." *Feminist Media Studies* 7, no. 1: 47–63.

Whelehan, Imelda. 1995. *Modern Feminist Thought: From the Second Wave to "Post-feminism"*. New York: New York University Press.

2 Postfeminist clothing

Anti-feminism or diversification of the narratives of emancipation?

Dorota Anna Gozdecka

Introduction

Feminist discourse appears to have reached a state of crisis, manifesting itself in diverse areas. As McRobbie has pointed out, new feminism has been pitched against 'old feminism' (McRobbie 2011, 179), white feminism against intersectional feminism (Harnois 2005), and different 'waves' of feminism against each other (Sanders 2007, 8). In our increasingly diverse world, the word 'feminism' is contested and criticised from outside and within.

Nothing symbolises the conflict of different feminist approaches better than diverse feminist discourses over women's clothes. What women should and should not wear has been not only a subject of a heated discussion, but of legal regulation, too. The most famous examples involve banning of religious garments in the name of feminism, including the most recent controversy over a burkini that has been banned due to allegedly covering too much of the body to be respectful of secularism and gender equality (Agerholm 2017). The ban has led to the police intervening and telling women who were 'overly' dressed to remove their clothing (Cockburn 2016). On the very opposite side of this debate is the regulation adopted by the majority of social media platforms banning the showing of the female nipple (Dumas 2016) and resulting in multiple campaigns to reverse the bans (Hunt 2017).

These two extremes of either too much or too little of the body being covered show not only the ongoing overregulation of women's bodies (Whisner 1982), but also a conflict over different ideas of feminism and its relationship with women's clothing. To be sure, these two are not the only examples of debate on the legal regulation of women's bodies and their clothing. Somewhere in-between these two extreme poles, there is also a debate over contemporary entertainers, such as burlesque and cabaret performers, whose clothing is also subject to regulation and has been seen as a manifesto against feminism due to its sexually charged nature (Ferreday 2008; Siebler 2015).

This chapter analyses how the question of postfeminism is linked with the regulation of women's clothing. It asks whether women wearing what are perceived as 'traditional', 'religious', or 'oversexualised' garments can be judged as 'anti-feminist', or perhaps the opposite? It attempts to show how an intersectional context (Vakulenko 2007) is important in reconciling different ways of being a woman and different ways of dressing as a feminist. It argues that in the contemporary, complex landscape of feminism there are many ways of expressing oneself as a feminist and that, despite their alleged incompatibility, all these different ways of dressing can be appreciated as feminist becomings, rather than mutually exclusive and anti-feminist stances.

Firstly, I will begin the chapter by discussing the above-mentioned three examples of women's garments (or lack thereof) that have been a subject of feminist critiques. To further my argument, I argue that feminist expression in clothing shows emancipatory expression that challenges majoritarian standards of what it means to be a woman. Such expression allows for the expression of one's identity as a woman, even if it challenges essentialist notions of what a woman should or should not wear to be a 'woman' or to be a 'feminist'. Secondly, I will follow with a discussion on what postfeminism is in this context and whether it goes against dominant feminism, or perhaps whether it is just another way of being a feminist. Finally, I will propose a theoretical solution based on a postmodern understanding of postfeminism and aim to reconcile these diverse and seemingly irreconcilable narratives of being a woman.

Overdressed or underdressed?

Overregulation of women's bodies is vast and touches many aspects, with clothing being just a fraction of the overwhelming desire to control what women's bodies should do or look like (Morgan 1991; Shorter 2017). One of the most visible conflicts over women's clothing and its alleged feminist, anti-feminist, or postfeminist nature has concerned women's choice to wear religious garments. Ever since Okin released her essay on feminism and multiculturalism (Okin 1999), the subject of culture and religion affecting women's rights has been vividly discussed (e.g. Philips and Saharso 2008; Bilge 2010; Gozdecka and Jackson 2011). Women who have voluntarily worn a hijab, niqab, or burqua have been accused of promoting Islamic fundamentalism, being unreasonable (Gunn 2005), and standing against gender equality (Evans 2006). Women manifesting their identity through a religious dress code have been portrayed as a proxy for 'non-democratic' religion, and their clothing put in contrast with secularism, understood as a cluster of many things, including feminism. On numerous occasions, women's own arguments concerning their religious choices were simply invalidated and considered irrelevant (Wing and Smith 2006). The equal liberty of women to practice their religion was more often than not put into opposition with their emancipation (Motha 2007). Soon enough, multiple bans on wearing 'conspicuous religious symbols' started to spread, particularly in Europe, targeting women wearing various Islamic head-covering garments. To be sure, legal cases decided before the European Court of Human Rights (ECtHR) were brought by Lucia Dahlab, Leyla Şahin, Sefika Köse, Belgin Dogru, or S.A.S. (*Dahlab v Switzerland* 2001; *Sąhin v Turkey* 2005; *Şefika Köse v Turkey* 2006; *Dogru v France* 2009; *S.A.S. v France* 2014) and the debate followed.

The applicants in all of these cases brought their complaints on the grounds of infringement of the right to manifest their own religion under Article 9 of the European Convention on Human Rights.

In these cases, without exception, the Court held that institutional policies prohibiting the wearing of religious garments were compliant with democratic principles and met the requirements of proportionality and necessity. In most of the cases, except to some extent *S.A.S. v France*, the ECtHR constructed the hijab and similar religious garments as symbols incompatible with the values of European democracies, primarily gender equality. This framing is seen particularly in *Dahlab*, which presented the garments themselves as allegedly fundamentalist and anti-feminist. In *Dahlab*, the Court framed the hijab itself as an essentially anti-feminist symbol encouraging contempt for women:

> [t]he applicant's pupils were aged between four and eight, an age at which children wonder about many things and are also more easily influenced than older pupils. In those circumstances, it cannot be denied outright that the wearing of a headscarf might have some kind of proselytizing effect, seeing that it appears to be imposed on women by a precept which is laid down in the Koran and which, as the Federal Court noted, is hard to square with the principle of gender equality. It therefore appears difficult to reconcile the wearing of an Islamic headscarf with the message of tolerance, respect for others and, above all, equality and non-discrimination that all teachers in a democratic society must convey to their pupils.
>
> (*Dahlab v Switzerland* 2001, para 13)

Adopting a generalised image of Islam (Evans 2006) and equating the applicant's religious views with intolerance, inequality, and contempt for gender equality, the Court denied the applicant any agency in manifesting her identity through her choice of garments (Evans 2006). But, as many have pointed out, the image of hijab as an anti-feminist clothing was based on a homogenous and narrow image of gender equality (Rebouche 2008) and on an essentialising image of Islam in the public sphere (Meerschaut and Gutwirth 2008). It also relied on a presumed rather than actual relationship between Islam and gender equality (Marshall 2008).

This framing was eventually modified, although not to the final satisfaction of the applicant in *S.A.S. v France*, where the ECtHR made an effort to approach the choice of religious garments in a more nuanced way, stating that:

> The Court takes the view, however, that a State Party cannot invoke gender equality in order to ban a practice that is defended by women – such as the applicant – in the context of the exercise of the rights enshrined in those provisions, unless it were to be understood that individuals could be protected on that basis from the exercise of their own fundamental rights and freedoms.
>
> (*S.A.S. v France* 2014, para 119)

Despite this progress in the understanding of a woman's autonomy in expressing her identity, the ban on full-face veiling was found to be legitimate for the protection of the right of others and the conditions of 'living together' (Marshall 2008, S.A.S. v France, para. 157), which would allegedly be in danger should such garments be permitted in public. The appearance of face coverings in public has resulted in the expansion of the notion of the 'public sphere', encompassing not only the political sphere but all situations of 'living together' with others. While such a construction of the public sphere is problematic for many reasons (Gozdecka 2015), its relationship with feminism is particularly troublesome. The notion of the public sphere construed by the Court in these cases fails to examine the reasons why women would defend particular garments and oversimplifies the relationship between secularism and feminism by ignoring the context in which women insist on manifesting their religious identity and the physical places where that occurs.

The question of baring the body in the pursuit of feminism has been subject of a similarly heated debate between feminists and anti-feminists. The Free the Nipple! movement has emerged as a response to the strict regulation of showing female areola and nipples in photos published on social media (Bock et al. 2017; Rúdólfsdóttir and Jóhannsdóttir 2018). The bans initially applied to all such images, including those of breast-feeding (Bock et al. 2017). Parallel movements have also emerged outside the social media context where feminist protest groups around the globe, such as GoTopless in the United States (Steinfeld 2017) and Femen in the Ukraine (Stauffer 2016, 7–9), have used nudity to draw attention to gender inequality.

While many have applauded the Free the Nipple! movement as feminist in terms of standing against the patriarchy (Rúdólfsdóttir and Jóhannsdóttir 2018) or the masculine gaze more generally (Megarry 2017), some have quickly criticised it. In their feminist defence of the campaign, Rudolfsdottir and Johannsdottir have pointed out that the Free the Nipple! campaign is a feminist response to the constant pressure of navigating between free expression of one's female sexuality and at the same time not falling into the social perception of being 'slutty' (Rúdólfsdóttir and Jóhannsdóttir 2018, 4–5) when revealing one's body.

Meanwhile, some commentators such as Patterson and Stauffer have been more critical of the campaign and pointed out that campaigns of this kind are an expression of a narrow understanding of white feminism (Patterson 2016; Stauffer 2016). Taking yet another approach, Barnard has criticised selfies more generally, including Free the Nipple! selfies as an expression of weak postfeminist empowerment, which is merely a substitute for effective empowerment (Barnard 2016, 81).

To be sure, law has also been involved in the dispute, and currently a decision in a case brought by Sonoku Tagami, from the GoTopless organisation, is pending before the US Supreme Court (*Sonoku Tagami v City of Chicago* 2017). The main question is whether women have equality when it comes to the right to be topless. The case follows an arrest of Sonoku in 2014 by

Chicago police during a GoTopless protest, for violating the city's public nudity ordinance (*Sonoku Tagami v City of Chicago* 2017, 2–3). A similar case has also been lodged in New Hampshire and is awaiting decision (Casey 2018). Tagami argued the breach of the First Amendment and the right to freedom of expression, saying that the right to take their shirts off should be available to all persons regardless of gender. The US Court of Appeals found no breach of the First Amendment, saying that freedom of expression is protected only for conduct that is 'inherently expressive' and that public nudity is not an 'inherently expressive' act (*Sonoku Tagami v City of Chicago*, 4). The Court also argued that protection from nudity is a legitimate purpose in itself that passes the O'Brien test, establishing the allowed limitations of freedom of expression:

> Put more succinctly, the interest at stake here 'is societal disapproval of nudity in public places and among strangers,' (...), so the prohibition 'is not a means to some greater end, but an end in itself,' (...) Chicago's ordinance has a similar pedigree. It has existed in one form or another for decades. Like other laws of this type, its essential purposes – promoting traditional moral norms and public order – are both self-evident and important enough to survive scrutiny under the O'Brien test.
>
> (*Tagami v Chicago*, 7)

In the case of Facebook censorship, while no legal action has yet been brought, users have begun to paste male nipples on female breasts to challenge the censorship. Facebook rules have been updated in 2015 and currently the rules state that: 'We also restrict some images of female breasts if they include the nipple, but we always allow photos of women actively engaged in breastfeeding or showing breasts with post-mastectomy scarring' (Facebook). In 2016, breast cancer detection awareness material was posted by replacing female breasts and nipples with a male model's nipple (Cook 2016). Facebook has routinely removed breast cancer awareness videos in different countries, including the famous case of an animated Swedish video (Agence France-Presse 2016).

Another controversial example related to female nudity is the regulation of performative art and its dress codes. The prime example of such expression is neo-burlesque performance that routinely experiences shutdowns and legal suits. In comparison with Free the Nipple! protests, neo-burlesque performance puts greater focus on the expression of women's sexuality as a protest against the control of women's sexuality or it being construed solely for male pleasure. Due to its focus on women's sexuality and sexual power, it is positioned as a feminist expression of pleasure. Neo-burlesque performances have been shut down multiple times, particularly often in the United States. Most recently, a show with a burlesque performer Lillian Bustle was closed down for violating obscenity laws in New Jersey in late March 2018 (McDonald 2018). Neo-burlesque relies heavily on sexual identities and sexuality in its diverse forms of expression, including comical, political, or classically inspired neo-burlesque.

As with responses to Free the Nipple! protests, there is no agreement within feminist scholarship whether the practice of neo-burlesque is a feminist, anti-feminist, or postfeminist expression. As mentioned earlier, I insist that feminist clothing allows for the fullest and most fulfilling way in which woman's identity can be expressed against any constraints that predefine any aspect of that identity as feminist, be it sexual, gender, religious, or other. Such identity may be complex, intersectional, and emphasise religious identity, or equally sexual identity. The complexity may be even greater if we imagine multiple identities and axes of emancipation occurring all at once. This would be the case with a transgender woman performer who is disabled and religious and struggling to express her identity regardless of predefined notions of attractiveness, womanhood, and so forth. Such a performer's expression through her choice of clothing may communicate different feminist messages in different contexts and the context will determine whether and how they can be seen as empowering or emancipatory.

An understanding of burlesque as both feminist and anti-feminist corresponds with the struggle within feminism to expand feminist approaches (Abrams 1995). Some scholars, such as Ferreday, insist that neo-burlesque can be adapted to speak back to hegemonic ideals of beauty, feminism, and queer theory (Ferreday 2008, 7). Others, however, like Siebler, insist that most neo-burlesque performances do not reflect feminist theory and instead reinforce what she calls 'powerlessness', 'voicelessness', and 'posing for the purpose of heterosexual male titillation' (Siebler 2015, 565). Some, however, argue that neo-burlesque, at least in some varieties, is simultaneously anti-feminist and feminist and engages with politically subversive concepts of sexuality and gender (Boucher and French 2011, 9). This understanding of burlesque as both feminist and anti-feminist corresponds with the struggle within feminism to expand feminist approaches beyond essentialisation of sexual activity as always defined by male aggression (Abrams 1995). It has resulted in the emergence of 'sex-positive' feminism, which seeks to validate female sexuality and sexual expression (Abrams 1995). Those who see neo-burlesque within the 'sex-positive' category (Gilmore and Wheeler 2012) see it as a form of sexual empowerment that allows women to define their sexual expression (Regehr 2012). Those who criticise it see it as speaking to traditional gender tropes and reinforcing the male gaze (Siebler 2015).

As shown above, whether overdressed or underdressed, a woman's struggle to best express her identity through wearing, or not wearing, specific garments is still a heated subject of legal and feminist debate. While scholars disagree on the merits of each of these expressions of feminism, sexuality, or religiousness, they all have in one way or another characterised these diverse expressions as 'postfeminist'. Therefore, below I will engage with a meaning of postfeminism used in these scholarly critiques and propose my own understanding of postfeminism that has the capacity to include all of these, sometimes contradictory, expressions of feminism. I will argue that within our contemporary pluralistic societies, we need to allow for recognition of the context in which a woman's struggle to express herself takes place and becomes 'feminist', and will offer a theoretical solution that can take into account such context.

Postfeminist, anti-feminist, or feminist (un)clothing?

There are several understandings of postfeminism that reverberate in scholarly approaches to the matter of clothing and its regulation. While most scholars use the word 'postfeminist' in the discussion on these very diverse forms of female expression, their understandings differ substantially.

Most scholars analyse these particular choices of (un)clothing by relying on McRobbie's definition of postfeminism as a state when feminism is seen to have already achieved its goals and become redundant (McRobbie 2004, 2008, 2011). Rudolfsdottir and Johannsdottir paraphrase Scharff in saying that within this understanding of postfeminism 'young women are considered the primary "beneficiaries of increased opportunities" and have only themselves to blame if they fail to take advantage' (Rúdólfsdóttir and Jóhannsdóttir 2018, 4–5). McRobbie herself has further elaborated on the relationship between feminism, anti-feminism, and postfeminism in her article from 2011 where she adds that:

> (…) feminism is associated with old and unglamorous women (…). This encourages a 'disidentification' with feminism on the part of young women. Indeed, it is a mark of the cultural intelligence of young women who renounce or disavow the need for a new sexual politics (…)
>
> (McRobbie, 2011, 180)

McRobbie contends that postfeminism results in the weakening of active feminism and the position of women, and is in fact an anti-feminist movement of new 'glamourous' women versus the 'old unglamorous feminist'. Similarly, Faludi in her *Backlash against American Women*, characterises the postfeminist turn within feminism as anti-feminist (Faludi 2005). Rivers (2017) equates postfeminism with neoliberal discourse allowing women to have an illusion of having it all. She uses the example of Emma Watson's revealing photos and Watson's retaliation to the critique of those photos (Rivers 2017, 71–72). Watson had expressed amazement at the fact people thought she could not be a feminist and, as she phrased it, 'have boobs' (Reuters 2017). Rivers, however, was not convinced by Watson's response, which she saw as the 'reductive view that all choice is feminist' (2017, 72) and fitting into a more general neoliberal discourse promoting white, middle class individualism.

Boucher and French (2011) observe, however, that the definition of postfeminism is more complex and does not necessarily mean departure from the ideals of feminism. They insist that two understandings of postfeminism in fact dominate. In addition to McRobbie's and Faludi's equation of postfeminism with anti-feminism and the postfeminist agenda with a 'disrespectful response to second wave feminism' (Boucher and French and 2011, 9), the term can also mean a celebration of 'plurality and difference within contemporary feminist discourses and extends the political goals of the second wave to incorporate race, ethnicity, sexuality and class' (Boucher and French 2011, 9). This understanding of postfeminism is particularly important if contemporary feminism is to respond to the variety of feminisms and develop an understanding that feminism may mean different things for different women from diverse backgrounds, such as ethnic (Harnois 2005, 824) or religious (Gökarıksel and Smith 2017).

Acknowledging that different feminisms exist is important because, as Harnois shows, different concerns are considered emancipatory by different women depending on their contexts (Harnois 2005). If we fail to acknowledge such differences, they can be easily dismissed or ignored under the umbrella of one version of feminism – primarily white, middle class, individualist feminism (Patterson 2016; Stauffer 2016). When one type of feminism serves as the yardstick for what the feminist agenda in the contemporary world should look like, postfeminism can indeed only appear as a danger and an essentially anti-feminist development. This is because such a pluralist and diversified agenda no longer corresponds to the concerns of primarily white, middle class women.

A singular understanding of what feminism should entail and whether women should cover their faces or bare their breasts in the name of feminism may be a tempting approach, but it ignores all other concerns and erases them in the name of speaking for 'all women', without really understanding the reality lived by 'all women'. Stauffer shows how a singular understanding of feminism, while promoting an allegedly feminist agenda, can in fact result in exclusion and straightforward discrimination, as in cases of Femen's protests targeting Muslim women at Tunisian embassies throughout Europe (Stauffer 2016, 8). Women whose concerns and emancipatory paths are different from a mainstream vision of feminism can easily be othered and dismissed. Their concerns may be seen as a critique of what McRobbie calls 'old women' and as potentially dangerous for feminism. This fear, however, appears justified only provided that the notion of feminism has a homogenous and hegemonic meaning, fixing what feminism should mean and how it should be lived. For such a version of feminism, religious or racial concerns, or equally sexual satisfaction concerns, remain beyond the scope of the traditional feminist struggle.

The goal of this chapter is not to question the validity of the feminist concerns of the first and second wave or dismiss the importance of one type of feminism in favour of another. Instead, alongside French and Boucher, I assert that contemporary postfeminism should not be viewed as a danger to traditionally defined feminism, but instead as a diversifying and complementing narrative that is based on 'rejection of essentialist identity categories in favour of indeterminate gendered and sexual identities' (Boucher and French 2011, 9). Such an understanding of postfeminism, I believe, could respond to multiple identity, race, and ethnicity politics within contemporary feminism and be more receptive to intersectional concerns preventing the othering of one feminist narrative by another.

It also allows for the recognition of the context in which the emancipatory struggle arises. Whether it is a religious identity struggling for recognition within a sterilely defined secularism or a big-bodied performer's sexuality struggling for recognition in a landscape where women's sexuality is firstly frowned upon, and secondly attached to a specific body type, the context of the struggle matters and makes it different from the primarily choice based, neoliberal feminism. Postfeminist struggle is always a struggle against the erasure of diverse and contextualised expressions of one's identity as a woman and a feminist, including the struggle against the erasure done by one feminist identity against another. Understanding postfeminism in the way proposed here does not assume that there is no anti-feminism, but that anti-feminism is something entirely different from postfeminism. Anti-feminism is based on challenging and trying to turn entirely away from diverse feminist narratives (Gökarıksel and Smith 2017). While anti-feminism attempts to side track, ignore, or straightforwardly attack women's different concerns, postfeminism, in the understanding I propose, accommodates the multiple concerns of multiple feminisms, and as such is essentially a continuation of the feminist narrative, albeit in a modified way.

In such a postmodern, flexible understanding of postfeminism, all seemingly contradictory understandings of female (un)clothing can be simultaneously viewed as feminist struggles dependent on the context and diversity of female concerns that they stem from. To show how these seemingly diverse ways of fighting for freedom of (un)clothing, like Free the Nipple! movement, neo-burlesque performance, and the fight to freely wear religious garments can be simultaneously seen as feminist empowerments, I will use my theoretical model of *otherwise than becoming*. I have previously used this model in my analysis of the plurality of discourses of emancipation in the context of religious freedom (Gozdecka 2015) and will use it below to show how emancipatory discourses can coexist without erasing and othering each other and how the context of these struggles is crucial for understanding feminist emancipation. Othering one feminism with the narrative of another feminism results in the rejection of some forms of expression and the marginalisation of some struggles, while others are glorified. Such an antagonistic approach contributes to the rise of anti-feminism, which benefits from suggestions that some ways in which women express themselves are less feminist than others.

Otherwise than becoming or responsibility for different emancipatory paths

To reconcile different emancipatory drives within contemporary postfeminism and bring them closer to the concerns of different women, we need to think of feminism as a diverse narrative responsive to the concerns of other women. To save feminist struggles for emancipation from the risk of being synonymous with one type of feminism and perpetuating stagnant discourses, we need a method of navigation between different emancipatory narratives. When we tie feminism to a uniformly understood struggle then the discourse offers no more than a totalising ontology, marginalising all women whose concerns do not conform to what feminism is 'meant' to be.

In my previous work (Gozdecka 2015), I turned to Emmanuel Levinas to unpack the emancipatory potential of human rights and free them from the ontological traps he identified. I have done so, based on the assumption that emancipation, embedded in the original narrative of human rights, requires a dynamic, rather than static, understanding of rights and freedom. Drawing on Levinasian principles in *Otherwise than Being* (Lévinas 1981), *Totality and Infinity* (Lévinas 1969), as well as his short essay, 'The Rights of Man and The Rights of the Other' (Lévinas 1994), I sought an escape from the totalising ontological categories embedded in the notion of rights and freedom. While Levinas has been criticised by feminists (Manning 1991), I believe that regardless of that critique the understanding of freedom offered in his theory is helpful for opening up a postfeminist space and conceptualising the freedom of other women as entirely different from one's own freedom.

In *Otherwise than Being*, Levinas remarks:

> The freedom of another could never begin in my freedom, that is, abide in the same present, be contemporary, be representable to me. The responsibility for the other cannot have begun in my commitment, in my decision. The unlimited responsibility in which I find myself comes from the hither side of my freedom, from a 'prior to every memory,' an 'ulterior to every accomplishment,' from the non-present par excellence, the non-original, the anarchical, prior to or beyond essence.
>
> (Lévinas 1981, 10)

If emancipation is a dynamic journey from unfreedom towards greater freedom (Gozdecka 2015, 157–167) and if different feminisms employ different emancipatory narratives, then we must abandon imagining the freedom of the other as mirrored on what freedom means to 'me' or to 'us'. Journeys to freedom by others cannot be reflected in the comfort of the ontological mirror. Freedom as to what other women wear or refuse to wear cannot be judged by what freedom of expression means to 'me' or to 'us'. As Levinas ascertains, the freedom of the other must remain unrepresentable to me and thus needs to transcend my essence. In other words, it requires acceptance prior to ontology. The freedom of the other, just as the other herself, cannot be fixed as an ontological category but instead must be freed from ontological rigidity by the responsibility that comes before my own freedom. It requires the patient facing of the other and responsibility awoken by the face of the other. For Levinas, it is the nakedness of the face that pierces all order in the world and allows the conscience to respond ethically (Lévinas 2003, 32).

In the context of (un)clothing, it requires facing the woman in hijab, facing the woman without a bra, and facing the woman in garter belts as someone whose struggle for freedom I may never entirely understand but for which I am answerable. If I fail to do so, all that my freedom and my feminism can offer is a fixed, rigid, and unchangeable notion of 'freedom', which in fact becomes 'unfreedom' for other women, as it was in the case of Femen protesters in front of Tunisian embassies. If different emancipatory journeys are to coexist then we need to avoid 'treating the person as an object by submitting (…) her (the unique, the incomparable) to comparison, to thought, to being placed on the famous scales of justice, and thus to calculation' (Lévinas 1994, 96). When a static and ontologically fixed meaning of freedom is taken, nothing prevents a 'possible war between multiple freedoms, or a conflict between reasonable wills' (Lévinas 1994, 96). In this war, one feminism takes a superior position over the other as the one that is recognisable to the self. The effort to reconstruct the emancipatory logic requires imagining responsibility of the self for the other woman's journey from unfreedom towards her freedom. Using Levinasian responsibility for construing the notion of emancipation prevents establishing culturally, racially, or socially static structures that define what feminism is and for what freedom it wishes to fight. Accepting this idea of freedom places the other woman before the self in an act of inexhaustible responsibility, it is the *otherwise* part *of Otherwise than Being*.

Since the Levinasian conception suffers from several difficulties (Badiou 2001; Smith 2009, 68–71), it is necessary to supplement the model to allow for the recognition of multiple emancipatory journeys in the proposed meaning of postfeminism. While we already accept that the freedom of other women may be different than the freedom of the self, Levinasian ethical responsibility can be fulfilled only in the presence of a third person, which allows for politics to take shape. As he elaborates:

> This 'thirdness' is different from that of the third man, it is the third party that interrupts the face to face of a welcome of the other man, interrupts the proximity or approach of the neighbour, it is the third man with which justice begins.
>
> (Lévinas 1981, 150)

It is the third person who motivates the self to the act of responsibility. Yet, it is precisely the third person who makes it difficult to imagine which journey is emancipatory. If it is the third person who motivates the self, how is it possible to reconcile responsibility for the freedom of all the others that become visible in the presence of different third persons? How can responsibility respond to the marginalisation of some, but not all, others? How can we define which journey is emancipatory and which is not? What makes the struggle to bare breasts emancipatory in the *otherwise than becoming* version of postfeminism? Criticised for an ethical and purely philosophical focus (Badiou 2001; Smith 2009, 68–71), Levinasian responsibility as the foundation of freedom may lead to the impossibility of emancipation simply due to the difficulty of defining the context in which such freedom is to be recognised. If taken alone, responsibility fails to address the question: Who is the one for whom I am responsible? Whose emancipation is my ethical duty? Can a woman in full covering claim emancipation when women have fought for centuries to free themselves from restrictive garments such as corsets, head coverings, and so on? How can I be responsible for a burlesquer in a g-string and a garter belt when women have protested against being the subjects of sexual objectification? What about Sonoku Tagami in her topless protest? Is she simply perpetuating the male gaze? How can they self-imagine them all as engaged in an emancipatory journey?

If we work on the assumption that in contemporary societies, axes of feminist emancipation are very diverse and can coexist; we also have to acknowledge that sometimes where one emancipatory journey ends, another begins. But, conceptualising this relationship is hard with the Levinasian *Otherwise than Being*. The existence of different others necessitates being more precise when it comes to the presence of the third person, or the conditions in which freedom is possible. Among the diverse axes of emancipation, different aspects such as the local situation, the cases considered, the type of issue, and the choices made by the agents themselves (Balibar 2013, 22) will matter in building the context. The other woman whose freedom and emancipation I am responsible for is always a minority and not simply in the numerical sense. A transgender, black, big-bodied neo-burlesque performer with disability will struggle with several contexts in which she may seek emancipation. These contexts will also change geographically, with different places taking different approaches to matters of transgender identities, racial equality, recognition of disability rights, constructing female attractiveness, and female sexuality. Each of these contexts will matter in defining the emancipatory struggle and recognising the other feminism and our responsibility for it.

While a minority may be numerical, they are not necessarily those who are less numerous, but instead those who are underrepresented in an established norm (Deleuze and Guattari 1980, 105). Deleuze and Guattari tie the notion of being in a minority with the notion of becoming. They privilege becoming over being as a more dynamic and flexible structure that offers the potential of deterritorialising the majoritarian norm (Deleuze 1986). Becoming offers a potentiality of deterritorialisation and refers to the 'potential of individuals or groups to deviate from the standard' (Patton 2005, 407). Such an approach relates to the fact that individuals and groups never truly conform to the standard, as Patton shows (2005, 407). Deleuze's minoritarian politics keeps the notion of minority fluid, dynamic, and applicable to endless combinations and variations. Becoming is thus 'individual or collective struggles to come to terms with events and intolerable conditions and to shake loose, to whatever degree possible, from determinants and definitions' (Biehl and Locke 2010, 317).

Williams (2005) illustrates that while seemingly different, Deleuze and Levinas share certain fundamental ethical concepts when it comes to facing the other. For Levinas, transcendence and responsibility are possible only when we encounter the face of the other. For Deleuze, what matters is not, in fact, the face as an object but a special relation of movement beyond that which has already been identified (Williams 2005). For Deleuze, life is open to constant new becomings. In their radical new conceptualisation of ontology, Deleuze and Guattari conceive of the notion of the rhizome (Deleuze and Guattari 1980, 3–25). The rhizome promises to rise above constraints of ontology and go beyond fixing forms and subjects. The Deleuzian ontology of the rhizome is anti-foundationalist in envisioning the possibility of constantly emerging points of growth and change. It is in that sense similar yet different from the Levinasian challenge to ontological categories. The rhizome defies structures and is not synonymous with the being that Levinas tried to overcome. It defies rigidities and envisions that points of growth might be stimulated in any part of the rhizomatic structure. Rhizome embeds the becoming – its purpose is to resist the rigidity of structures:

> At the same time, something else entirely is going on: not imitation at all but a capture of code, surplus value of code, an increase in valence, a veritable becoming, a becoming-wasp of the orchid and a becoming-orchid of the wasp. Each of these becomings brings about the deterritorialization of one term and the reterritorialization of the other; the two becomings interlink and form relays in a circulation of intensities pushing the deterritorialization ever further. There is neither imitation nor resemblance, only an exploding of two heterogeneous series on the line of flight composed by a common rhizome that can no longer be attributed to or subjugated by anything signifying.
>
> (Deleuze and Guattari 1980, 10)

The process of deterritorialisation involves constant renegotiation. The becoming minoritarian enjoys the possibility of positioning the force that is becoming against the majority and deterritorialising the majoritarian standard. It is the becoming against whatever the standard may be. A dynamic understanding of freedom, which focuses on becoming rather than being, is able to build a context that can help in recognising emancipation as a becoming in endless configurations and ongoing new deterritorialisations. In that process, the freedom changes all the time and the journey from unfreedom to greater freedom is redefined constantly.

It is becoming, not being, that corresponds to the matrix of contemporary different axes of emancipation. When combined in *otherwise than becoming*, Levinasian responsibility secures an approach to the freedom of other women as a responsibility for what is different from our understanding of freedom, while Deleuzian becoming preserves the transformative, dynamic relation between unfreedom and freedom. Becoming is rhizomatic – it might be an emancipatory journey of one person, one ideal, community, or a collective of ideals away from whatever constraints are put on them. These constraints may even be the self's own notion of freedom.

Otherwise than becoming allows us to be responsible for other women who are about to become, who contest their position and renegotiate their constraints. The notion of responsibility for freedom as a rhizomatic becoming allows the accommodation of endless categories of people, movements or groups that think of feminist deterritorialisations differently and that have arisen in different contexts. Contemporary feminist revolutionaries whose freedoms we are responsible for exist in a perpetual state of a flux. Their becoming can be initiated in any place and at any point, in any of the structures that surround them. These structures may even arise from old feminist struggles, once they have become a new structure themselves. When this happens, a new feminist emancipation arises and takes on a new form – a new point of growth within the structure and the new force of becoming.

Postmodern postfeminism based on otherwise than becoming sees a woman wearing a veil contesting a norm that constrains veiling in her country and a woman in a different societal structure contesting veiling as a majoritarian standard as equally valid feminist struggles. A woman in secular France choosing this garment as an expression of identity and a woman in Saudi Arabia who struggles with losing the garment will both be engaged in emancipatory struggles, precisely because of the constraining context in which these struggles emerge and become new 'becomings'. It recognises a burlesquer removing nearly all her garments in the search for sexual power, and the same burlesquer contesting pornography as derogatory for women as engaged in legitimate struggles against two differently defined structures. While such a flexible approach is hard for most to imagine, it allows for the presence of context and the understanding that one emancipatory journey cannot contain all journeys. It acknowledges the importance of context, power relations, and existing societal structures that differ and generate different becomings, different paths towards freedom, and also different responsibilities. This proposed vision of postfeminism is open to the possibility that emancipation cannot be forged once and for all or defined a priori. Who, where, and struggling to emerge out of what must remain open to interpretation and renegotiation. The capacity of feminism to be emancipatory ends when it attempts to control, question, or even constrain other women from achieving their emancipation.

Conclusions

This chapter has shown that the diversity of female struggles to wear clothing that defies societal norms can indeed be seen as a postfeminist effort. The understanding of postfeminism suggested here has, however, rejected the contention that postfeminism is something that embodies a rejection of feminism, but is instead a term that can signify a diversification of narratives of emancipation. With the help of my theoretical construction of *otherwise than becoming*, I have reconstructed the notion of postfeminism to be more inclusive and open to the diversity of emancipatory journeys within contemporary feminism. The proposal is as modest as it is radical in its attempt to reinject emancipatory potential into feminism and to bring feminism closer to those women who continue being marginalised within the dominant theoretical frameworks of feminism. I am aware that the feasibility of this reconstruction and reconciliation, and the further philosophical dilemmas that it might raise, requires further attention. As it currently stands, it may serve as a roadmap to a different way of thinking about the coexistence of diverse feminist struggles. Once women have won the freedom to be topless on French beaches, this proposal allows us to imagine that burkini wearers on the same beaches are engaged in an equally valid struggle to express a different feminist journey to freedom. It proposes a version of postfeminism that is less susceptible to creating immutable structures and limiting the emancipation of other women. In the world facing diverse feminist struggles in the legal arena, this *otherwise than becoming* understanding of postfeminism can find its place at the heart of legal uncertainty – in the interpretation of phrases used by the Courts such as 'a democratic society' (*Dahlab v Switzerland* 2001; *S.A.S. v France* 2014) or 'essential purposes' (*Tagami v. Chicago* 2017). It is within these legal debates that we can and should ask: 'Where lies our responsibility for the other women's freedom and what is their becoming deterritorialising?' This question is as relevant for postfeminism in its search for identity as it is for law when dealing with postfeminist axes of multiple emancipations.

References

Abrams, Kathryn. 1995. "Sex wars redux: Agency and coercion in feminist legal theory." *Columbia Law Review* 95, no. 2: 304–376.

Agence France-Presse. 2016. "Facebook bans 'offensive' Swedish breast cancer awareness video." *The Guardian*, October 20, 2016. https://www.theguardian.com/technology/2016/oct/20/facebook-bans-swedish-breast-cancer-awareness-video-for-being-offensive.

Agerholm, Harriett. 2017. "Burkini ban: Geneva says women must bare arms and legs." *The Independent*, December 11, 2017. https://www.independent.co.uk/news/world/europe/burkini-ban-geneva-bare-arms-legs-a8102701.html.

Badiou, Alain. 2001. *Ethics: An Essay on the Understanding of Evil*. London, New York: Verso.

Balibar, Etienne. 2013. "On the politics of human rights." *Constellations* 20, no. 1: 18–26.

Barnard, Stephen R. 2016. "Spectacles of self(ie) empowerment? Networked individualism and the logic of the (post)feminist selfie." In *Communication and Information Technologies Annual (Studies in Media and Communications, Volume 11)*, edited by Laura Robinson, Jeremy Schulz, Shelia R. Cotten, Timothy M. Hale, Apryl A. Williams, and Joy L. Hightower, 63–88. Emerald Group Publishing Limited. https://www.emeraldinsight.com//book/10.1108/s2050-206020159

Biehl, João, and Peter Locke. 2010. "Deleuze and the anthropology of becoming." *Current Anthropology* 51, no. 3: 317–351.

Bilge, Sirma. 2010. "Beyond subordination vs. resistance: An intersectional approach to the agency of veiled Muslim women." *Journal of Intercultural Studies* 31, no. 1: 9–28.

Bock, Mary Angela, Paromita Pain, and JhuCin Jhang. 2017. "Covering nipples: News discourse and the framing of breastfeeding." *Feminist Media Studies*: 1–17. https://www.researchgate.net/profile/Paromita_Pain/publication/316320605_Covering_nipples_news_discourse_and_the_framing_of_breastfeeding/links/5a36a17caca27247ede1be81/Covering-nipples-news-discourse-and-the-framing-of-breastfeeding.pdf.

Boucher, Georgie, and Sarah French. 2011. "Postfeminist pleasure and politics: Moira Finucane and The Burlesque Hour." *Australasian Drama Studies* 58: 193–211.

Casey, Michael. 2018. "Topless beachgoers: Ban is unconstitutional, discriminatory." *The Seattle Times*, January 31, 2018. https://www.seattletimes.com/nation-world/new-hampshires-highest-court-will-hear-topless-case.

Cockburn, Harry. 2016. "Burkini ban: Armed police force woman to remove swimwear on Nice beach." *The Independent*, August 24 2016. https://www.independent.co.uk/news/world/europe/burkini-swimwear-ban-france-nice-armed-police-hijab-muslim-a7206776.html.

Cook, Jesselyn. 2016. "Breast cancer awareness video sidesteps censorship rules in an ingenious way." *The Huffington Post*, April 22 2016. https://www.huffingtonpost.com/entry/breast-cancer-video-censorship_us_571a4b5be4b0d0042da9031b?guccounter=1.

Dahlab v Switzerland, European Court of Human Rights, Decision, Application no. 42393/98, 15 February 2001.

Deleuze, Gilles. 1986. *Kafka: Toward a minor literature* (Vol. 30). London, Minneapolis: University of Minnesota Press.

Deleuze, Gilles, and Felix Guattari. 1980. *A Thousand Plateaus: Capitalism and Schizophrenia*. London, New York: Continuum International Publishing Group.

Dogru v France, European Court of Human Rights, Judgment, Application no. 27058/05, 4 March 2009.

Dumas, Daisy. 2016. "How Facebook decides which female breasts you can see." *The Sydney Morning Herald*, 16 March 2016. https://www.smh.com.au/technology/how-facebook-decides-which-female-breasts-you-can-see-20160315-gnjdub.html.

Evans, Carolyn. 2006. "Islamic Scarf in the European court of human rights." *The Melbourne Journal of International Law* 7: 52–73.

Facebook. "Community standards." https://m.facebook.com/communitystandards/encouraging-respectful-behavior/, accessed 21 April 2018.

Faludi, Susan. 2005 (1991). *Backlash: The Undeclared War against American Women*. New York: Crown Publishing Group.

Ferreday, Debra. 2008. "'Showing the girl' The new burlesque." *Feminist Theory* 9, no. 1: 47–65.

Gilmore, Stephanie, and Leigh Ann Wheeler. 2012. "Getting "down and dirty" at the Berks: A conversation about feminism, queer politics, and the many meanings of sexual performance." *Journal of Women's History* 24, no. 2: 171–197.

Gökarıksel, Banu, and Sara Smith. 2017. "Intersectional feminism beyond US flag hijab and pussy hats in Trump's America." *Gender, Place & Culture* 24, no. 5: 628–644.

Gozdecka, Dorota Anna. 2015. *Rights, Religious Pluralism and the Recognition of Difference: Off the Scales of Justice*. Oxon, New York: Routledge.

Gozdecka, Dorota A., and Amy R. Jackson. 2011. "Caught between different legal pluralisms: Women who wear Islamic dress as the religious 'other' in European rights discourses." *Journal of Legal Pluralism and Unofficial Law* 64: 91–120.

Gunn, Jeremy T. 2005. "Fearful symbols: The Islamic headscarf and the European court of human rights." Strasbourg Consortium: Freedom of Conscience and Religion at the European Court of Human Rights. http://www.strasbourgconsortium.org/document.php?DocumentID=3846.

Harnois, Catherine E. 2005. "Different paths to different feminisms? Bridging multiracial feminist theory and quantitative sociological gender research." *Gender & Society* 19, no. 6: 809–828.

Hunt, Ellen. 2017. "Male or female? Genderless Nipples account challenges Instagram's sexist standards." *The Guardian*, January 19 2017. https://www.theguardian.com/world/2017/jan/19/genderless-nipples-generates-50000-followers-on-instagram.

Lévinas, Emmanuel. 1969. *Totality and Infinity: An Essay on Exteriority*. Pittsburgh, PA: Duquesne University Press.

———. 1981. *Otherwise than Being or Beyond Essence*. Dordrecht: Kluwer Academic Publishing.

———. 1994. "The rights of man and the rights of the other." In *Outside the Subject*, edited by Emmanuel Lévinas. Stanford, CA: Stanford University Press.

———. 2003. *Humanism of the Other*. Urbana, Chicago: University of Illinois Press.
Manning, Robert John Sheffler. 1991. "Thinking the other without violence? An analysis of the relation between the philosophy of Emmanuel Levinas and feminism." *The Journal of Speculative Philosophy* 5, no. 2: 132–143.
Marshall, Jill. 2008. "Women's right to autonomy and identity in European Human Rights Law: Manifesting one's religion." *Res Publica* 14, no. 3: 177–192.
McDonald, Terrence T. 2018. "N.J. city shuts down burlesque show, citing obscenity laws." *The Jersey Journal*, 29 March 2018. https://www.nj.com/hudson/index.ssf/2018/03/jersey_city_shuts_down_burlesque_show_citing_obsce.html.
McRobbie, Angela. 2004. "Post-feminism and popular culture." *Feminist Media Studies* 4, no. 3: 255–264.
———. 2008. "Young women and consumer culture: An intervention." *Cultural Studies* 22, no. 5: 531–550.
———. 2011. "Beyond post-feminism." *Juncture* 18, no. 3: 179–184.
Meerschaut, Karen, and Serge Gutwirth. 2008. "Legal pluralism and Islam in the scales of the European Court of Human Rights: The limits of categorical balancing." In *Conflicts between Fundamental Rights*, edited by Eva Brems, 431–465. Antwerp: Intersentia.
Megarry, Jessica. 2017. "Under the watchful eyes of men: Theorising the implications of male surveillance practices for feminist activism on social media." *Feminist Media Studies*: 1–16. https://www.tandfonline.com/doi/full/10.1080/14680777.2017.1387584.
Morgan, Kathryn Pauly. 1991. "Women and the knife: Cosmetic surgery and the colonization of women's in bodies." *Hypatia* 6, no. 3, 25–53.
Motha, Stewart. 2007. "Veiled women and the affect of religion in democracy." *Journal of Law and Society* 34, no. 1: 139–162.
Okin, Susan Moller. 1999. *Is Multiculturalism Bad for Women?* Princeton, NJ: Princeton University Press.
Patterson, Laura. 2016. "Whiteness in contemporary feminist campaigns: Free the nipple." College of Arts & Sciences Senior Honours Theses, University of Louisville, Paper 100, 1–47.
Patton, Paul. 2005. "Deleuze and democracy." *Contemporary Political Theory* 4, no. 4: 400–413.
Philips, Anne, and Sawitri Saharso. 2008. "Guest editorial. The rights of women and the crisis of multiculturalismus." *Ethnicities* 8, no. 3: 291–301.
Rebouche, Rachel. 2008. "Substance of substantive equality: Gender equality and Turkey's headscarf debate." *The American University International Law Review* 24: 711–737.
Regehr, Kaitlyn. 2012. "The rise of recreational burlesque: Bumping and grinding towards empowerment." *Sexuality & Culture* 16, no. 2: 134–157.
Reuters. 2017. "Emma Watson on Vanity Fair cover: 'Feminism is about giving women choice'." *The Guardian*, March 6 2017. https://www.theguardian.com/film/2017/mar/05/emma-watson-vanity-fair-cover-feminism.
Rivers, Nicola. 2017. *Postfeminism(s) and the Arrival of the Fourth Wave: Turning Tides*. Cham: Palgrave Macmillan.
Rúdólfsdóttir, Annadís G., and Ásta Jóhannsdóttir. 2018. "Fuck patriarchy! An analysis of digital mainstream media discussion of the #freethenipple activities in Iceland in March 2015." *Feminism & Psychology* 28, no. 1: 133–151.
Sąhin v Turkey, European Court of Human Rights, Grand Chamber Judgment, Application no. 44774/98, 10 November 2005.

Sanders, Lise Shapiro. 2007. "Feminists love a Utopia." In *Third Wave Feminism*, edited by Stacey Gillis, Gillian Howie and Rebecca Munford, 3–15. London: Palgrave Macmillan.
S.A.S v France. 2014. European Court of Human Rights, Judgment, Application no. 43835/11, 1 July 2014.
Şefika Köse and 93 Others v Turkey, European Court of Human Rights, Decision, Application no. 26625/02, 24 January 2006.
Shorter, Edward. 2017. *Women's Bodies: A Social History of Women's Encounter with Health, Ill-health and Medicine*. Oxon, New York: Routledge.
Siebler, Kay. 2015. "What's so feminist about garters and bustiers? Neo-burlesque as post-feminist sexual liberation." *Journal of Gender Studies* 24, no. 5: 561–573.
Smith, Nick. 2009. "Questions for a reluctant jurisprudence of alterity." In *Essays on Levinas and Law: A Mosaic*, edited by Desmond Manderson. Basingstoke: Palgrave Macmillan.
Sonoku Tagami v City of Chicago et al., United States Court of Appeals, Seventh Circuit, No. 16–1441, 8 November 2017.
Stauffer, Emily. 2016. "Free the nipple: A white feminist movement." *Essay Contest 2017*. 1. https:ir/lib.uwo.ca/essay-contest-2017/1.
Steinfeld, Jemimah. 2017. "Uncovering the nipple cover-up: The battle to give the female nipple equal rights as one woman heads to the Supreme Court. Plus, a cut-out-and-keep male nipple for social media use." *Index on Censorship* 46, no. 3: 114–116.
Vakulenko, Anastasia. 2007. "'Islamic headscarves' and the European convention on human rights: An intersectional perspective." *Social & Legal Studies* 16, no. 2: 183–199.
Whisner, Mary. 1982. "Gender-specific clothing regulation: A study in patriarchy." *Harvard Women's Law Journal* 5: 73–120.
Williams, James. 2005. *The Transversal Thought of Gilles Deleuze: Encounters and Influences*. Manchester: Clinamen Press Ltd.
Wing, Adrien Katherine, and Monica Nigh Smith. 2006. "Critical race feminism lifts the veil? Muslim women, France, and the headscarf ban." *UC Davis Law Review* 39: 743–790.

3 Narratives of belonging

Religion, the gendered body, and claims of autonomy and authenticity

Kati Nieminen and Sanna Mustasaari

Introduction

Feminism is in constant movement. Since the late twentieth century, the concept of postfeminism has been used in many, often contradictory ways. Simplifying a complex matter, interpretations of postfeminism fall roughly in two categories: for some, postfeminism indicates a time after feminism, announcing 'if not the death then at least the redundancy of feminism' (Genz and Brabon 2009, 3). For others, postfeminism is another phase, or a wave, of feminism, a 'process of ongoing transformation', relating to postmodern, anti-foundationalist movements (Genz and Brabon 2009, 4; see also Brooks 1997, 1–4; Heilmann 2011). The evolution of feminism to postfeminism should not, however, be understood as a smooth transition from a previous phase to the next one on a continuum of linear progression. Rather, postfeminism breaks up any monolithic feminist thinking, reminding us of the fact that feminism has never had a universally accepted agenda. Thus, 'postfeminism encourages feminism to develop an understanding of its own historicity' (see Genz and Brabon 2009, 3–13, 112; Zalewski 2000, 31–32, 53).[1] In this chapter we attempt to do just that: to exercise feminist self-reflection and analyse the ways in which feminism may contribute to reifying a particular narrative of 'us'.

For us, postfeminism is an invitation to stay sensitive to questions such as whose interests claims of authenticity and autonomy promote, and to recognise that the question of power persists at the centre of feminist thought. Both the challenge and the political potential of postfeminism lies in its 'critical engagement with earlier feminist political and theoretical concepts and strategies' (Brooks 1997, 4). In this chapter we discuss postfeminism as a form of feminism that engages with two painful and yet invaluable postmodern lessons. There is no 'original' or 'authentic' subject from which the 'different' or the 'deviant' deviates, and that the universal, neutral, genderless, and colourless liberal subject of law is everything but. This realisation, still under-acknowledged, invites us to re-evaluate the seemingly self-evident in law. In this chapter we take this challenge seriously and turn the inspecting gaze, for a change, away from 'the Other' and questions such as to what extent pluralism should be tolerated or encouraged, towards the way the law participates in producing homogeneity among 'us'. We take postmodern feminism to acknowledge its own existence within and as part of narrative reality, which means that it admits the impossibility of making statements from any ahistorical, neutral, or objective perspective and that it recognises that it too takes part in the reproduction of our social world by producing stories of who we are.

We discuss how the autonomy and authenticity of 'us' as gendered and ethnic subjects are reproduced in two examples, which raise questions about religion, gender equality, and integration. The first situation is the discussion that followed the Swedish politician Yasri Khan's refusal to shake hands with a female journalist. The central question was the limits of acceptable difference in treatment of men and women in a rather personal area of conduct – the way a person may greet another. The issue was also about whether a different greetings based on gender constitutes inferior treatment, and thus an insult not only towards the specific woman in question (regardless of what she herself thinks about the issue), but towards all women. The second example is the recent European Court of Human Rights (EctHR) case *Osmanoğlu and Kocabaş v. Switzerland*[2] concerning Muslim parents' request that their daughters are exempted from mixed-gender swimming classes. The applicants were Muslim parents who wanted to have their daughters exempted from mixed swimming lessons, as attending them was against their religious convictions on modesty. According to the parents, the refusal to grant an exemption violated their freedom of religion as protected by Article 9 of the European Convention on Human Rights. Both examples illustrate the ways in which the cultural differences draw upon constructions of gendered and sexualised bodies.

Our aim is to challenge the taken-for-granted perspective of the Western legal subject, which evaluates the 'Other'. By studying the notions of 'authenticity' and 'autonomy' embedded in our examples, we seek to examine how postmodern feminist perspectives may contribute to making visible the ways in which 'us' and 'the Other' are produced in mundane, everyday practices and within the law. We approach our examples as narratives and ask how authenticity and autonomy are constructed in the narratives of belonging, which delineates the boundaries of the national community. Our examples illustrate how the imagined national communities (Anderson 2006) are being reproduced in 'narrative acts of self-definition', '[t]urning the scraps and patches of daily life into "signs of national culture"' (Bhabha 2002, 297).

Narratives may normalise chronologies and causality to such an extent that alternative narratives go unnoticed (Brooks and Gewirtz 1996, 17). In this process the law may play a crucial role, since, as Gilkerson (1992) argues, law as a social institution tells stories about people's relationships with others. The term 'narrative' can be understood in many ways, but here we use it in the sense of story; typically narratives position characters and events in space and time in order to make sense of events. Thus, according to Bamberg (2012, 77) 'narratives attempt to explain and normalize what has occurred; they lay out why things are the way they are or have become the way they are'. In the following we analyse the ways in which autonomy and authenticity are narrated in our two examples, and how these narratives construct gendered and ethnic subjectivities.

'In Sweden we shake hands'

In April 2016, a heated debate over greeting traditions occupied news media headlines in Sweden as Yasri Khan, a Green Party MP and candidate for the Central Committee, refused on religious grounds to shake hands with journalist Ann Tiberg in a television show. Instead of shaking hands Khan put his right hand on his heart and nodded his head. The leaders of Green Party condemned Khan's act, insisting that everyone should be treated equally in Sweden, and doubted his suitability for a position of trust due to his religious convictions. Khan later resigned from his post as an MP.

How should the meaning of a handshake be understood? Is it a question of personal autonomy and the right to draw one's physical boundaries or about acknowledging the other person's autonomy and equality? Or is it perhaps an innocuous and rather trivial matter of custom? We can construct two competing narratives about the meaning of the handshake, based on which concept of autonomy we assume. In the first narrative, Khan's refusal to shake hands with women is a signal of disrespect towards all women and is considered as utterly intolerable by the community, the 'us' in the Swedish public space. A comment made by Prime Minister Stefan Löfven captures this narrative: 'In Sweden, we shake hands, that goes for both women and men'. For Löfven, refusing to shake hands with a woman was disrespectful because it indicated that Khan did not regard women and men as having equal value.

Irrespective of Khan's intentions, or the experience of the individuals whom Khan greeted with this Islamic gesture, this narrative holds that treating women and men differently in this way violated the Swedish normative understanding of autonomy. By contrast, shaking hands recognises the autonomy of other individuals and signals gender equality.

What, then, was disrespectful in the gesture? Was the problem that women and men were being treated differently, and no gender-specific customs are acceptable (dress code, opening of doors, helping to carry bags etc.)? The debates did not appear to criticise Khan simply because he treated men and women differently. Rather, the problem seemed to be that his discomfort to shake hands with women drew a line between the genders in an inappropriate place. Khan broke the cultural code of how and where sexuality can be made visible or recognised in the public sphere of the nation. Refusing to greet women with a handshake sexualised what was regarded a culturally neutral way to greet people in Sweden. He was seen to impose a sexualised, corporeal identity on a Western, Swedish woman in a public place, who during the past decades had fought for – and accomplished – the right to present in the public sphere as a free and autonomous agent. This narrative illustrates how identities are constructed: the question of who has the right to define the proper code of conduct in the public sphere and what a gesture means becomes a struggle between identities – the Swedish, liberal 'we' and the foreign, barbarian, and backward 'Other'.

However, a counter-narrative can represent Khan's act as an expression of his own autonomy. Autonomy can be understood as granting individuals the right to define their own bodily limits and to choose the physical encounters they wish to engage with. Thus, Khan's choice should be respected. One could then conclude that his greeting gesture was respectful and in line with his own convictions, and that unwanted physical contact should not be imposed on anyone regardless of their gender.

A third narrative about authenticity can be reconstructed from the handshake debate. The heated discussion initiated by the brief encounter between Khan and Tiberg captures how the gesture became 'ethnified'. Ethnification refers to (in media and journalism studies) to a 'one sided dominant (…) focus on a person or group as an *ethnic Other*' emphasising their difference from a presumed 'us' (Eide 2010, 66). Ethnification results in members of ethnic minorities having a lesser national identity even if they have citizenship and/or have been born in the country (Friedman 1998, 236). Khan, despite having been elected as a representative of 'the people', faced a situation where his Swedishness was questioned by the single line from the Prime Minister: 'In Sweden we shake hands'. Thus, Khan's discomfort with shaking hands with women was contrasted with Swedishness. The gesture of placing one's hand on one's heart instead of shaking hands was not regarded as a mere greeting gesture, but as an indication of Khan's inauthenticity as a Swede and his inability to represent the Swedish people. The incontestable statement that 'in Sweden we shake hands' essentialises Swedishness as an identity category and illustrates the way in which identity can become a form of social control, policing the boundaries of 'Swedishness' (Phillips 2010, 5).

The handshake issue continues to be contentious in Sweden. As well as being discussed in the media, the handshake issue has also been debated in court. In 2010 Sweden's Discrimination Ombudsman (DO) won a case against the National Public Employment Agency, which was found guilty of discrimination for expelling a Muslim man from a job training programme and withdrawing his benefits because he refused to shake hands with women (Vinthagen Simpson 2010). More recently, the DO sued a company that cut a female applicant's job interview short when it became known that she would not shake hands for religious reasons (*The Local* 2017). A similar case decided by the Lund District Court in Sweden concerned a Muslim man who was dismissed by Helsingborg municipality for not shaking hands with his female colleagues (*The Local* 2016). The Court decided in favour of the Municipality because it did not find sufficient evidence to support neither direct nor indirect discrimination (Johansson 2017a, 2017b).

Not all 'handshake cases' make it to court: Another Swedish example concerns a teacher who decided to resign after she was told that she must shake hands with her colleagues if she wanted to continue working. Her male colleagues felt 'tremendously discriminated against by her', as instead of shaking hands, she would put her hand on her heart and bow (Roden 2016).

While above examples show that the handshake debate in Sweden has raised concerns over national identity and proper Swedishness, legally the question is still approached from the perspective of discrimination and minority rights. In Switzerland, on the other hand, similar cases are increasingly framed explicitly in terms of national identity and shared values. Swiss authorities have ruled that having a religious conviction is not a sufficient reason for refusing to shake hands with a teacher – a Swiss tradition allegedly signalling 'respect' and 'decency' (Basel Landschaft 2016; *The Guardian* 2016). The school's decision to grant an exemption for two teenage Muslim boys from shaking their teacher's hand was overruled by Swiss education authorities, according to whom 'The public interest with respect to equality between men and women and the integration of foreigners significantly outweighs the freedom of conscience of the students' (Samuels 2016). The boy's parents were fined, and the citizenship process of the family was suspended (*The Guardian* 2016).

What makes the 'handshake debate' interesting for the purpose of this chapter is that the apparently mundane gesture of shaking hands brings all sorts of messiness to the surface. It makes visible the ways in which the gendered body and sexuality are present in the everyday practices without them being noticed until something interrupts the steady flow of day-to-day life. The interruption, in this case, was rather insignificant: a gesture was replaced by another one. And yet, looked at from a postfeminist angle, it suddenly revealed that our everyday interactions are not as neutral as we thought and made visible the ways in which national identity and belonging are entangled with gendered and ethnified ideas about autonomy and authenticity.

'It is common in Switzerland to see partially nude bodies'

Our next example continues to explore the ways in which the everyday narratives of belonging are reiterated in institutional (legal) practices. We discuss the ECtHR case of *Osmanoğlu and Kocabaş* (2017) examining how the national identity is narrated in a legal setting.

Referring to their freedom of religion protected by the Article 9 of the Convention, the Swiss parents requested that their daughters be exempted from compulsory swimming lessons, as mixed swimming lessons were against their Islamic religious conviction relating to modesty. The Swiss authorities had refused the exemption stating that it could only be granted based on medical reasons or after reaching puberty – suggesting that at puberty female and male bodies become sexual bodies that can or should be separated from each other. As result, the applicants were fined for not allowing their daughters to participate in swimming lessons. The ECtHR (§94-106) found that the interference with the parents' freedom of religion was justified as its aim was to guarantee the pupils' socialisation and the public interest of general cohesion and integration of minorities. The Court accepted the Swiss government's assertion that the aim of the swimming lessons was not merely to teach the pupils to swim, but also to behave in line with the 'local customs and mores' (§97). As part of its proportionality test the Court took into account that the Swiss state had sought a fair balance by offering the applicants the option to wear burkinis (§101). Decisive in the case was the wide margin of appreciation concerning matters relating to the relationship between state and religion, and the significance to be given to religion in society (§105).

The concept of integration played a key role in the argumentation of the parties and of the ECtHR. *Osmanoğlu and Kocabaş* includes a summary (§28–30) laying out two key cases in Swiss case law. According to the summary, in 1993 the Swiss Federal Supreme Court examined the question of exemption from mixed swimming lessons for religious reasons. At that time, the Federal Supreme Court ruled that given the principle of proportionality, the education of children in accordance with the parents' religious convictions took precedence over the compulsory swimming lessons, particularly because swimming constituted only a small part of the teaching of sport. Regarding integration, the Federal Supreme Court considered that the duty of immigrants is limited to adhering to the Swiss law. At that time, it was decided that the parents were not required, in any legally meaningful way, to adapt to all local customs and practices. In 2008, however, the Federal Supreme Court 'amended its case law, having regard to the sharp increase in Switzerland's Muslim population' (*Osmanoğlu and Kocabaş* §29). Integration was now considered by the Swiss government and courts to mean something more profound than simply adhering to the Swiss laws.

According to D'Amato (2010, 137), in Switzerland the meaning of integration has been open to both a liberal and conservative interpretation. The liberal interpretation is that integration means encouraging immigrants to participate in mainstream society, while the conservative interpretation emphasises the need for mandatory and coercive measures. In 2003, a populist right wing Swiss People's Party (SVP) dramatically changed the way integration was understood in Swiss politics, and made way for new expectations for immigrants from outside of Europe, as well as new legal criteria they have to fulfil to facilitate their integration. According to D'Amato (2010, 139), the ultimate aim of the new integration paradigm is to restrict the number of immigrants outside of European Union/European Free Trade Association. The underlying idea is that these third country nationals have inherent deficits regarding their capacity to integrate to the Swiss society due to their culture, language, and religion. These developments indicate that 'integration has undergone a political ideologisation and securitisation' and transformed from 'a concept that includes emancipation, to a term that now comprises coercion and repression' (D'Amato 2010, 139). Can this shift in the way in which integration is understood in Switzerland be argued to have influenced the ruling of the Swiss Federal Supreme Court in 2008? It does appear that the logic of the government's argumentation was based on the implicit definition of integration as something that guards not only the national laws, but also the national values and customs – the national authenticity.

In *Osmanoğlu and Kocabaş* the Court did not address the applicants' argument that their children were primarily integrated outside of the swimming lessons, their religion being the only difference between them and the majority population. Most importantly, the Court did not engage with the applicants' claim that tolerance is an important part of integration, and that integration does not require homogeneity.[3] The Swiss government successfully established integration both as an interest of the Swiss society and as an individual right of the applicants' daughters. Thus the Court implicitly contrasted the rights of the parents and those of their children, so that the interests of the children and of the Swiss society were in line with each other. In the Court's own words, 'children's interest in an all-round education, facilitating their successful social integration according to local customs and mores, takes precedence over the parents' wish to have their daughters exempted from mixed swimming lessons' (§97).

The question remains, what explains the change in the way integration is now understood by the Swiss state? Reading the case *Osmanoğlu and Kocabaş* gives the impression that the decisive turn was the growing number of Muslim immigrants in Switzerland, resulting in more emphasis being placed on social cohesion and integration. The government directly referred to the fact that since 1993, 'the composition of the population had changed', as in 1990 there were 152,200 Muslims living in Switzerland, 310,000 in 2000, and in 2008 in estimation 400,000 (§69). According to the narrative reiterated in the ECtHR's ruling, in 2008 the Federal Court revised its previous case law in the light of the rapid increase in the Muslim population in Switzerland. The Federal Supreme Court now placed more weight on integration in the sense of respecting the local values and culture and decided that pupils attending mixed swimming classes was important from the perspective of socialisation and securing equal opportunities for girls and boys.

D'Amato's analysis helps to reconstruct an alternative narrative to the one that begins with the rising number of Muslims and ends with a greater emphasis on integration in the conservative sense, even assimilation. The alternative narrative begins with the outrage caused by the Federal Supreme Court's 1993 ruling allowing Muslim pupils to be exempted from mixed swimming lessons, and the rise of right-wing populism. According to D'Amato (2010, 140–141), an immediate reaction in Switzerland to the Federal Supreme Court's 1993 ruling was hostile:

> In a country in which the fear to be overrun by foreigners is deeply rooted in public discourse, a policy that allowed the recognition of differences was felt a provocation and turned out to be a red rug to right wing populist parties, inciting them to mobilise against liberal jurisdiction.

The rise of a conservative interpretation of integration can be seen as a natural effect of the rising number of the Muslim population – this was the government's storyline in *Osmanoğlu and Kocabaş*. However, it could also be understood as a result of right-wing populism. Thus, the question presented to the ECtHR could be framed in two completely different ways, steering the course of the Court's argumentation into two different paths: that of protecting the cohesion of the population (and therefore, ultimately, the democratic order) on the one hand, or that of protecting the minority rights and diversity (and therefore, ultimately, pluralism essential for the democratic order).

What looms in the background of the Court's argument is the threat of disintegration of the Swiss nation and its people. The applicants were unable to contest the underlying narrative of a threat to the authentic Swiss way of life due to the increasing Muslim population. Moreover, from the children's perspective, we argue that their own religion was narrated as a threat to their proper integration into the authentic Swissness and belonging in the Swiss community. In fact, the main subjects of *Osmanoğlu and Kocabaş*, the two children, are noticeably absent from the argumentation of the parties. They are present only through someone else's eyes: the parents', who fear that their children will be exposed to a sexualising gaze; and the government's, who denies the existence of such a gaze (or who insists that one must tolerate such a gaze?). The unquestioned line between the genders, for both parties, is drawn at puberty. The parents argued that despite the fact that their religion does not require the covering of the female body before puberty, they wanted to prepare their daughters for the requirements of their religion, and invoked their parental authority on the matter (2017 §45). Similarly, the government drew the line at the age of puberty, pointing out that the pupils could be exempted from mixed swimming lessons after reaching puberty (2017 §47). Both parties reproduce the idea that gender difference is linked to sexuality and corporeality, that sexuality begins at puberty, and that at that point, it is appropriate to separate girls and boys. Both parties also claim to have a say over the bodies of the children: the parents by referring to their parental authority over the girls, i.e. their autonomy as parents, and the state by assuming authority over the bodies of its subjects.

At the heart of the issue was, again, the body and the conflicting demands of covering and exposing it in the name of autonomy and authenticity. Both the parents and the state framed their concern over the children with reference to their future as authentic and autonomic members of communities. The parents wished to prepare the girls for becoming full members of their religion, whereas the state wanted to prepare them to be full members of the Swiss society. From the children's perspective, both autonomy and authenticity were something that they may or may not grow into in the future, depending on the success of their integration into their religious or in the nation-state communities. From the state's perspective integration required freeing the children from their religious background, which was regarded as a hindrance to full integration and belonging. But what was it exactly that made swimming lessons essential from the perspective of integration? The Court did not discuss this point explicitly, but the government pointed out that 'partially dressed bodies were frequently to be seen in Switzerland' for example on the beach or in the media, and that it is therefore 'all the more important that children learned from an early age to handle this aspect of communal life, in order to facilitate their development in society' (*Osmanoğlu and Kocabaş* §77).

The narratives of belonging fleshed out above squarely raise the question of intersectionality. For some time now intersectional feminism has invited us to recognise the myriad ways in which race, gender, class, and sexuality shape the experience of individuals, and that anti-discrimination laws are often insufficient for capturing the lived experience of people (see Conaghan 2009; Crenshaw 1989; Nash 2008).

While intersectional and postmodern feminism have a lot of common ground in terms of epistemology and their approach to power and knowledge, postmodern feminism rejects the notion of historically shared, group-based experience and instead 'deconstructs all group categories as essentialist' (Mann 2013, 64). Thus, it would be a mistake to try to capture the lived experience of any group of people, such as for instance Muslims living in Switzerland. As white Western feminists, we are unable to say much about their experience anyway. What we can do, however, relates to the second question raised by the narratives discussed above: *Osmanoğlu and Kocabaş* invites us to consider the way in which national identity is constructed in relation to 'the Other'. Our postfeminist reading of the case, sceptical of any cemented yet often implicit notions of autonomy and authenticity, makes once again visible those aspects of 'us' that are coercive and othering, and embedded in particular notions of autonomy and authenticity.

Conclusion

How might a postfeminist approach unsettle the narrative of 'us' reproduced in the law and legal practices, as well as in national 'debates' over religious customs and symbols? In this chapter we have discussed the handshake controversy and the litigation over compulsory mixed swimming lessons. We argued that they are examples of the ways in which narratives of belonging contribute to boundary maintenance between 'us' and 'the Other', by asserting specific notions of authenticity and autonomy. As our examples illustrate, the notions of autonomy and authenticity are embedded at the intersection of ethnified and gendered subjects, and therefore it is important to stay alert to the ways in which feminist rhetoric may contribute to reifying a particular narrative of 'us'. This is where critical self-reflection of (post)feminist thinking is needed. Postfeminist wariness of any intransigent conceptions of authenticity, autonomy, gender, equality, etc. allows resistance towards essentialising notions of 'us'.

Yasri Khan's authenticity as Swedish, and his ability to represent the 'Swedish people' was questioned because his greeting gesture was perceived as incompatible with authentic Swedishness. Thus, the debate brought to surface the otherwise invisible boundaries of the people of a nation. Along with authenticity, autonomy played a key role in the debate over the handshake. The reason Khan faced such an amount of opposition was that the refusal to shake hands with women was interpreted as a denial of women as autonomous subjects, and because by showing discomfort with touching a woman's hand, Khan sexualised a 'neutral' gesture of shaking hands.

Regarding the role the concept of integration played in the case of *Osmanoğlu and Kocabaş* we argued that the Court uncritically reiterated the government's narrative of belonging, in which the growing number of Muslims resulted in the need to emphasise the minority's duty to adhere not only to the Swiss law, but also its customs, values, and way of life. The narrative of a growing Muslim population threatening Swiss society reproduces the authenticity of 'us' (the Swiss), the inauthenticity of 'the Other' (Muslims). This narrative reproduces the idea that members of the society can be truly autonomous as individuals only when they are 'authentic' – Muslims, whether they have citizenship and whether they have been born into said society, remain 'the Other'. The autonomy, then, is granted to 'the people', who reproduce the authenticity of the nation, including the nation's norms concerning gender and sexuality.

The question remains, how would the European Court of Human Rights rule on a handshake case? The margin of appreciation doctrine would most likely have a decisive role in such a case. The doctrine has attracted criticism, particularly in cases concerning the relationship between national values and freedom of religion. Some aspects of the Court's approach suggest that the Court would be likely to favour the Government's assertion of what is 'necessary in a democratic society' (European Convention of Human Rights Article 9.2). In some cases, this has resulted effectively in protecting the majority's alleged perceptions and sentiments over the freedom of religion of minorities. For example, in *S.A.S. v. France*[4] concerning the ban on full-face veils in public, the Court asserted, referring to veiled Muslim women, that 'individuals who are present in places open to all may not wish to see practices or attitudes developing there which would fundamentally call into question the possibility of open interpersonal relationships (...)' (§122). Thus the problem identified by the Court was not so much the practical aspect of the veil complicating interpersonal interaction, but rather the 'attitude' against such interaction, that wearing a full-face veil allegedly communicates. Similar tendencies to address arguments drawing from national values and customs can be identified in *Osmanoğlu and Kocabaş*. Thus, it is not farfetched to predict that in a handshake case the Court would be inclined to consider a handshake as part of the 'minimum requirements of life in society' (*S.A.S. v. France* §140–141) or crucial for 'successful integration' (*Osmanoğlu and Kocabaş* §105), if the responding government would so argue.

In practical terms, a postfeminist approach to legal analysis can be useful for making visible the ways in which law reifies a particular notion of 'us'. A postfeminist reading of the (legal) narratives of belonging allows critical assessment of the underlying, seemingly self-evident conceptions that uphold ethnification and exclusion. The challenge to feminism is to stay alert to the appropriation of feminism, for example, for Islamophobic purposes. The examples discussed in this chapter invite us to stay self-reflective to the ways in which power relations are reproduced in feminist discourses, and to the ways in which autonomy and authenticity are constructed in them. This means that we take postmodern feminism to acknowledge its own existence within and as part of narrative reality.

Notes

1 For example, the question of what role feminist scholarship has played and still plays in reproducing heterosexism, racism, and Eurocentrism, has been addressed by queer theorists and postcolonial feminists.
2 10 January 2017, application no. 29086/12.

3 For comparison, it is interesting to note that in *S.A.S. v. France* (App. No.43835/11 2014) concerning the full-face veil ban, the applicant contested the idea that reciprocal exposure of faces is fundamental in the French society because not all minorities shared this view. In other words, implicit in her argument was the idea that minorities who do not share the view that reciprocal exposure of faces is fundamental in France, are an integral and inseparable part of the French society and that therefore it is not factually true that revealing of the face is considered fundamental by the society. The Court did not address this argument.

4 1 July 2014, application no. 43835/11.

References

Anderson, Benedict. 2006. *Imagined Communities: Reflections on the Origin and Spread of Nationalism*. London: Verso.

Bamberg, Michael. 2012. "Narrative Analysis." In *APA Handbook of Research Methods in Psychology: Volume 3, Data Analysis and Research Publication*, edited by Harris M. Cooper, Paul M. Camic, Debra L. Long, A.T. Panter, David Rindskopf, and Kenneth J. Sher, 85–102. Washington, DC: American Psychological Association.

Basel Landschaft. 2016. "Der Handschlag an Schulen wird durchgesetzt – ohne Wenn und Aber." September 19 2016. www.baselland.ch/politik-und-behorden/direktionen/bildungs-kultur-und-sportdirektion/medienmitteilungen/der-handschlag-an-schulen-wird-durchgesetzt-ohne-wenn-und-aber.

Bhabha, Homi K. 2002. "DissemiNation: Time, Narrative, and the Margins of the Modern Nation." In *Nation and Narration*, edited by Homi K. Bhabha, 291–322. London, New York: Routledge.

Brooks, Ann. 1997. *Postfeminisms: Feminism, Cultural Theory, and Cultural Forms*. London: Routledge.

Brooks, Peter, and Paul Gewirtz. 1996. *Law's Stories: Narrative and Rhetoric in the Law*. Ann Arbor: University of Michigan Press.

Conaghan, Joanne. 2009. "Intersectionality and the Feminist Project in Law." In *Intersectionality and Beyond: Law, Power and the Politics of Location. Intersectionality and Law*, edited by Davina Cooper, 21–48. Cavendish, London: Routledge.

Crenshaw, Kimberle. 1989. "Demarginalizing the Intersection of Race and Sex: A Black Feminist Critique of Antidiscrimination." *University of Chicago Legal Forum* 1: 139–167.

D'Amato, Gianni. 2010. "Switzerland: A Multicultural Country without Multicultural Policies?" In *The Multiculturalism Backlash: European Discourses, Policies and Practices*, edited by Steven Vertovec and Susanne Wessendorf, 130–151. London: Routledge.

Eide, Elisabeth. 2010. "Strategic Essentialism and Ethnification." *Nordicom Review* 3, no. 2: 63–78.

Friedman, Jonathan. 1998. "Transnationalization, Socio-political Disorder, and Ethnification as Expressions of Declining Global Hegemony." *International Political Science Review* 19, no. 3: 233–250.

Genz, Stéphanie, and Benjamin A. Brabon. 2009. *Postfeminism: Cultural Texts and Theories*. Edinburgh: Edinburgh University Press.

Gilkerson, Christopher P. 1992. "Poverty Law Narratives: The Critical Practice and Theory of Receiving and Translating Client Stories (Theoretics of Practice: The Integration of Progressive Thought and Action)." *Hastings Law Journal* 43, no. 4: 861–945.

The Guardian. 2016. "Swiss Halt Muslim Family's Citizenship Process after Refusal to Shake Hands." April 19 2016. www.theguardian.com/world/2016/apr/19/switzerland-suspends-citizenship-process-muslim-family.

Heilmann, Ann. 2011. "Gender and Essentialism: Feminist Debates in the Twenty-first Century." *Critical Quarterly* 53, no. 4: 78–89.

Johansson, Yvonne. 2017a. "Ny dom ger ingen svar – måste man ta kollegor i hand?" *Helsingborg*, April 10. www.hd.se/2017-04-10/ny-dom-ger-ingen-svar-maste-man-ta-kollegor-i-hand.

———. 2017b. "Man som vägrade skaka hand blev inte diskriminerad när han inte fick förlängt jobb." *Helsingborg*, April 10 2017. www.hd.se/2017-04-10/man-som-vagrade-skaka-hand-blev-inte-diskriminerad.

The Local. 2016. "Muslim Man Fired for Not Shaking Women's Hands" July 22 2016. www.thelocal.se/20160722/muslim-man-sues-over-handshake.

———. 2017. "Swedish Company Sued in Handshaking Row" April 3 2017. www.thelocal.se/20170403/swedish-company-sued-in-handshaking-row.

Mann, Susan Archer. 2013. "Third Wave Feminism's Unhappy Marriage of Poststructuralism and Intersectionality Theory." *Journal of Feminist Scholarship* 4: 54–73.

Nash, Jennifer. 2008. "Re-thinking Intersectionality." *Feminist Review* 89: 1–15.

Phillips, Anne. 2010. "What's Wrong with Essentialism?" *Distinktion: Scandinavian Journal of Social Theory* 11, no. 1: 47–60.

Roden, Lee. 2016. "Handshaking Row Causes Swedish Teacher to Leave Job." *The Local*, September 22 2016. www.thelocal.se/20160922/handshaking-row-causes-swedish-teacher-to-leave-school.

Samuels, Gabriel. 2016. "Muslim Schoolboys Who Refused to Shake Hands with Female Teachers Lose Appeal." *Independent*, September 21 2016. www.independent.co.uk/news/world/europe/muslim-schoolboys-handshake-female-teacher-refuse-appeal-lose-a7319986.html.

Vinthagen Simpson, Peter. 2010. "Job Agency Accepts 'Muslim Handshake' Fine." *The Local*, March 3 2010. www.thelocal.se/20100303/25320.

Zalewski, Marysia. 2000. *Feminism after Postmodernism: Theorising Through Practice*. London: Routledge.

Part II

The politics of law reform

4 Feminism and its absence in Pakistani legal discourse

Maliha Zia[1]

Introduction

Two recent incidents highlight the different approaches to feminism in current-day Pakistan.

In a recent interview, two well-known female actresses of Pakistan, Sanam Saeed and Amina Sheikh, were asked if they were feminists. Amina immediately laughed and stated that she had been criticised because she had always said she was not a feminist. Saeed asked 'What is a feminist?'. She then stated that if feminism was about fighting for women's rights, then she was a feminist. However, she went on to explain that she did not believe that men and women were equal and therefore others thought that she was not a feminist. Amina commented about feminism that 'the term has been so misused which is why we are confused'. Concluding, the host stated 'So basically you don't want to typecast yourself, don't want to pigeon-holed [sic] yourself' (Saeed & Sheikh 2018). Interestingly, in an earlier interview, Saeed had explicitly stated that men and women were equal and should have equal rights, but that she did not approve of 'men-hating, bra-burning and growing body hair as acts of feminism' (Nayeem 2018).

On 8 March 2018, the Hum Auretein Collective organised an Aurat (Women's) March to highlight several women's issues. Posters and banners were displayed with phrases such as 'Paratha[2] rolls not gender roles', 'Heat your own food' (translated), and 'Stop being menstrual-phobic' (*Dawn* 2018). The demands made at the Aurat March included an end to violence, reproductive justice for women and other sexual minorities, the recognition of all labourers, protection from sexual harassment in the workplace, and environmental and economic justice for all (Mushtaq 2018).

These incidents evidence the contradictory stances that women and girls have towards feminism in today's Pakistan. In the first incident, both actresses distanced themselves from feminism while recognising the feminist principle of equality. The second incident demonstrates a celebration of feminism, and the acceptance of core feminist principles, which challenge gender roles, patriarchy, and the gendered status quo. The contrasting approaches are indicative of the contradictions within the Pakistani feminist movement.

What is postfeminism and does it have any relevance in Pakistan? This chapter seeks to analyse the evolution of feminism within the developing, Islamic country of Pakistan and asks what role, if any, does postfeminism play? This chapter unpacks the situation of the Pakistani women's rights movement within the framework of feminism and feminist legal theory. It assesses the status of feminism and the relevance of postfeminism in Pakistan.

First, I will provide an outline of the theory of postfeminism that will be used for the purposes of this chapter. I then summarise the socio-political environment in Pakistan with specific reference to the status of women and the impact of 'Islamization'. This summary contextualises the discussion to follow. I will then look at the emergence of the feminist movement in Pakistan and current feminist ideologies. Lastly, I will examine the role of feminist legal theory, use of feminist legal strategies, and assess the relevance and place of postfeminism in Pakistan today.

Framing 'postfeminism'

Postfeminism discourses are contradictory in nature and contain both feminist and anti-feminist themes within its rhetoric. Whelehan remarks that while postfeminism may use 'feminist sentiments to justify certain behaviours or choices' (Whelehan 2010, 156), these sentiments no longer have links to 'their political or philosophical origins'. Gill states, 'In this postfeminist moment … feminist ideas are simultaneously incorporated, revised and depoliticised, and, I would add, attacked' (Gill 2007, 167).

Despite not having a clear definition, there are a number of core concepts that are linked to postfeminism. This includes a focus on the individual as opposed to the community. Adriaens and Van Bauwel posit that this is a 'logical consequence of our postmodern society that stands for neoliberalism and capitalism' (Adriaens & Van Bauwel 2014, 186). Thus, 'it is up to individual women to make personal choices that simply reinforce those fundamental societal changes' (Orr 1997, 34). Personal choices for women include whether to stay at home for her family or have a career (Lancioni 2006). Adriaens and Van Bauwel state that:

> Postfeminism can be conceptualized as a new form of empowerment or subjectivity, adjusted to the actual societal context. Agency, freedom, sexual pleasure, fashion, consumer culture, hybridism, humor, and the renewed focus on the female body are the elements of this new feminism. Postfeminists are considered to be sexual activists who use their body and attractiveness as an instrument to achieve societal and personal change.
>
> (Adriaens & Van Bauwel 2014, 192)

Based on the principle of personal choice, postfeminism identifies sexual pleasure and fun as critical resistance. This establishes a link between feminism and femininity, without losing integrity, as these women are exercising their choice as opposed to being exploited for their sexuality (Genz 2006; Adriaens 2009). Postfeminism not only posits that feminist struggles are outdated, it also emphasises 'how undesirable feminists themselves [are]'. That is, feminism is undesirable because it is about 'man-bashing bra-burners, created by the sexist forces in the media, and images of feminists as stereotypical second wavers who haven't changed in thirty years' (Kisner 2004, 135).

Adriaens and Van Bauwel have consolidated the arguments against postfeminism into three main critiques (Adriaens & Van Bauwel 2014, 174–195). First, postfeminists focus on the individual as opposed to feminist universal action and reject the gains made by feminism. For instance, Modleski (1991, 3) believes that rejecting the gains of the earlier feminist movement will have the effect of delivering us back into a prefeminist world. Second, postfeminism in popular culture and the media is another patriarchal tool. It is linked with male-owned, patriarchal companies who use postfeminism as a moneymaking gimmick. The third critique is that it is an anti-feminist narrative that undermines the 'merits of feminism' (Faludi 1991).

In assessing the relevance of postfeminism in Pakistan, it is necessary to understand the local paradigm. The political and social context of Pakistan includes Islam, culture, and patriarchy, and how feminism has operated within it. This chapter looks at the socio-political and Islamization of the state and society in Pakistan and its impact, before examining the role of feminism within this framework. The chapter will then unpack strategies used in Pakistan for advancing women's issues within the legal feminist framework.

Feminism in Pakistan

Pakistani feminism cannot be analysed within the schemas and waves of Western feminism. As Zia states, the debates in Pakistani feminist circles have focused on developing an 'indigenous feminist discourse' based on local realities and challenges (Zia 2018, 31). This section will briefly outline some important contextual factors that influence the status of women in Pakistan, before analysing the emergence of Pakistani feminism.

Socio-political environment and the status of women in Pakistan

Feminism in Pakistan developed within a distinct and complicated socio-political environment, including its unique politics, culture, religion, and history.

Gender roles are constructed through traditional social values based on women's ability to reproduce (Critelli 2012). In Pakistan, a woman is known through her relationship to men, which shifts over the course of her life, i.e. the roles of daughter, wife, and mother. These defining relationships result in the 'ownership' of women by men (Lari 2011, 19). This creates a normative framework where men have control over women's lives, using power and violence (Ibid). It allows men to set the standards within which women are 'allowed' to function. These frameworks control women's behaviour, mobility, control over resources, finances, and reproductive choices (Babur 2007), as well as sexuality (Lari 2011, 19). A woman's autonomy is further undermined by additional vulnerabilities, which may include caste, age, religion, region, and marital status.

Religion and culture play a key role in the perception and treatment of women in Pakistani society. Due to the deeply entrenched cultural and conservative religious structures, there is 'a distinct way in which gender issues are conflated with religious beliefs in Pakistani public discourse that often results in deeply disturbing rhetoric about women being tolerated and accepted as religious fact' (Rashid 2017).

Politics in Pakistan has not only contributed to the emphasis placed on religion and culture but has also exacerbated it. Pakistan has been a politically insecure state due to a constant barrage of domestic political upheavals resulting from the oscillation between democracy and military rule, as well as from regional and international confrontations (Khan 2013; Ahmed & Khan 2016). Religion has been strategically used for political aims as a defining 'ideology' of Pakistan, creating a 'Muslim' state (Chengappa 2001). Political leaders, including democratic leaders such as Zulfikar Ali Bhutto, and military dictators such as General Zia ul Haq have used the rhetoric of Islam either to seek legitimacy for their reigns or for popularity (Saigol 2016, 14). General Zia's regime (1977–1988) undertook an 'Islamization' process, which effectively criminalised the idea of a secular state.

Mixing religion and politics has created space for religious groups and religio-political parties to have a disproportionate influence on society, with long-lasting impacts particularly on women (Zia 2009, 30). Women are now seen as the repositories of culture, religion, and tradition, and those who discriminate against and commit violence towards women are demonised. The impact of General Zia's policies of Islamization has extended beyond society to state institutions including the legal system and judiciary. As a result, notions of the rule of law are derived from, and determined by, diverse and sometimes mutually exclusive jurisprudential standpoints including Anglo-Saxon Common Law, Islamic law (*Shariat*), and tribal/customary laws. These plural jurisprudences make Pakistan an arena of struggle between different and competing bodies of laws and bodies with different notions of the rule of law.

A history of the women's movement in Pakistan

While feminism in Pakistan has developed within the larger women's movement, it would be inaccurate to state that the women's rights movement in Pakistan was built only on feminist ideology and principles. The women's movement, within which today's feminist movements in Pakistan have evolved, can be identified as having three indigenous waves.

The first wave of the women's movement occurred in the nationalist struggle for Pakistan, and immediately after independence in 1947, where women primarily argued for the prioritisation of personal laws and a basic right to services (Zia 2018, 27).

The second wave occurred in the 1980s and 1990s, where the women's movement challenged the dictatorship of General Zia and his anti-women policies (Zia 2018, 27). At that time, there were only a handful of women who self-identified as 'feminists' or had exposure to 'feminism' (Saigol 2016, 14). They belonged to the urban middle class, and most of them had studied in Western universities. These women became some of the early founders and leaders of the infamous Women's Action Forum (WAF).[3] WAF emerged as one of the leading organisations in the struggle against the Zia regime and became the face of the women's movement in Pakistan for the next decade (Saigol 2016, 15). While other feminist groups did emerge, they did not achieve the same national stature as WAF for a variety of reasons. For example, the Sindhiani Tehreek movement was restricted due to its geographic limitations (Ibid). WAF provided (and still does) leadership on identifying issues and formulating feminist demands. Many of the women in WAF also were leaders of other different civil society groups and bodies. These wider groups became part of the women's movement and adopted WAF's political and legal agenda, albeit without many groups having an understanding of WAF's ideological and feminist underpinnings.

Shaheed identifies this second wave as having two phases (Shaheed 2010, 6). First, 'a period of intensely publicly visible activism' (Ibid), which was reactive to restricting and rescinding of women's rights and spaces as a result of General Zia's oppressive regime of 'Islamization'. And then a second, 'more diffused movement' from the 1990s onwards (Ibid), which saw the restoration of democracy for a relatively longer period, however flawed.[4] The second phase allowed for 'better negotiation, less confrontational tactics and greater engagement with the international arenas' (Ibid). This period also resulted in the proliferation of non-governmental organisations (NGOs) and the initiation of the 'commercialisation' of the women's movement (Saigol 2016, 21). Large numbers of people joined NGOs as a career and for the income, as opposed to joining as a commitment to an ideological struggle. This harmed the feminist movement as these workers gave up on advocating for the essential principles of feminism and equality for women (Saigol 2016, 23).

The third wave appeared post 9/11, when the women's movement across Pakistan once again grappled with notions of religious identity. Post 9/11 has seen a rise in scholarship (mostly by Pakistani diaspora living abroad) advocating for 'a religious citizenship as a viable alternative to liberal feminism' (Zia 2018, 8). This scholarship attempts to 'de-link liberal/secular feminism from the Muslim context in order to argue for the recovery of postsecularist, postfeminist and certainly, non-liberal re-consideration of Muslim women's subjectivities, experiences and even rights' (Zia 2018, 38). What is missing from this scholarship, however, is the narrative of the secular feminist movements in Pakistan and the lack of recognition of its role in the development of women's empowerment within the country (Zia 2018, 2).

In recent years, feminism expressed by younger feminist groups seem to share similarities with Western postmodernism, i.e. as they challenge the universalism of concepts such as knowledge, justice, and beauty (Parpart 1993,

439). They argue that these narratives reflect a reality 'embedded in the specific historical time and place in which they were created and are associated with certain political baggage' (Parpart 1993, 434). Thus, they recognise the differences between women, as opposed to the generalist universalism of women. These groups include collectives such as Girls at Dhabas, The Feminist Collective (which identifies itself as a leftist feminist group), and the Hum Aurtein Collective. These collectives acknowledge the work of the older generation but take their protests to other sites, primarily the social media, and where necessary, the streets.

Thus, in the Pakistani context, while there is a vibrant women's movement based on equality and non-discrimination for women, it cannot be said that there is an overarching feminist movement. Pakistani women who have identified themselves as feminist from the 1980s have been inclined to agree with this observation (Shaheed 2010, 4). It may therefore be more accurate to state that feminism in Pakistan has primarily flourished within the women's movement (Shaheed 2010, 5).

Current Pakistani 'feminist' movements and legal projects

While there has been little theorisation of contemporary feminism in Pakistan, there are primarily two different ideological movements. The two movements are secular liberal feminism (SLF) and modern Islamic feminism (Serez 2017, 62). These two movements emerge from the historical relationship with, and challenge to, religion in an Islamic country.

Secular liberal feminism

Secular liberal feminists believe in the strict separation between state and religion. That is, religion should not impact state laws, policies, institutions, and services. Essentially 'religious privilege must not influence government' (Zia 2017). Secular feminists argue that Pakistan has multiple realities including ethnicity, class, caste, gender, linguistic, and regional identities. Islam is one of those realities, not the sole or primary identity (Saigol 2016, 16).

SLF advocates for women's rights by using the human rights discourse (Jalal 1991; Khan 1994; Moghadam 1994, 2002, 2003; Shahidian 1994; Jilani 1998). It views feminism as an extension of universal human rights (Serez 2017, 64) and uses concepts such as nationality, as well as gender-neutral notions about privileges, diversity of the public domain, equality, and justice. SLF looks at 'structural and legal factors to explain the status of women' (Zia 2018, 24). To achieve equality and universal human rights, they strongly believe in the need for secular democracy (Ahmed-Ghosh 2008, 106).

SLF is often criticised by opponents as being imposed by the West and subscribing to anti-religious, cultural, and moral values (Ahmed-Ghosh 2008, 107). Serez also notes that SLF may exclude 'people who value the teachings of the

Qu'ran, primarily the lower, middle and upper-middle strata of society' (Serez 2017, 65). Thus, as Jalal declares, it is a 'convenience of subservience' catering primarily to elite and upper-class women (Jalal 1991). For example, SLF tends to exclude women in lower-economic classes because those women usually have close religious associations, and results in a lack of buy-in by those classes (Shaheed 2002, 378; Zia 2009).

However, its proponents state that the theory is fluid enough to allow for a construction of a human rights discourse 'within a culturally and politically appropriate setting, without imposing western ideals and values' (Ahmed-Ghosh 2008, 107).

Modern Islamic feminism

Modern Islamic feminism works within the Islamic framework for the recognition of women's rights by asking men to uphold the rights and responsibilities of women as provided in the Quran[5] (Badran 2001; Serez 2017). In contrast with secular feminism, which arguably developed as a social movement, Islamic feminism emerged out academic discourse (Badran 2011). Modern Islamic feminism identifies religion as the core characteristic of people.

Islamic feminists differentiate between religion, customs, and culture. While they challenge anti-women customs and practices, they do so within a religious framework. They identify certain customs (such as honour killings) as un-Islamic and falsely justified under religion. However, Islamic feminists do not challenge the religion itself as being patriarchal (Zia 2009). These feminists do not blame Pakistan's Sharia laws for discrimination against women, but instead blame men and patriarchal traditions (Serez 2017, 64). They posit that the Quran is not the problem, but the patriarchal interpretations of it (Ibid). Thus, they seek to carry out reinterpretations of the Quran and other religious texts, with the objective of 'detangling outmoded cultural ideas and patriarchal practices from what are considered to be the authentic Quranic norms and divine messages of revelation' (Zia 2018, 19). Rashid identifies several NGOs and women in Pakistan as 'Islamic modernists' (Rashid 2006), including Riffat Husain and Farida Shaheed. These women have had success in the use of modern interpretations of the Quran and religion to advocate for women's rights.

The movement is not without its detractors. Critiques of Islamic feminism say that there is a 'disconnect in the discourse on women's status in Islam with the reality of Muslim women's lives' (Ahmed-Ghosh 2008, 104). They argue that Islamic feminism does not engage with the discussion about whether the rights of Muslim women are unconditionally equal to men's (Zia 2018, 22). It therefore does not challenge 'the patriarchal obstacles directly' (Zia 2018, 33). Further, Badran argues that secular feminism is more inclusive than Islamic feminism because SLF allows the rights of both Muslims and non-Muslims to be considered, whereas Islamic feminism is exclusionary and ignores the issues faced by non-Muslims (Badran 2001).

Feminist legal projects

Both the women's and feminist movements in Pakistan have been engaged with the law since the 1970s, when they challenged General Zia's discriminatory and anti-women laws. Interestingly, this was one time when women from many different groups, including those now identifiable as Islamic feminists and SLF, came together to challenge General Zia's discriminatory laws, resulting in successful collective action. A core focus for the women's movement has been on the law, largely because of the involvement of several lawyers in the early leadership of WAF including Asma Jahangir, Hina Jillani, and Shahla Zia.

Both feminist movements have critically engaged with the law. Secular feminists have highlighted the 'masculinity of the law' and the lack of response to women's issues. In the Pakistani context, the power holders are male who have had the most influence on the law, basing it on 'male conceptions of problems and harm' (Zia, Mirza & Ahmad 2015, 72). The absence of women in the superior courts, and a fluctuating and minority representation of women in early years of formulating laws, has resulted in laws that embody 'men's understanding of women, women's nature, their experiences, and capacities, as opposed to women's definitions [informing] law and legal language' (Ibid).

> The demolition of the myth of neutrality of laws has increased the awareness of how laws help in sustaining the unequal power relations between men and women, from the fundamental level of the family to the highest levels of decision-making.
>
> (Mahbub ul Haq Human Development Centre 2000, 76)

The male perspective influences the content and interpretation of the law. For example, the definition of rape only refers to penile rape on a female vagina (Zaman & Zia 2013),[6] which reflects a man's perspective. The definition does not include anal and oral rape, which feminists argue should be included in the definition of rape (Amnesty International 2011). Feminists have extensively discussed this 'male dominance' and its impact on women, society, and law (Zia 2001; Lari 2011; Zia & Zaman 2011; Zaman & Zia 2013; Zaman 2014; Qaisrani, Liaquat & Khokhar, 2016).

The male perspective is also reflected in case law, which emphasises distinct gender roles, particularly within the family, based on Islamic and patriarchal principles. For example, the Federal Shariat Court's judgement in *Malik Tanveer Khan vs. Amber Liaqat* 2009 CLC 1210 held that a woman seeking a divorce was considered not to be 'obedient' and was told not to be a 'fault finder, malignant critic', and instead to protect her husband's privacy and provide 'cover' to his 'shortcomings and secrets'. In particular, it was noted that 'in Islam it is binding upon the wife to guard the secrets of her husband' (2009 CLC 1210, para 13). Due to such interpretations, the emerging case law continues to emphasise the importance of protecting women who are 'the weaker segment of society' (2017 MLD 1567 Lahore High Court) and must be given 'preferential treatment' (2011 CLC 1498 Lahore High Court). However, the unwritten caveat is that this protection is available, as long as she fulfils her expected gender role (Zaman 2014; Zaman & Zia 2018 Qureshi 2018).

Although not explicitly, Islamic feminism also engages with the law in Pakistan. In particular, their influence can be observed in how judges interpret and respond to cases involving women using Islamic arguments as evidence and support. For example, in the judgement of *Mukhtar Ahmad Shaikh vs. Government of Pakistan* PLD 2009 65, the Federal Shariat concludes that Section 151(4) of the Evidence Act 1984[7] is discriminatory. Section 151(4) states that in case of rape or attempted rape, it is relevant that the 'prosecutrix was of generally immoral character'. This allows for a female victim's history to be used to discredit her. In Shaik, the court held that the section

> is discriminatory on the basis of sex and violates Article 25(C) of the Constitution as it purports to impeach the credit of a woman, and above all it negates the concept of 'gender equality' as enshrined in the Holy Quran.
>
> (para 10)

The court instructed the government to repeal it. The court based its arguments on Islamic principles stating, 'We are of the view that a woman is placed in a more exalted and respected position than a man in Islam' (para 6) and that

> The Holy Qur'an places women on a much higher pedestal than ever known in any society. She is not considered as an agent of devil nor treated as a chattel in Islam. She has all the property rights. She has similar rights as of man in matters of marriage and divorce. The penal laws of Islam treat her equally with man.
>
> (para 8)

In spite of their differences, there is some consensus between the two feminist movements about strategies to use to engage with the law. Bartlett identifies that these strategies can be roughly divided into three common overarching methods: asking the 'woman' question, feminist practical reasoning, and consciousness-raising (Bartlett 1990).

Of these three methods, 'asking the woman' question (Clougherty 1996) is a key strategy used to question existing laws and to inform the drafting of laws.[8] This method was employed to challenge the Zina Ordinance 1979, purportedly passed for the protection of women. Both feminist movements highlighted the long-term negative impact of these laws on various aspects of women's lives, including its use as a controlling mechanism over women. After the amendment to the Zina Ordinance 1979, identifying bias in the law has remained a crucial element in both feminist movements, particularly of the SLF, as evidenced by several research reports (Commission of Inquiry for Women 1997; Zia & Butt 2012). Islamic feminism has based its arguments on different and more liberal interpretations of the Quran and other religious sources, emphasising the religious protections available to women.

Both Pakistani feminist movements have critiqued the law, its implementation, and women's experience in the justice sector time and again over the years (Zia 1998; Khan & Zaman 2012; Zaman & Zia 2013; Zaman 2014). However, it is the SLF which has successfully advocated for the passage of laws on human rights standards under Article 25 of the Constitution, which allows for special laws to be passed for women and children. Islamic feminists have supported SLF where it has been consistent with Islamic arguments. Thus, the activities of the feminist movements have resulted in the passage of pro-women legislation based on the principles of formal equality. Laws have been passed addressing several issues including sexual harassment, honour killings, rape, sexual abuse, incest, domestic violence, forced marriage, anti-women customary practices, acid crimes, and child marriages. Their implementation nevertheless remains weak, thus not translating into substantive equality between men and women. Law has been one tool successfully used by the women's and feminist movements to protect women's rights. While debate continues about which basis for feminism is to be preferred, Islamic law or secular law, it is essential to recognise that feminism (although this may not be explicit) is very much part of the ongoing wider discourse in Pakistan and continues to be of relevance.

The relevance of postfeminism to the Pakistani feminist framework

Feminism is under-theorised generally in Pakistan (Zia 2018, 10). As a result, there has been little discourse and academic writing on the applicability of postfeminism within Pakistan feminism.

Some of the concepts of postfeminism resonate with both feminist movements. Islamic modern feminism might welcome it, basing its support on a mix of concepts of identities, choice, and autonomy. Islamic feminists, with all its diversity of thought and debate (Najmabadi 1993; Yamani 1996; Badran 2001), argue that issues of choice, autonomy, and empowerment are present within the Quran. These postfeminist concepts might be used to challenge patriarchy as a tool of subjugation of women and the claim that Islam does not support or need patriarchy (Wadud 1999; Barlas 2002). Mahmood represents the view that women's choice and agency is consistent within the Islamic framework (Mahmood 2004). She asserts that women's docility should not read as an abandonment of agency but more as a 'malleability' (Mahmood 2004, 29). She brings the struggle for women's rights within an Islamic framework. She asserts that challenging social norms is to believe that it is an act of voluntary obedience to God and not men or patriarchal systems (Mahmood 2004, 575). She contends that one can create a space for the exercise of agency within one's relationship to transcendental power. These feminists advocate for choice, autonomy, and empowerment within Islamic feminism, using their agency to challenge the traditional, conservative, and patriarchal interpretations of Islam (Moghissi 2011).

While SLF explicitly rejects patriarchy, in recent years their focus on patriarchy as the main site of power has decreased. Instead, they see other sites of power in the daily life of women. This might resonate with a postfeminist approach that suggests that feminism is no longer relevant (McRobbie 2004). This refocusing can be observed also by the activities of several NGOs, who have diversified their work to focus on gender inequality and formal structural reforms. SLF also identifies that notions of autonomy, choice, and empowerment are worthy goals to be attained. Indeed, SLF has been successful in ensuring a continued focus on these goals within the women's movement, yielding significant successes over the past 17 years, such as in the passage of many pro-women laws including the ones on domestic violence, rape, and sexual harassment (Times of Islamabad 2016).

However, there remains a major difference between the two movements with regard to any adoption of postfeminist concepts. Islamic feminism might be understood to adopt postfeminism in that it rejects 'feminism', believing feminism to be a more Western concept and it is not needed due to the protections provided by religion. SLF, on the other hand, while it has displayed a decreased focus on patriarchy, is still led by core feminist principles and believe in its continued relevance in contemporary Pakistan. SLF agrees that there remains much work to be done on the implementation of key feminist concepts before they see real change for women. They maintain the need for feminism and thereby reject postfeminist perspectives, including that feminism is redundant or has moved onto a new phase (Becker 2000, 399–408).

While threads of postfeminist thoughts are visible, postfeminism and its focus on individual action as opposed to development of a collective political identity is inconsistent with the current legal strategies being used by feminist and women's movements in Pakistan. Postfeminism does not 'ask the women question', politicise the oppression of women, and create a clear ideology for action, including in law. Thus, the recognised need for feminist interventions in Pakistan makes it clear that the work of feminism is not over. Pakistan has not reached a postfeminist stage and postfeminism is not relevant within current Pakistani feminist legal discourse.

Key legal challenges

There are four key challenges for contemporary Pakistani feminism in law today, none of which can be effectively addressed through postfeminist concepts such as choice, empowerment, and autonomy.

First, while the feminist and women's movement have been influential in the passage of several pro-women laws, they have not been as successful in addressing the bias within society or the justice sector (Detho & Junejo 2017). This is evidenced by situations where police refuse to register cases involving women (Zaman 2014, 29), or where parliamentarians and right-wing parties use women as a bargaining chip in parliament. Where this occurs, women's issues are dropped from the agenda or proposed laws are diluted. The language of the courts evidences a continued bias and perpetuation of women's gendered roles. For example, in one case where the wife left the marital home due to domestic violence, the court deliberated on whether the 'plaintiff is a disobedient wife and deserted without any reason at the instigation of her father, or the defendant was a cruel person who ousted plaintiff' (2013 MLD 537, para 3). The court, ignoring the domestic violence, went on to say that the wife had so much hatred towards the respondent that 'we can safely gather … that it was the attitude of the petitioner which made her desert her husband's house', and thus, being found to be a disobedient wife, she did not have a right to claim maintenance from her husband (2013 MLD 537, para 8).

Second, the focus on women's rights alone has limited the capacity of contemporary feminist movements to achieve conscious reform to address deep, systemic bias. Reform to women's rights have been supported by the burgeoning number of NGOs and donors, who slowly de-politicise the discourse on 'feminism' to a safer and gentler focus on 'gender'. A focus on gender includes both men and women, which leads to a situation where the emphasis on women disappears (Saigol 2016, 21). Core feminist ideologies and discussion on concepts such as patriarchy become diluted within the development context.

Further, all programs and projects are expected to integrate gender into their work, resulting in it becoming a 'mechanical, robotic exercise' (Saigol 2016, 23–24). Within the development sector, to use its language, legislation has become a measurable outcome and indicator. Legislative reform is more easily attained than attitudinal change. NGOs and donors began using legislation as a 'goal' and 'success' indicator in short-term projects, and did not allow for proper processes and analysis. The process of legislative drafting is often not properly followed (Zia 2014, 1–2). This is not to say that proper drafting processes are never used, but that failures are widespread enough to have become a frequent practice.

For example, the drafting of a law or amendment is often based on three stages: a desk review, a few focus group discussions at the policy level, and a seminar or focus group discussion to gain a stamp of approval at the end. Issues such as funding, time, lack of proper analysis of the issue, and the need to concede several aspects due to challenges from within parliament have compromised the process, and thereafter the law. For example, the Sindh Child Marriages Restraint Act 2013 has declared child marriages punishable but has not made it invalid. As a result, the victims of child marriage must apply for divorce as opposed to an automatic invalidation of those marriages. This re-victimises those who must go through another tenuous court process, with the onus being on the child to end the marriage (Detho & Junejo 2017). The de-politicised version is popular with governments and donors who strive to show a 'progressive' or 'moderate' Islam.

Third, Zia contends that the formation of an identity for the feminist movement within a religious paradigm has been another challenge (Zia 2009). The frantic, reactive activism needed by the women's movement in its early days led to a lack of clarity on the issue of its relationship with a religious identity. Few groups or organisations such as WAF took a direct political stance on religion, which declared itself to be a secular organisation. This lack of clarity and the subsequent co-option of the liberal women's agenda by Islamic feminists has led to the formation of a new brand of feminism rooted in a predominantly religious identity, further leading to constant debates and struggles (Zia 2009).

Fourth, another challenge has been the major criticism of the Pakistani feminist movement that it excludes women from other groups, particularly with regard to class (Jalal 1991). While groups such as WAF do consist of predominantly educated, middle-class Muslim women, there have been concrete efforts to ensure that the voices of women from diverse groups are heard and that WAF is responsive to them. As Shaheed notes, 'The women's movement expanded to embrace the voices and causes of differently situated women, especially with respect to class but other identities as well, developing understanding of the somewhat cumbersome term "intersectionality"' (Shaheed 2010, 5). However, intersectionality seems not to have found its way permanently onto the Pakistani feminist agenda. For example, while the women's movement criticised the Zina Ordinance for discriminating against women, they focused on Muslim Family Laws. There was little focus on whether women belonging to other religious minorities were protected by their personal laws, except by a few organisations.

The challenge of intersectionality in Pakistani feminism is further highlighted by issues such as forced conversion, which primarily impacts religious minorities. This issue has only relatively recently appeared on the Pakistani feminist agenda. There have been several cases of forced conversion brought before the courts, particularly in the province of Sindh (Hadi 2014). In many cases, the girls/women declare that they have married of their own free will and choose to go with their 'husbands'. The courts have let the women/girls go with their husbands, no matter their age or the circumstances of the case (Zia, Mirza & Ahmad 2015, 92–93). While in some of the cases, the couple may truly have married on their own accord, several of the cases are unclear, with suspicious and controversial circumstances.

For example, initial reports from eye-witnesses from the Supreme Court case of Rinkle Kumari highlighted her distress and desire to go home with her mother at the initial hearings (PILER 2012). While during the trial, the girls and women are often isolated and placed in Dar-ul-Amans (shelter homes) for them to be able to make their decision without pressure of those around her, in Rinkle's case, her 'husband' and her family were both allowed to visit. In other cases, the girl is sent home with her husband and remains with him during the trial, leaving her susceptible to threats, intimidation, and coercion (Zia, Mirza & Ahmad 2015, 92–93). Thus, either a young girl or woman is forced to be in isolation during a potentially traumatic time in her life, or she is sent back to her alleged abductor/rapist (Ibid).

The specific situations of the girls or women also contribute to the situation, including characteristics such as age, religion, economic status, and class status. There are also socio-political issues including the fear that religious minorities experience in regions where they remain insecure due to violence inflicted against them, exploitation, and lack of access to resources, opportunities, and justice. Religious minority members often also belong to lower economic classes, while perpetrators belong to powerful groups (e.g. landlords and politicians).

Thus, in some cases, the police have refused to register complaints of such cases in order to please a powerful perpetrator and his family (Schaflechner 2018, 286).

Newer feminist collectives have emphasised the need to ensure diversity and an inclusionary approach to be able to hear women's voices speak their own truth. This has been demonstrated by the Hum Aurtein's inclusion of veiled women on their banner, which older feminist groups would never allow as they see the veil as a sign of oppression.

The question arises as to how feminist movements in Pakistan might proceed, in order to achieve its objectives. The women's and the feminist movements have been working to challenge barriers to women's equality using a variety of methods, with varied levels of success. I posit that the lack of understanding of feminist principles and tools has contributed to these less than ideal outcomes. A lack of feminist ideologies, foundations, and understanding of on-the-ground practical realities and needs negatively impacts the feminist work by all those involved. For example, the lack of understanding and articulation of the basis of the recommended changes in laws results in giving away essential rights and protections at the negotiating table. The lack of feminist legal methods has hampered the feminist and women's movements ability to respond adequately to the case of forced conversion. If the judges in any of the cases had asked the 'women' question when dealing with these cases, the outcomes may have been more appropriate for women.

What becomes clear is that feminism is neither redundant nor dead in Pakistan. On the contrary, there is a great need for feminism to lead the path towards the creation of a cohesive collection action based on core feminist principles and goals to challenge the current status quo.

The feminist movement must take stock of its own positionality within the women's movement in Pakistan. Acknowledging the debate between the two feminist movements, they must nevertheless identify areas of collaboration where a collective political identity must be developed. There is precedence of collaboration in the amendment/repeal of the Zina Ordinance 1979. Feminists must also recognise the newer sites of discourse such as social media and find ways to create an effective voice here as well. Social movements on women issues, such as the worldwide #MeToo and #TimesUp movements, as well as the growing number of recently formed Pakistani feminist collectives online, demonstrate the positive impact of an online collective identity. It is essential for the feminist movement to recognise the power of collective action in person, as well as online, to be more politically effective.

Conclusion

This chapter has sought to situate Pakistani women within the framework of feminism and feminist legal theory. It asked whether Pakistan has entered a postfeminist phase.

The confusion of Sanam and Amina over the word 'feminist' in the example given at the beginning of the chapter indicates that concepts of feminism have not yet become a norm in Pakistan. Laws passed, with their flaws, have yet to be properly implemented. As a consequence, feminist narratives must be introduced within the justice system to effectively implement a real change.

This chapter argues that the de-politicisation of feminism through Islamic challenges, donor demands, proliferation and commercialisation of NGOs, and the ideology of development, appeasement, and inclusiveness, has damaged the natural growth and development of indigenous feminism (Saigol 2016, 22; Zia 2018, 33, 114, 120). With the influence of the Islamic modern feminist movement, more radical Islamic groups and identities are better able to challenge any secular opposition to them. The Islamic/cultural narrative of protection of women within the confines of Islam is problematic if it does not also challenge patriarchy, the very basis of gender inequality.

Is Pakistan postfeminist? The feminism of SLF does not seem to fall within some aspects of the postfeminist framework. While Islamic feminism could borrow some of the concepts of postfeminism to strengthen and broaden its own theories, particularly those related to choice, autonomy, agency, and empowerment, postfeminism is not useful in addressing the contemporary challenges faced by the Pakistani feminist movement as a whole. Postfeminism fails to ask the 'woman' question, which is still so important in tackling key challenges for feminists in Pakistan.

Pakistan must develop feminist legal methods within its own indigenous and localised context, to be able to play an effective role within the legal framework. It must first conduct an analysis of the existing framework and responses to women's issues to create an effective feminist strategy, which can challenge the status quo. Without this strategy, the feminist movement will appear uncoordinated and unable to articulate its specific demands. Thus, I conclude that Pakistan is most definitely not in a postfeminist phase.

Notes

1 Maliha Zia is a lawyer and women's rights activist, researcher, and trainer in Pakistan. She currently holds the position of Associate Director at the Legal Aid Society.
2 Pakistani bread commonly made at home.
3 WAF is a non-partisan, non-hierarchical, and non-funded voluntary alliance functioning in several cities in Pakistan. It is supportive of all aspects of women's rights and related issues, irrespective of political affiliations, belief system, or ethnicity.
4 General Pervez Musharraf held power from 2001 to 2008 after a coup against Prime Minister Nawaz Sharif in 2001.
5 The Holy Book of Islam.
6 The offence of rape was removed from the Zina Ordinance 1979 and placed into the Pakistan Penal Code 1860. Section 375, Pakistan Penal Code 1860.
7 Article 151 (4) Qanun-e-Shahadat Order 1984. This section has since been repealed.
8 Asking the 'woman' question includes asking what impact a certain law, policy, or clause has on women. 'It seeks: 1) to identify bias against women implicit in legal rules and practices that appear neutral and objective, 2) to expose how the law excludes the experiences and values of women, and 3) to insist upon application of legal rules that do not perpetuate women's subordination' (Clougherty 1996).

References

Adriaens, Fien. 2009. "Post Feminism in Popular Culture: A Potential for Critical Resistance?" *Politics and Culture* 4: https://politicsandculture.org/issue/2009-issue-4/.

Adriaens, Fien, and Sofie Van Bauwel. 2014. "Sex and the City: a Postfeminist Point of View? Or How Popular Culture Functions as a Channel for Feminist Discourses." *Journal of Popular Culture* 47, no. 1: 174–195.

Ahmed-Ghosh, Huma. 2008. "Dilemmas of Islamic and Secular Feminists and Feminisms." *Journal of International Women's Studies* 9, no. 3: 99–116.

Ahmed, Zahid, and Zeb Khan. 2016. "Direct and Indirect Impacts of Terrorism on Youth in Pakistan." *Journal of the Research Society of Pakistan* 53, no. 1: 235–249.

Amnesty International. 2011. *Rape and Sexual Violence: Human Rights Law and Standards in the International Criminal Court.* London: Amnesty International Publications.

Babur, Zaheed-ud-din. 2007. *Violence against Women in Pakistan: Current Realities and Strategies for Change.* Burg: European University Centre for Peace Studies.

Badran, Margot. 2001. "Understanding Islam, Islamism, and Islamic Feminism." *Journal of Women's History* 13, no. 1: 47–52.

———. 2011. "From Islamic Feminism to a Muslim Holistic Feminism." *IDS Bulletin. Special Issue: Gender, Rights and Religion at the Crossroads* 42, no. 1: 78–87.

Barlas, Asma. 2002. *Believing Women in Islam: Un-reading Patriarchal Interpretations of the Quran.* Austin: University of Texas Press.

Bartlett, Katharine T. 1990. "Feminist Legal Methods." *Harvard Law Review* 103, no. 4: 829–888.

Becker, Penny, E. 2000. "Boundaries and Silences in a Post-Feminist Sociology." *Sociology of Religion* 61, no. 4: 399–408.

Chengappa, Bidanda M. 2001. "Pakistan: The Role of Religion in Political Evolution." *Strategic Analysis* 24, no. 12, www.idsa-india.org/an-mar-3.01.html.

Clougherty, Lydia A. 1996. "Feminist Legal Methods and the First Amendment Defence to Sexual Harassment Liability." *Nebraska Law Review* 75, no. 1: 1–26.

Commission of Inquiry for Women. 1997. *Report of Commission of Inquiry for Women, Pakistan.* Islamabad: Pakistan Law Commission.

Critelli, Filomena M. 2012. "Voices of Resistance: Seeking Shelter Services in Pakistan." *Violence Against Women* 18, no. 4: 437–458.

Dawn News. 2018. "These Posters from the Aurat March Say Everything You Wish You Could", 9 March 2018. Pakistan, https://images.dawn.com/news/1179620.

Detho, lqbal, and Jamil Junejo. 2017. *Research on Pro-Women Laws: An Analysis of the Implementation Gaps.* Karachi: Strengthening Participatory Organisation Publication.

Faludi, Susan. 1991. *Backlash: The Undeclared War against Women.* London: Vintage.

Genz, Stéphanie. 2006. "Third Way/ve. The Politics of Postfeminism." *Feminist Theory* 7, no. 3: 333–353.

Gill, Rosalind. 2007. "Postfeminist Media Culture: Elements of a Sensibility." *European Journal of Cultural Studies* 10, no. 2: 147–166.

Hadi, Rabeea, and Muhammad Ullah. 2014. *Violence against Women in Pakistan: A Qualitative Review of Reported Incidents January – December 2014.* Islamabad: Aurat Foundation Publication.

Jalal, Ayesha. 1991. "The Convenience of Subservience: Women and the State in Pakistan." In *Women, Islam and the State*, edited by Deniz Kandiyotti, 77–114. London: Macmillan.

Jilani, Hina. 1998. *Human Rights and Democratic Development in Pakistan.* Lahore: Human Rights Commission of Pakistan.

Khan, Nighat Said. 1994. "Reflections on the Question of Islam and Modernity." In *Locating the Self: Perspectives on Women and Multiple Identities*, edited by Nighat Said Khan, Rubina Saigol and Afiya Shehrbano Zia, 77–95. Lahore: ASR Publications.

Khan, Hidayat. 2013. "Pakistan's Contribution to Global War on Terror after 9/11." *IPRI Journal* 13, no. 1: 37–56.

Khan, Ayesha, and Sarah Zaman. 2012. *The Criminal Justice System and Rape: An Attitudinal Study of the Public Sector's Response to Rape in Karachi*. Karachi: War against Rape (WAR) and Collective for Social Science Research Publication.

Kisner, Amber E. 2004. "Negotiating Spaces for/through Third-Wave Feminism." *National Women's Studies Association Journal* 16, no. 3: 124–153.

Lancioni, Judith. 2006. "Murder and Mayhem on Wisteria Lane: A Study of Genre and Cultural Context in Desperate Housewives." In *Reading Desperate Housewives: Beyond the White Picket Fence*, edited by Kim Akass and Janet McCabe, 129–143. London: I. B. Tauris.

Lari, Maliha Z. 2011. *Honour Killings*. Pakistan and Compliance of Law 201, no. 1: 2.

Mahbub ul Haq Human Development Centre. 2000. *Human Development in South Asia 2000. The Gender Question*. Oxford: Oxford University Press.

Mahmood, Saba. 2004. "Women's Agency within Feminist Historiography." *The Journal of Religion* 84, no. 4: 573–579.

McRobbie, Angela. 2004. "Post-Feminism and Popular Culture." *Feminist Media Studies* 4, no. 3: 255–265.

Modleski, Tanya. 1991. *Feminism Without Women: Culture and Criticism in a 'Postfeminist' Age*. New York: Routledge.

Moghadam, Valentine M. 1994. *Identity Politics and Women: Cultural Reassertions and Feminisms in International Perspective*. Boulder, CO: Westview Press.

———. 2002. "Islamic Feminisms and Its Discontents: Toward a Resolution of the Debate." *Signs* 27, no. 4: 1135–1171.

———. 2003. *Modernizing Women: Gender and Social Change in the Middle East*. Boulder, CO: Lynne Rienner Publishers.

Moghissi, Haideh. 2011. "Islamic Feminism Revisited." *Comparative Studies of South Asia, Africa and the Middle East* 31, no. 1: 76–84.

Mushtaq, Ayesha. 2018. "Aurat March Shakes the Patriarchy in Pakistan." *Pakistan, Women's Own*, 10 March 2018, https://womensownpk.com/2018/03/10/aurat-march-shakes-patriarchy-pakistan/.

Najmabadi, Afsaneh. 1993. "Zanha-yi millat: Women or Wives of the Nation." *Iranian Studies* 26, no. 1–2: 51–71.

Nayeem, Bushra. "Sanam Saeed Has Two Different Narratives on Feminism and Here Is How." Pakistan, *Daily Pakistan*, 6 April 2018, https://en.dailypakistan.com.pk/lifestyle/sanam-saeed-has-two-different-narratives-on-feminism-and-here-is-how/.

Orr, Catherine M. 1997. "Charting the Currents of the Third Wave." *Hypatia: Special Issue: Third Wave Feminisms* 12, no. 3: 29–45.

Pakistan Institute of Labour Education and Research (PILER). 2012. *Rinkle Kumari Case*. International Dalit Solidarity Network, https://idsn.org/wp-content/uploads/user_folder/pdf/New_files/Pakistan/Rinkel_Kumari_case_-_2012.pdf.

Parpart, Jane L. 1993. "Who Is the 'Other'?: A Postmodern Feminist Critique of Women and Development Theory and Practice." *Development and Change* 24, no. 3: 439–464.

Qaisrani, Ayesha, Sadaf Liqat and Elishma N. Khokar. 2016. *Socio-economic and Cultural Factors of Violence against Women in Pakistan*. Working paper # 158, Pakistan:

Sustainable Development Policy Institute, www.sdpi.org/publications/files/Socio-economic&Cultural-Factors-of-Violence-against-Women-in-Pakistan(W-158).pdf.

Qureshi, Zainab. 2018. "The Construction of Consent in Rape Adjudication in Pakistan." In *Disputed Legacies: The Pakistan Papers*, edited by Neelam Hussain. New Delhi: Zubaan Books.

Rashid, Tahmina. 2006. *Contested Representation: Punjabi Women in Feminist Debate in Pakistan*. Karachi: Oxford University Press.

Rashid, Ammar. 2017. "Theology of Patriarchy." *Daily Times*, 20 March 2017, Pakistan, http://dailytimes.com.pk/opinion/21-Mar-17/a-theology-of-patriarchy.

Saeed, Sanam, and Amina Sheikh. 2018. Speaking to HSY "Djuice presents Tonite with HSY." 16 April 2018, Season 4, Episode 6, Hum Television Network, aired on 15 April 2018.

Saigol, Rubina. 2016. *Feminism and the Women's Movement in Pakistan Actors, Debates and Strategies*. Islamabad, Friedrich-Ebert-Stiftung.

Schaflechner, Jurgen. 2018. "Forced Conversion and (Hindu) Women's Agency in Sindh." *South Asia Chronicle* 7, Südasien-Seminar der Humboldt-Universität zu Berlin: 275–317.

Serez, Annie. 2017. "Feminism in Pakistan: Dialogues between Pakistani Feminists." *Laurier Undergraduate Journal of the Arts* 3, no. 1: http://scholars.wlu.ca/luja/vol3/iss1/.

Shahidian, Hamid. 1994. "The Iranian Left and 'The Woman Question' in the Revolution of 1978–1979." *International Journal of Middle East Studies* 26, no. 2: 223–247.

Shaheed, Farida. 2002. "Women's Experiences of Identity, Religion and Activism in Pakistan." In *The Post-Colonial State and Social Transformation in India and Pakistan*, edited by S. M. Naseem and K. Nadvi. Karachi: Oxford University Press.

———. 2010. "The Women's Movement in Pakistan: Challenges and Achievements." In *Women's Movements in a Global Era*, edited by Amrita Basu, 100–126. New York: Routledge Press.

Times of Islamabad. 2016. "24 New Pro-women Laws Passed in Pakistan in 3 Years." Islamabad, https://timesofislamabad.com/25-Nov-2016/24-new-pro-women-laws-passed-in-pakistan-in-3-years.

Wadud, Amina. 1999. *Quran and Woman: Rereading the Sacred Text from a Woman's Perspective*. New York: Oxford University Press.

Whelehan, Imelda. 2010. "Remaking Feminism: Or Why Is Postfeminism So Boring?" *Nordic Journal of English Studies* 9, no. 3: 155–172.

Yamani, Mai. 1996. "Introduction." In *Feminism and Islam: Legal and Literacy Perspectives*, edited by Mai Yamani, 69–86. New York: New York University Press.

Zaman, Sarah. 2014. *Forced Marriages and Inheritance Deprivation: A Research Study Exploring the Substantive Structural Gaps in the Implementation of Anti-Women Practices (Criminal Law Amendment) Act 2011*. Islamabad: Aurat Foundation.

Zaman, Sarah, and Maliha Zia. 2013. *Women's Access to Justice in Pakistan*. Working Paper submitted to the Committee on Women's Access to Justice, at the 54th CEDAW Session.

———. 2018. "How much Rape is Rape: Understanding Normative Assumptions within Rape Victimology in Pakistan." In *Disputed Legacies: The Pakistan Papers*, edited by Neelam Hussain. New Delhi: Zubaan Books.

Zia, Afiya S. 2009. "The Reinvention of Feminism in Pakistan." *Feminist Review* 91, no. 1: 29–46.

———. 2017. "The Secular Myth." *Dawn News*, 24 May 2017, Pakistan www.dawn.com/news/1334995.
———. 2018. *Faith and Feminism in Pakistan*. Lahore: Folio Books.
Zia, Maliha. 2014. "Legislative Initiatives on Women in Pakistan – Need for Self-Critique and Reassessment." *Legislative Watch Newsletter*, no. 43 (January–May 2014), 1–2.
Zia, Maliha, and Sarah Zaman. 2011. *Sexual Violence and the Law*. Karachi: War Against Rape Publication.
Zia, Maliha, and Riffat Butt. 2012. *NGO Alternative Report on CEDAW*. Islamabad: Aurat Foundation Publication.
Zia, Maliha, Angbeen Mizra and Zahra Ahmad. 2015. *Judge's Facilitators Toolkit: Delivery of Justice, Issues Faced by Gender and Religious Minorities*. Karachi: Legal Aid Society Publication.
Zia, Shahla. 1998. "Some Experiences of the Women's Movement: Strategies for Success." In *Shaping Women's Lives; Laws, Practices & Strategies*, edited by Farida Shaheed, 371–414. Lahore: Shirkat Gah.
———. 2001. "Women and the Law in Pakistan." *Mahbub ul Haq Human Development Review* 1, no. 2, 145–184.

Case List

Malik Tanveer Khan v. Amber Liaqat (2009 CLC 1210).
Rukhsana Jabeen v. Additional District Judge (2011 CLC 1498 Lahore High Court).
Mst. Ishrat Bibi v. Muhammad Arshad (2013 MLD 537).
Mukhtar Ahmad Shaikh v. Government of Pakistan (PLD 2009 Federal Shariat Court 65).

5 Interrogating ourselves, again

Women's human rights and the feminist practice of critical self-assessment[1]

Mariana Prandini Assis

Introduction

Subject-making is a challenging political endeavour because it necessarily entails a logic of inclusion and exclusion. Four different events, which took place in various parts of the world and in distinct historical moments, bring to light this thorny issue that lies at the centre of feminisms.

Paris, 1789. French Revolutionaries eschewed from questioning prevailing ideas about sexual difference and gender roles that inscribed women as 'passive citizens'. Olympe de Gouges courageously challenged this definition not only with her extensive public intervention in debates on women's rights, but perhaps most importantly, with her performance. Olympe's public appearance and writing were an exercise of the rights she vindicated for her sex: by taking part in public life, she performed the role of the active citizen that she had been denied by the state (Rancière 2004). However, while challenging the sexual difference deployed to justify women's exclusion from citizenship, Olympe necessarily and paradoxically reinscribed the gendered subject (Scott 1997).

Mexico, 1975. The United Nations invited Domitila Barrios de Chungara, an indigenous leader from the Bolivian mines, to participate in the World Conference of the International Women's Year. There, Domitila struggled to navigate a space where men were portrayed as enemies and the dominant discourse distinguished between women's issues and all the rest (anti-imperialist struggles, socioeconomic problems, genocide of indigenous peoples, colonial legacy, and so forth). Articulating political claims from her lived experience, Domitila was interested in talking about her unpaid domestic work, as well as her husband's exploitation in the mines, indigenous people's access to natural resources and land, and the unjust and predatory economic system that deprived them of their traditional modes of life. For Domitila, these were 'women's concerns', just as much – or perhaps even more so – than the calls made in the name of gender equality at that same place by other feminists such as Betty Friedan (Viezzer 2014).

Beijing, 1995. People from all over the world gathered in China at the Fourth World Conference on Women. Dianne Otto, an Australian international law and human rights scholar, acting as a representative of the Lesbian Caucus, attended a meeting of the African Caucus with the aim of convincing participants 'to lobby their state's representative to support the recognition of "sexual orientation" as an unacceptable ground of discrimination in the Platform for Action of the UN's Fourth World Conference on Women' (Otto 2007, 346). As Dianne sat in that room and listened to various accounts of how poverty, armed conflicts, and the International Monetary Fund's structural adjustments programmes impacted women's lives in the African continent, she looked for words that would make the quest for self-determination in sexual matters meaningful in that context. Dianne felt overwhelmed by the limits of the identification as women, and as feminists, which she shared with the others who were at that same space (Otto 2007).

São Paulo, 2005. Participants gathered for the final plenary of the *X Encuentro Feminista Latinoamericano y del Caribe* (Latin American and Caribbean Feminist Meeting),[2] in Brazil. For the first time in the history of the *Encuentro*, an issue could not be decided by consensus and counting individual votes was necessary. The issue at hand was whether transgender women should be allowed in the next meeting. The majority of the participants agreed that it was not one's biological features, but rather one's feeling and identity that should determine her acceptance as a woman in the *Encuentro* (Adrião and Toneli 2008). The final decision was considered controversial by many feminists in the region. At a feminist conference in Salvador a month later, I heard a well-known figure remark, 'Next year, it will rain men in the *Encuentro Feminista*.' Since 2015, transgender women have entered the space of the *Encuentro*, actively participating in feminist activism in the region, and a special commission has been established to consider the inclusion of transgender men, intersex, and non-binary persons in the next meetings.

These examples show that historically, feminisms have struggled to include women in spaces and frameworks (of rights, material production, and knowledge) through a gendered identity based on (naturalised) sexual difference. In developing demands for inclusion, feminists have constructed the subject of their politics, necessarily butting against essentialism. The essentialised feminist political subject has been created and recreated with ever-changing exclusions.[3] Building from this ongoing reflection in feminist theory (Grosz 1990; Wong 1999; Brown 2000; Lloyd 2005), I explore in this chapter the problems with essentialism in international law and, particularly, human rights discourse.

I pursue Judith Butler's admonition that 'it is the presupposition of the category of woman itself that requires a critical genealogy of the complex institutional and discursive means by which it is constituted' (Butler 1988, 530). Therefore, I examine the construction of the category[4] 'women' in the discourse of 'women's human rights' and its evolving meanings in the field of international human rights law. I argue that 'women's human rights' reinstates the very difference of the gendered subject that it aimed to question in the first place, creating new exclusions of its own. Examining the construction of 'women' as the subject of human rights requires us to acknowledge that not only are there a variety of feminist projects, but also that they often compete with one another.

I argue that interrogating feminist political subjects is a central endeavour of feminisms, an endeavour that follows from their characteristic call for critical self-assessment. Such a call will never be completely answered, especially in women's human rights, as it requires a restless 'critical operation' (Scott 2004). This chapter attempts to demonstrate this continual movement and critical core: looking back at past discourses and achievements to call into question and disrupt the frameworks of the present, thus paving the way for imagining new (and more inclusive) futures (Scott 2004, 18). The future for a critical feminist approach to human rights, needs to be founded upon the recognition of their ever-present marginalising and exclusionary potential. If postfeminism is a discursive formation that 'displaces or replaces feminism altogether' (Butler 2013, 42) because feminism as a project is finished, then I reject those postfeminist claims.

The chapter is organised in four parts. In the first section, I lay down the theoretical frame to confront essentialism in the realm of feminist human rights politics. Next, I present a brief historical account of feminist intervention in international and human rights law. Then, I highlight how this intervention relied upon essentialist constructions of subject and agenda. Finally, I argue that a corrective to essentialism does not lie in embracing a postfeminist argument that rejects feminism (Butler 2013, 44). The answer demands rather that we take the feminist call for critical self-assessment seriously, not only by scrutinising the subjects produced by feminisms, but also by acknowledging feminisms as a 'discursive field of action' (Alvarez 2014), sustained through ongoing and competing formulations.

Essentialism in feminist politics

The participants of the *Encuentro Feminista* in São Paulo raised and disputed questions such as: Who is a woman? Who can be a feminist? On what grounds are these identities constituted? What makes someone part of the group and what grants her legitimacy to speak for and within it? These questions point to the limits of collective identification. Similarly, Dianne Otto's difficulty in finding a common language, as women and feminists, demonstrates such limits. The simple fact that Dianne shared the international space of a conference on women with others did not necessarily mean they also shared worldviews, interests, or political claims. The clashes between Domitila Barrios de Chungara and Betty Friedan equally expose the fragility of the assumption that a politically assembled identity always reveals an underlying commonality of experiences and needs.

Throughout history, to successfully make political and legal claims, feminists had to speak on behalf a specific group with shared needs and interests – women. For this reason, feminist politics has always struggled with the necessity of thinking essentially because 'it was imperative if feminist political claims were to be treated as rightful' (Lloyd 2005, 58).

At the same time, essentialism has always been problematic for a feminist politics. Elizabeth Grosz (1990, 334) teaches us that 'essentialism [...] refers to the attribution of a fixed essence to women. [...] to the existence of fixed characteristics, given attributes, and ahistorical functions which limit the possibilities of change and thus of social reorganization'. The problem with essentialism is thus multifaceted: it is ahistorical; it mistakes social relations for fixed attributes, which impose constraints to social changes; it ignores geographical, racial, and class differences among women, both within and across cultures (Grosz 1990).

The difficulty then is that, while feminist politics has always had to pursue its demands in the name of an essential political subject, it cannot ignore the traps and dangers that follow from it. To confront this problematic, it is important, first, to clarify that the essential collective identities constituted are not ahistorical: 'women' are produced and mobilised within a historical and political context, as the events recounted in the opening paragraphs of this chapter illustrate.

Second, it is necessary to acknowledge that shared experiences do not reveal a pre-existing collective entity, but rather produce such an entity, as 'narratives of experience are seen to *produce* rather than to reveal reality' (Lloyd 2005, 60). This process is always marked by the inclusion of some and the exclusion of many – the singling out of a set of attributes that will make up the collective political subject.

Because of their very nature then, these narratives require 'a double move: the theorization of the "essentialist spaces from which we speak" (as women, say) and the opening up to scrutiny of the *historical processes and practices that shape these narrative spaces into particular scripts*' (Lloyd 2005, 60). Otherwise, we risk turning collective identities into essentialised entities that become the reason of the social struggle per se, rather than a tool for the achievement of social transformation. The stable political subject does not precede politics, rather it is the initiator of politics (Lloyd 2005, 58). As such, the creation of the political subject is a requirement for political action, which cannot be reduced to pursuing the public recognition of that subject.[5]

In feminist legal theory and politics, the essentialised meaning of gender difference is not fixed; it has been based on biology and natural characteristics, or in psychological traits, such as empathy and nurturance (Wong 1999, 275). In the next section, I will provide the historical background out of which the essentialised female subject of human rights was constructed, because attention to the problem of essentialism is necessary in human rights politics.

Judith Butler has argued that

> when we struggle for rights, we are not simply struggling for rights that attach to my person, but we are struggling to be conceived as persons. [...] we are struggling not only to be conceived as persons, but to create a social transformation of the very meaning of personhood.
>
> (Butler 2004, 32)

Therefore, struggles for rights are not individual undertakings nor are they mere translations of political demands into legal language. They operate on a deeper and structural level, unleashing critical interventions 'into the social and political process by which the human is articulated' (Butler 2004, 32). Struggles for human rights narrate the dominant understanding of who counts as a human and who is denied such characterisation. They therefore serve not only to critique the exclusive status quo collective identity against which they fight, but also to create the opportunity for its radical transformation towards more inclusive meanings. This is why any critical approach to human rights struggles needs to always question who their constituted subject is.

Feminisms confront international human rights law

An examination of the historical encounter between 'women' and 'human rights' is necessary to assess the political work done thus far by the category 'women's human rights'. The mobilisation for the inclusion of women's and gender issues into the mainstream of human rights discourse, norms, and institutions confronted feminist activists and scholars with the challenge of what (and consequently who) to put in, and what/who to leave out. This section argues that within the field of international human rights law, feminism has become largely identified with a narrow political and legal agenda focused on bodily security, encompassing violence against women, rape, and sex trafficking.

International law has historically operated under the assumption of a male–female dichotomy, understood as a synonymy for sex/gender, and according to which women were categorised, along with colonised people, as dependent subjects in need of protection (Otto 2013). From the beginning of the era of the League of Nations (1920–1946), some international feminists rejected this protective scheme, demanding equality and recognition of women's rights in areas such as labour regulation.[6] There were important feminist interventions in the international legal domain throughout the next few decades, leading to some key developments. These included the establishment of the Commission on the Status of Women as early as 1946 and the adoption by the United Nations (UN) of the International Convention on the Elimination of All Forms of Discrimination against Women (CEDAW) in 1979.

While these efforts were somewhat scattered, in a more organised effort beginning in the 1980s, feminist activists struggled for recognition within the realm of international human rights. They critically observed that human rights discourse had emerged as gender neutral, and they engaged in a dispute over a new framing inclusive of women and their specific grievances. In 1985, a World Conference on Women took place in Nairobi, creating momentum for expanded activism. In 1992 and 1993, advocates gathered on different occasions 'to prepare sections as well as intermittent phrases for inclusion in the draft of the Declaration and Programme of Action to be adopted at the Vienna World Conference on Human Rights' (Ashworth 1999, 263). In 1994, the Inter-American Convention on the Elimination of Violence against Women was adopted by the Organization of the American States and in 1995, the fourth World Conference on Women took place in Beijing.

During the 1990s, transnational feminist activists and women's rights advocates entered mainstream human rights institutions aiming to make women's issues, including, but not limited to, gender-based violence, a priority for the international agenda. Indeed, a variety of problems have long been articulated through human rights language, and around which women and feminist activists mobilised. These encompassed 'issues of economic justice, labour standards, public health, occupational safety, and environmental protection' (Orford 1998, 195), as well as indigenous rights and sovereignty (Viezzer 2014). The 1990s was thus a turning point in feminist mobilisation within the international human rights system, known as the decade when the recognition of human rights for women enabled the 'mainstreaming of feminism', as Canadian feminist Ariane Brunet remarked at the Vienna World Conference (Miller 2004, 20). While this mainstreaming could have taken different routes, it remained trapped in 'dualistic conceptions of sex/gender' (Otto 2013) and led feminists to carry 'a brief only for women' (Halley 2006). Essentialism played an important role in this outcome.

As the diversity of human rights issues brought forward by women as part of the feminist agenda faded away in the 1990s, it was replaced by a single focus on violence against women and, particularly, sexual harm (Miller 2004). This focus not only targeted violence against women and rape, but also various forms of sexual labour framed as 'slavery' (Bernstein 2007). Very diverse perspectives, agendas, and issues, advanced by equally varied advocates pursuing multiple feminist projects and located in different geopolitical spaces, began to converge into one single frame.[7]

Violence against women thus recently prevailed as the main and almost sole focus of the women's human rights agenda. According to Alice Miller (2004), there were two different entry points at that time in the struggle for women's human rights: either equality and non-discrimination, or violence.[8] The issue of violence had not been a salient item on the international and particularly United Nations agenda for many decades, while equality had permeated feminist intervention in the international arena since at least the League of Nations. This shift took place because women's issues adopted 'the form of the mainstream human rights paradigm of the time: a focus on the body suffering from acts committed by the state' (Miller 2004, 23).

Miller (2004) argues that three different histories intersected, allowing for violence against women to become visible to key human rights actors and bodies. First, sexual harm provided the gender-specific version of violence, an issue already relevant for human rights bodies and practitioners, although equal attention was not dedicated 'to remedies and enabling conditions' of such harm (Miller 2004, 19). Particularly important for the emerging focus on violence against women was the campaign to include sexual assault as an element of genocide and crimes against humanity in the international criminal law framework (Halley 2008).[9]

Second, 'the history of mainstream human rights' failure to take on economic and social rights until recently' (Miller 2004, 19) concealed a social justice agenda that had been an important part of many struggles for women's rights in the international arena. Claims that socioeconomic rights are not enforceable and only constitute moral aspirations contributed to the denial of international legal status to demands such as rights to public health or social security. In addition, the hyper visibility given to harms to the bodily integrity of individual women did not challenge the socioeconomic issues that underlie and contextualise gendered violence.

Third, 'the history of health and human rights, as well as an older, troubled history of sexuality and health' (Miller 2004, 19) provided the vocabulary and tools for the description of violence against women (VAW) as a serious medical issue. This description enabled the creation of a highly individualised and pathologising structure of attention to victims,[10] which also meant that alternative social and structural explanations for gender-based violence were generally ignored.

The feminist focus on sexual and bodily integrity succeeded in highlighting some women's issues, thus opening the existing human rights framework to allow for the recognition of violence against women as a rights violation. This recognition contributed to reframing the prevalent public and private division in international law, also prompting discussions on state accountability and responsibility (Chickin 1999). Nonetheless, this focus carried its own problematic assumptions leading to some unintended political consequences. The '"hyper-attention" to sex perversely operated to exclude attention to other aspects of harm' (Miller 2004, 18–19), while also producing a particular portrayal of the female bearer of rights – a localised and racialised victim – for whom feminist activists would speak in the international arena.

An abundant critical literature shows that the victim subject is a relatively recent transnational phenomenon, occurring in the legal discourse springing from both the West and the Third World (Kapur 2002), as it travelled throughout the globe along with feminist legal politics in its struggle against violence. Distinct strands of feminist assessments of the human rights system and the mechanisms necessary for accommodating women's specific grievances – albeit positioning themselves differently in relation to the same issue (such as, for example, female genital mutilation) – equally presupposed the existence of the 'Exotic Other Female (as something "out there")' (Engle 1991, 1512). The category of the helpless victim of 'dysfunctional and exceptionally patriarchal cultures and states' (Razack 1995, 46) became the proxy for women seeking international legal forms of protection such as asylum on the basis of gendered experiences of domestic violence.

At the same time, the construction of women's identities in civil war settings as 'victims of rape' also dominated the field, curtailing their sexual, military, and political agency, and replacing a focus on gender with a focus on sex (Engle 2005a). A similar process of invisibilisation of the actual subject along with victimisation took place in the feminist engagement with the regulation of trafficking in international law, producing the 'myth of trafficking in women, structured around the figure of the passive and unknowing innocent' (Doezema

2005, 67). The anti-trafficking activists' approach was marked by 'a "matronizing" stance towards sex workers' with the consequent denial of the latter's self-ascribed identity (Doezema 2005, 73).

Moreover, the discourse on sexual harm and violence against women reinscribed the male–female dichotomy (Otto 2013) underlying international law since its inception. At work here was the influence of a specific feminist justice project that ties feminism to the essential distinction between two genders of male and female, consequently reinforcing heterosexuality (Halley 2004, 67). This project is also characterised by positing some kind of ontological subordination of female to male, and always supporting females (Halley 2004).[11] Sexuality as a distinct domain of women's subordination was the idea justifying the unification of 'women's distinctive suffering in globalization and in "culture" under the rubric "violence against women", where rape, not market exchange, is the paradigm violent act' (Halley 2004, 79). A feminist universalist worldview that targeted rape with humanitarian law and international criminal law as 'part of a global *war against women*' (Halley 2008, 6) emerged from the developments described here and became the hegemonic paradigm to address violence against women.

The narrow definition of women's human rights also often became attached to old colonial and racial stereotypes circulating in the transnational sphere. For example, the dominant narrative in relation to women's human rights emerging from the legal and justice processes following civil wars in Rwanda and Sierra Leone 'represent[ed] African women not only as victims of armed conflict but as rape victims of a militarized African masculinity' (Mibenge 2013, 7). Such a narrative is problematic because, first, it 'essentializes women as a monolithic victim group and gender as a unitary ground of discrimination' (Mibenge 2013, 7), and second, it fuels the colonial stereotype of African men as indomitable sexual beasts.[12] In failing to acknowledge some locations of resistance, it also makes invisible the multiple sites of power besides the state. By relying on a universal victim subject that does not accommodate the multi-layered and diverse experiences of women (Kapur 2002), this frame fuelled the civilising mission of international law (Koskenniemi 2001).

While one may claim that the stereotyped and often racialised representation of the female victim was an unintended consequence of the feminist campaigns, Alice Miller (2004, 28) points to the contrary. She argues that the rights reports from the 1980s written by feminist activists focused on individual stories and were grounded in limited, 'non-political' claims. She shows how these reports framed a victim devoid of agency and in need of protection. The frame adopted to claim women's human rights placed a focus on 'bodies, pathology, and suffering', rather than simultaneously stressing other dimensions of justice claims, such as equality, democratic participation, and individual agency (Miller 2004, 29). Feminists were then placed in the difficult position of dealing with two existing sexual hierarchies.[13] First, it deems some victims more legitimate than others (Miller 2004). Second, it ascribes false consciousness to those rejecting the 'victim label' (Doezema 2005). In addition to producing the somewhat simplistic portrayal of the victim who needs protection and care and is unable to speak for herself, that frame also contributed to the depoliticisation of the targeted problem, obscuring the understanding that gendered violence is a structural matter.

This framework reduces the scope of the entire 'women's human rights' catalogue to enable the 'protection of bodily integrity'. With this critique, I do not aim to belittle the harms suffered by women or to deny that they deserve legal response. However, the political project of securing women's safety from violence as a human right should be pursued as part of a larger effort, one that critically interrogates its frames. Such critical interrogation needs to encompass questions about both which feminist political subjects and feminist justice projects are included in the frame.

The international women's right to freedom from violence and the problem of essentialism

Having critiqued the minimalist agenda taken by many mainstream women's rights struggles, I now want to underscore the political problem of the gendered subject that is created by representing women as bearers of the (negative) right to a life free of violence.

The dominant transnational campaign for women's human rights came to be characterised by both cultural and gender essentialism (Kapur 2002), as it relied on violence – particularly sexual violence (and sex as violence, in the case of sex workers) – to give content to its agenda. Moya Lloyd has asserted that 'to accrue legitimacy for feminist political demands these demands had to be couched in terms of the needs of a distinct constituency, women' (Lloyd 2005, 59). The question of whether such a political constraint is necessary deserves critical scrutiny. A closer look at the essentialisms characterising the mainstream feminist human rights approach, as outlined thus far, demonstrates what and whose needs are politically prioritised.

In the brief history of the international women's human rights campaign outlined in the previous section, essentialism came to figure at the centre, not only through the attribution of a fixed essence to women as sexualised and passive subjects of human rights, but also through the limitation of what women's human rights mean and entail – a right to a life free of gender-based forms of violence. As the dominant feminist project for women's human rights made violence against women the number one priority, it essentialised the victim in ways that disavowed engagement with the complexities of personal history (Mibenge 2013), as well as with histories that do not follow the dominant script (Doezema 2005).

Essentialism presents itself in the women's human rights politics in two forms: the subject of rights (women) and the content of these rights (sexual violence). This dual essentialisation is problematic for at least three reasons. First, gender-based violence is crystallised, in an ahistorical way, as the specific harm defining women's vulnerability and violability. Second, the discourse that every woman is always a potential victim of violence tends to erase women's other social markers (race, ethnicity, class, gender identity, sexual orientation, location, and so on), therefore neglecting the operation of interlocking systems of oppression (Collins 1990). Finally, and perhaps most importantly, the dual essentialisation entails a form of feminist politics oriented by a logic of humanitarianism.

The problem with humanitarianism and consequently with the discourse of women's human rights that follows the humanitarian logic is that it reduces the human to a suffering body, who needs to be protected and saved, thus foreclosing the critical engagement that characterises feminisms (Scott 2004). The humanitarian frame generates different categories of the human positioned in a hierarchical spectrum organised upon the duality of choice and coercion (Doezema 2005). There are those who are free and autonomous, and those who are oppressed and in need of liberation. Indeed, the logic of humanitarianism distinguishes 'between those who are subjects (the witnesses who testify to the misfortunes of the world) and those who can exist only as objects (the unfortunate whose suffering is testified to in front of the world)' (Fassin 2007, 517). When vindicated through this logic, human rights claims lose their critical potential to question the very basic notion of who counts as human, while also establishing a dangerous hierarchy between victim and spokesperson. Feminists who pursue the goal of women's rights enter this hierarchy in the position of free human beings who seek to rescue and liberate other women, portrayed as helpless victims.

However, is the problem with the discourse of women's human rights located in the particular historical frame of humanitarianism that it has acquired? Is it therefore redeemable through the recognition of both women's diversity and the relationships of power that operate within feminisms themselves? Or is the problem located on a deeper level? Is the problem that women as a category for rights claims 'does not simply report a pre-linguistic experience, but constructs that experience as well as the limits of its analysis' (Butler 1988, 530), therefore excluding subjects and issues that should also be of feminist concern?

(Feminist) critique comes to the rescue of feminisms: new futures for women's human rights

The radical potential of human rights claims should not be lost. We should not see women's rights as static or encompassing a definitive list. Maintaining women's human rights in a manner that is open to contestation and revision must be a part of the feminist human rights project itself.

In face of the need to overcome the exclusionary barriers imposed by hegemonic human rights institutions and framing, feminist activists have focused on a single experience among many others that mark women's lives, namely violence. In doing so, they produced an essential characterisation of the female victim as rights' bearer. If we follow the path from violence against women to the more contemporary campaign against trafficking and prostitution, the trope of victimisation remains not only dominant but still pervasive. As contemporary analysis of 'governance feminism' (Halley, Kotiswaran, Shamir, and Thomas 2006) shows, this version of feminist justice project rules institutions, produces norms, governs various realms of our lives, and wants to do so (Halley 2004, 65). 'Governance feminism' has succeeded in framing the regulation of sexual harassment, child sexual abuse, pornography, and sexual violence – both on national and international levels – and advocates the expansion of its regulatory agenda (Halley 2004), despite the critique that it does so at the expense of various other socio-political interests.

The overwhelming attention given to this female victim legitimates and reinforces a narrow approach to women's human rights. Yet, such a narrow approach is something feminists generally argue against.

What I have just described is the paradox of women's human rights. This paradox resonates with the paradox unleashed by feminist critiques of essentialism.

> [I]f women cannot be characterized in any general way, if all there is to femininity is socially produced, then how can feminism be taken seriously? [...] If we are not justified in taking women as a category, then what political grounding does feminism have? [...] Are these the only choices available to feminist theory – an adherence to essentialist doctrines, or the dissolution of feminist struggles into localized, regional, specific struggles, representing the interest of particular women or groups of women?
>
> (Grosz 1990, 341–342)

I claim that the paradox above needs to be overcome. This can be done first by historicising the essentialism in women's human rights struggles. Second, by pursuing the critical self-assessment that such historicising demands. Both tasks are not only aligned with the idea that feminisms are forms of critique (Scott 2004), but in fact they are constitutive of critique itself.

In what follows, I examine some other relevant elements for this debate, and faithful to the spirit of this chapter, I avoid giving any ultimate solution for the problems outlined thus far. Moya Lloyd argues that the division between essentialism and constructivism, or constation and performativity, which runs through feminist thought, is misleading. For Lloyd (2005, 69),

> [E]very declaration of what a woman is, is simultaneously a performative production of that being and every time that demands are made on behalf of women (as a whole or specific groups of them), there is a provisional reification of what it means to be a woman ('the victim of rape', 'a mother', and so forth).

In this sense, the relevant issue to address is not essentialism per se, but rather the act of freezing in history and protecting from critical scrutiny the essentialisms we develop out of political necessity in very specific historical contexts. In making her claim, Moya Lloyd (2005) is interested in pushing forward an agenda of agonistic politics for feminism, in which, by acknowledging that its (essentialised) subject is always an unavoidably partial and fallible construction, feminisms need to constantly interrogate and destabilise that very identity.

I believe that this is one part of the critical self-assessment demanded by feminisms. When making political claims that require mobilising a collective identity, for example when vindicating rights for groups previously denied legal recognition, it is of utmost importance to leave those identities open, contested, and contingent – knowing that they are nothing more than a partial and historical essentialism. As such, this critical reflection may lead to a radical re-articulation of the collective identity, in an endless spiral in which critique produces a new essentialised formation that, once scrutinised, is again abandoned for the emergence of a new one.

However, the second part of feminisms' critical self-assessment entails understanding that just as women do not have a unified identity, feminisms are not unitary, but rather a highly contested political space. Feminisms are so contested that it is more accurate to talk about a 'feminist discursive field of action' (Alvarez 2014). Understanding feminisms as one of many 'discursive fields of action' describes 'much more than mere collections of organizations focused on a specific issue' (Rodrigues and Assis 2017, 158). Discursive fields of action assemble 'a vast array of individual and collective actors as well as social, cultural, and political places' (Alvarez 2014, 18). Being dynamic, the discursive fields of action are historically configured and reconfigured, which means that 'both their more politically and culturally visible sectors, as well as the nodal points articulated within them, vary throughout time' (Alvarez 2014, 18). Moreover, these fields are structured

> (i) formally and informally, through political-communicative networks, or better said, reticulated nets or meshes; (ii) discursively, through languages, meanings, worldviews at least partially shared through a kind of political grammar connecting actors who identify with them, even if these are almost always disputed, and (iii) through an enmeshment of interlocutions.
>
> (Alvarez 2014, 18–19)

Along these lines, the discursive fields of action are various and clustered around a wide range of issues, with the feminist being only one of them. Another important characteristic of these fields is how they relate theory and practice. These fields are spaces where ideas are not only generated, but also lived, practiced, and embodied. In other words, there is an experimental and experiential element to the fields, because those who are part of them put in practice the circulating thoughts and propositions, and experiment with possibilities and limits. Moreover, the fields are not devoid of internal struggles, dissent, or contradictions. On the contrary, they are fluid spaces, reconfigured because of changes in alliances, internal disputes, and transformations both within and without, in connections and conflicts with other fields (Alvarez 2014). Finally, the discursive fields are influenced and even shaped by other nets or meshes, in a productive interaction with their counterparts.

Understanding feminisms as a 'discursive field of action' is necessary because it highlights the variety of projects, ideas, positions, and imaginable futures that contend with one another. Rather than a unified universality, the feminist discursive field of action is an ongoing, endless contestation of theories and practices, actors, and discourses that formulate women as their subjects. Not only is the identity of the feminist subject a contested one, thus open to critical interrogation, but, and perhaps even more importantly, the identity of feminism itself is also in dispute. These two issues are in fact intertwined: certain feminisms produce certain 'feminist subjects', which are coherent with their feminist justice projects.

The question is then what those of us who identify with strands of feminisms that disagree with what has been accomplished in the name of women's human rights should do. Should we embrace a postfeminist argument that posits the 'pastness' of feminism (Tasker and Negra 2007) and has been strongly appropriated by neoconservative work (Halley 2006, 59), fuelling a neoliberal subjectivity (Butler 2013)? My answer is no. I believe, with Joan Scott, that the answer lies in 'conceiving of feminism as a restless critical operation, as a movement of desire' (2004, 19). Here, desire refers to 'a mutating historical phenomenon, defined as and through its displacement' (Scott 2004, 19). This formulation gives us a path that does not subscribe to the postfeminist script and makes a critique of essentialism possible.

Conclusion

Feminisms, understood as a field of discursive action oriented by 'restless critical operation' (Scott 2004), are as alive and necessary today as they have ever been. The formulation of critiques in contemporary times, rather than signalling the death of feminist political projects, means that we are taking these projects seriously. In other words, feminisms contain in themselves the call to suspend our current feminist assumptions and interrogate ourselves about the doings and undoings of the essential categories we forge and deploy in our struggles for rights, political space, recognition, and so on.

In order to assess the category of women's human rights and imagine the different paths it might take, it is not necessary to posit the end of feminisms, but rather to recover their critical force, giving away the idea of a 'utopian project of complete emancipation' (Scott 2004, 19). Such a critical force entails historicising: it 'uses the past to disrupt the certainties of the present and so opens the ways to imagining a different future' (Scott 2004, 18). It entails, also, rescuing the other possible paths we left behind on our way to where we stand now – for example, by reclaiming global socioeconomic justice as an integral part of women's human rights. This would involve acknowledging that the violence perpetrated by multinational corporations against indigenous lands and communities is a form of violence against indigenous women, that neocolonial exploitation is a women's rights issue, and that the relationship between women within the movements has always to be a horizontal one, no matter what position they occupy.

The dominant version of women's human rights, as I argued throughout this chapter, abdicated the force of critique in favour of a stable and all-encompassing emancipatory script that could politically succeed in changing hegemonic human rights institutions. It is now time to imagine new futures – futures that are not postfeminist, but rather feminist to the very core, for they are critical of their own history and aware of the necessary contingency of any essentialism we deploy.

Notes

1 I would like to thank the blind reviewers for the comments and suggestions to improve this chapter. The editors, and particularly Anne Macduff, were also extremely generous in their various revisions and advice. This chapter would not have been published without their assistance. Finally, my dear friend Ana Carolina Ogando, with her close reading, pointed out many of the blind spots and inconsistencies, encouraging me to improve my writing and analysis. I am grateful to her. Any mistakes and deficiencies are obviously on me.

2 Interestingly enough, it was a group of Latin American feminists who had met in Mexico City amid the confrontation with the Friedan-led Feminist Caucus in 1975 who initiated the *Encuentro Feminista Latinoamericano y del Caribe*, in 1981 (Olcott 2017, 242).

3 As Joan Scott explains, this is a context dependent process: 'the terms of exclusion are also variable and contradictory, based in different epistemologies, and this variability and contradiction result in fundamentally different conceptions of the "women" whose rights are being claimed' (Scott 1997, 14).

4 I have suggested in a previous work that

> categories are relevant in different specialized fields: they play a central role in social science, public policy and [...] in transnational activism. For academics observing and explaining the world, categories enable them to make sense and organize a messy reality, identifying groups of people and things that share specific features and can then be aggregated for data analysis (Bakewell 2011, 24). In the field of public policy, categorization also serves to organize reality, but here they have a much more concrete impact. It is through categorization that policy makers grant specific entitlements to certain groups while excluding others (Bakewell 2011, 24). [...] As the case of violence against women shows, categorization is also an important tool for activists. It was through the development of a category that the transnational network against violence could name a problem and give a face to it.
> (Assis 2017, 1515–1516)

5 For example, when the Black Lives Matter movement creates its political subject – all black people who have been murdered for their skin colour – their political purpose is not, and should not be, to recognise that subject, but to fight racism and white supremacist ideology that made the creation of the subject necessary in the first place.

6 Along these lines, in July 1926, Lady Margaret Rhondda proposed to Alice Paul, the chair of the International Advisory Committee of the American National Woman's Party, the idea of an equal rights treaty, following the model of the American Equal Rights Amendment (ERA). Paul, a leading feminist lawyer, not only immediately took up Rhondda's suggestion and drafted the treaty, but also spent most of the next decade campaigning in the international sphere for its support by feminist organisations and its adoption by international bodies, such as the Pan-American Union, the League of Nations and the International Labor Office (Miller 1994, 220–221).

7 Interestingly enough, in her analysis of the feminist involvement in the legislative process leading to the establishment of the International Criminal Tribunals

for the former Yugoslavia (ICTY) and for Rwanda (ICTR) and the International Criminal Court (ICC), Janet Halley points to the fact that feminists' 'organizational style was overwhelmingly coalitional, resulting in a literary "trace" of feminist work that is almost devoid of manifest internal conflict' (Halley 2008, 2). Thus, Halley finds a single structuralist-feminist worldview animating the argumentation and rule preference in relation to the formation of those tribunals and, particularly, the criminalisation of wartime rape, with no expression of internal conflict or dissent.

8 It is also important to acknowledge the role played by liberalism in leading violence, and particularly sexual violence (understood as the denial of ownership of one's body), to be seen as the core of women's oppression (Doezema 2005, 69).

9 As a result of this large international campaign,

> many new mechanisms and norms came into being [...], including: the incorporation of gender crimes in the statutes/practice of the ad hoc War Crime Tribunals, the creation of a UN Special Rapporteur on Violence against Women, a UN Declaration on the Elimination of Violence against Women, and the integration of gender into the definition of crimes and expertise of the judges for the International Criminal Court (ICC).
>
> (Miller 2004, 23)

10 For an insightful account of how the medicalisation and consequent pathologisation of violence against women took place in the United States, as well as its dreadful consequences, see the work of Kristin Bumiller (2008).

11 As Halley (2004, 66) has argued, these three essential elements worked to configure the disciplinary boundaries of what may be characterised as feminist and what lacks such qualification, while also providing to feminism a 'paranoid structuralism' (Halley 2004, 62) that presupposes the need for feminism always, and everywhere.

12 In addition to these problems, similar accounts also ended up serving strategic interests in the domain of international relations. Critics (Abu-Lughod 2002; Ayotte and Husain 2005; Engle 2005b) have demonstrated this to be the case of the so-called War on Terror, when the rescue and liberation of Muslim women (from aggressive and brutalised Muslim men), buttressed by the values of equality, freedom, and democracy and provided the gendered narrative that would allow 'might' to have the appearance of 'right'.

13 Drawing from Gayle Rubin, Alice Miller defines sexual hierarchies as

> systems of legitimacy both tacit (shaming) and explicit (legal) that arise in various contexts (country, culture, whatever the unit of imagination) and that prioritize certain forms of reproductive, marital, and heterosexual activity above other sexual behaviors and identities, eventually forcing these marginalized behaviors outside the pale of rights claiming.
>
> (Miller 2004, 36)

References

Abu-Lughod, Lila. 2002. "Do Muslim Women Really Need Saving? Anthropological Reflections on Cultural Relativism and Its Others." *American Anthropologist* 104, no. 3: 783–790.

Adrião, Karla Galvão, and Maria Juracy Filgueiras Toneli. 2008. "Por Uma Política de Acesso Aos Direitos Das Mulheres: Sujeitos Feministas Em Disputa No Contexto Brasileiro." *Psicologia & Sociedade* 20, no. 3: 465–474.

Alvarez, Sonia E. 2014. "Para Além da Sociedade Civil: Reflexões sobre os Campos Feministas." *Cadernos PAGU* 12, no. 43: 13–56.

Ashworth, Georgina. 1999. "The Silencing of Women." In *Human Rights in Global Politics*, edited by Ken Booth, 259–276. Cambridge: Cambridge University Press.

Assis, Mariana Prandini. 2017. "Violence against Women as a Translocal Category in the Jurisprudence of the Inter-American Court of Human Rights." *Revista Direito & Práxis* 8, no. 2: 1507–1544.

Ayotte, Kevin J., and Mary E. Husain. 2005. "Securing Afghan Women: Neocolonialism, Epistemic Violence, and the Rhetoric of the Veil." *NWSA Journal* 17, no. 3: 112–133.

Bakewell, Oliver. 2011. "Conceptualising Displacement and Migration: Processes, Conditions, and Categories." In *The migration-displacement nexus: Patterns, Processes, and Policies*, edited by Khalid Koser and Susan Martin, 14–28. Oxford and New York: Berghahn Books.

Bernstein, Elizabeth. 2007. "The Sexual Politics of the "New Abolitionism"." *Differences* 18, no. 5: 128–151.

Brown, Wendy. 2000. "Suffering Rights as Paradoxes." *Constellations* 7, no. 2: 208–229.

Bumiller, Kristin. 2008. *In an Abusive State: How Neoliberalism Appropriated the Feminist Movement against Sexual Violence.* Durham, NC: Duke University Press.

Butler, Judith. 1988. "Performative Acts and Gender Constitution: An Essay in Phenomenology and Feminist Theory." *Theatre Journal* 40, no. 4: 519–531.

———. 2004. *Undoing Gender.* New York; London: Routledge.

Butler, Jess. 2013. "For White Girls Only? Postfeminism and the Politics of Inclusion." *Feminist Formations* 25, no. I: 35–58.

Chickin, Christine. 1999. "A Critique of the Public/Private Dimension." *European Journal of International Law* 10, no. 2: 387–395.

Collins, Patricia Hill. 1990. *Black Feminist Thought: Knowledge, Consciousness, and the Politics of Empowerment.* Boston, MA: Unwin Hyman.

Doezema, Jo. 2005. "Now You See Her, Now You Don't: Sex Workers at the UN Trafficking Protocol Negotiations." *Social & Legal Studies* 14, no. 1: 61–89.

Engle, Karen. 1991. "Female Subjects of Public International Law: Human Rights and the Exotic Other Female." *New England Law Review* 26: 1509–1526.

———. 2005a. "Feminism and Its (Dis)contents: Criminalizing Wartime Rape in Bosnia and Herzegovina." *The American Journal of International Law* 99, no. 4: 778–816.

———. 2005b. "Liberal Internationalism, Feminism, and the Suppression of Critique: Contemporary Approaches to Global Order in the United States." *Harvard International Law Journal* 46: 427.

Fassin, Didier. 2007. "Humanitarianism as a Politics of Life." *Public Culture* 19, no. 3: 499–520.

Grosz, Elizabeth. 1990. "Conclusion: A Note on Essentialism and Difference." In *Feminist Knowledge: Critique and Construct*, edited by Sneja Gunew, 332–344. London; New York: Routledge.

Halley, Janet. 2004. "Take a Break from Feminism?" In *Gender and Human Rights*, edited by Karen Knop, 57–81. Oxford: Oxford University Press.

———. 2008. "Rape at Rome: Feminist Interventions in the Criminalization of Sex-Related Violence in Positive International Criminal Law." *Michigan Journal of International Law* 30, no. 1: 1–123.

Halley, Janet, Prabha Kotiswaran, Hila Shamir, and Chantal Thomas. 2006. "From the International to the Local in Feminist Legal Responses to Rape, Prostitution/Sex Work, and Sex Trafficking: Four Studies in Contemporary Governance Feminism." *Harvard Journal of Law & Gender* 29: 335–423.

Kapur, Ratna. 2002. "The Tragedy of Victimization Rhetoric: Resurrecting the Native Victim Subject in International/Postcolonial Feminist Legal Politics." *Harvard Human Rights Law Journal* 15: 1–38.

Koskenniemi, Martti. 2001. *The Gentle Civilizer of Nations: The Rise and Fall of International Law 1870–1960.* Cambridge, New York: Cambridge University Press.

Lloyd, Moya. 2005. *Beyond Identity Politics: Feminism, Power and Politics.* London: SAGE.

Mibenge, Chiseche Salome. 2013. *Sex and International Tribunals: The Erasure of Gender from the War Narrative.* Philadelphia: University of Pennsylvania Press.

Miller, Alice M. 2004. "Sexuality, Violence against Women, and Human Rights: Women Make Demands and Ladies Get Protection." *Health and Human Rights* 7, no. 2: 16–47.

Miller, Carol. 1994. "'Geneva – The Key to Equality': Inter-War Feminists and the League of Nations." *Women's History Review* 3, no. 2: 219–245.

Olcott, Jocelyn. 2017. *International Women's Year: The Greatest Consciousness-raising Event in History.* Oxford, New York: Oxford University Press.

Orford, Anne. 1998. "Contesting Globalization: A Feminist Perspective on the Future of Human Rights." *Transnational Law & Contemporary Problems* 8: 171–98.

Otto, Dianne. 2007. "The Gastronomics of TWAIL's Feminist Flavourings: Some Lunch-Time Offerings." *International Community Law Review* 9, no. 4: 345–352.

———. 2013. "International Human Rights Law: Towards Rethinking Sex/Gender Dualism and Asymmetry." In *The Ashgate Research Companion to Feminist Legal Theory*, edited by Vanessa Munro, 197–216. Farnham: Ashgate Publishing.

Rancière, Jacques. 2004. "Who Is the Subject of the Rights of Man?" *South Atlantic Quarterly* 103, no. 2–3: 297–310.

Razack, Sherene. 1995. "Domestic Violence as Gender Persecution: Policing the Borders of Nation, Race, and Gender." *Canadian Journal of Women and the Law* 8: 45–88.

Rhode, Deborah L. 1989. *Justice and Gender: Sex Discrimination and the Law.* Cambridge, MA: Harvard University Press.

Rodrigues, Cristiano, and Mariana Prandini Assis. 2017. "Academic Feminism and Exclusion in Brazil: Bringing Back Some of the Missing Voices." In *Gender Studies and the New Academic Governance: Global Challenges, Glocal Dynamics and Local Impacts*, edited by Heike Kahlert, 153–175. Wiesbaden: Springer VS.

Scott, Joan. 1997. *Only Paradoxes to Offer: French Feminists and the Rights of Man.* Cambridge, MA: Harvard University Press.

———. 2004. "Feminism's History." *Journal of Women's History* 16, no. 2: 10–29.

Tasker, Yvonne, and Diane Negra. 2007. "Introduction: Feminist Politics and Post-feminist Culture." In *Interrogating Postfeminism: Gender and the Politics of Popular Culture*, edited by Lynn Spigel and Angela McRobbie, 1–26. Durham, NC: Duke University Press.

Viezzer, Moema. 2014. "Si Me Permiten Hablar: Testimonio de Domitila, Una Mujer de Las Minas de Bolivia." In *Tejiendo de Otro Modo: Feminismo, Epistemología Y Apuestas Descoloniales En Abya Yala,* edited by Yuderkys Espinosa Miñoso, Diana Marcela Gómez Correal and Karina Ochoa Muñoz, 389–398. Popayán: Editoral Universidad del Cauca.

Wong, Jane. 1999. "The Anti-Essentialism v. Essentialism Debate in Feminist Legal Theory: The Debate and Beyond." *William & Mary Journal of Women and the Law* 5, no. 2: 273–296.

6 Postfeminism and the possibilities of post-essential politics

Anne Macduff

Introduction

Feminist legal scholars might be wary of 'postfeminism' for many reasons. One reason might be that the term conveys many meanings. 'Postfeminism' is associated with the position that feminism is no longer necessary (McRobbie 2004), either because women have achieved equality, do not see themselves as victims of oppression, and/or do not hate men. This position is also called 'neo-feminism', or 'choice-feminism' (Budgeon 2015, 304) or indeed 'anti-feminism'. Yet 'post-feminism' is also a position taken by feminists working with a range of theories loosely labelled as 'postmodern'.[1] Postmodern theories question the assumption that there is a fixed, essential subject position from which to articulate women's experience. For clarity, this chapter refers to this second notion of postfeminism as 'postmodern feminism'.

Another reason feminists are wary is because both meanings appear to undermine a feminist politics. Neo-feminism undermines feminist politics because it views it as unnecessary. Postmodern feminism undermines feminist politics because it challenges the identity category at its core, the subject 'woman'. Without the category 'woman', it is assumed that there is no position from which women can politically rally for law reform.

While the argument that feminist politics is no longer necessary is swiftly rejected by substantial scholarship outlining continued gender inequality, legal feminists need to take seriously the argument that postmodern feminism undermines a feminist politics. Has postmodern feminism rendered the politics of legal feminists impossible? Does the absence of a unified, women's experience mean that there are no firm foundations upon which to argue for law reform? These questions need to be resolved if postmodern feminism is to remain relevant to contemporary feminist legal scholars. Feminist legal scholars need to have both the theoretical tools to challenge the gendered limits of the law, and the practical tools to transform the law and social reality (Drakopoulou 2000a, 208–209). This aim of this chapter is to start to address these questions.

This chapter argues that postmodern feminism can support a feminist politics of law reform through theorising a 'post-essential politics'.[2] The chapter begins with a section that briefly explains postmodern feminism and its critique of essentialism. It outlines the 'crisis of subjectivity' that followed (Drakopoulou 2000a, 199), and explains why some legal feminists argue that postmodern feminism undermines the possibilities of a feminist politics of law reform.

The second section examines the claim that an effective politics requires the solidarity of individuals who share a unified subject position. It deploys Bell's theory of 'interest convergence' (Bell 1980), developed in the context of critical race theory, to reject this claim. Following Bell, this section argues that political gains are not achieved through a unified politics, but rather through an alignment of interests with the dominant majority. To demonstrate the power of this theory in a feminist context, this section uses interest convergence to critically analyse the Child Support Act 1988 (Cth) in Australia. While some feminists might argue that this is a pessimistic direction in which to go, it is not necessarily the case. If one understands politics as an ethical commitment, then Bell's theory provides the impetus to rethink the possibility of a 'post-essential politics' (Hunter 1996, 156).

The third section explores how Chantal Mouffe's political theory of 'agonism' (Mouffe 1992, 1993, 1999, 2000) is a way of understanding political action that does not rely on a unified subject position. This section concludes with a brief exploration of how Mouffe's theory might be useful for postmodern feminists seeking to engage in law reform through a strategy of coalition.

This chapter harnesses postmodern feminism to spark a 'reorientation of the feminist project in law' (Drakopoulou 2000b, 71). Far from undermining a feminist politics of law, this chapter suggests that postmodern feminism has capacity to breathe new life into it.

The problem with essentialism and the subjectivity crisis

To begin, this section broadly outlines the key concepts informing postmodern feminism and its critique of essentialism. It then explores the crisis of subjectivity which followed, and its implications for a politics of feminist law reform.

Feminism has, over time, drawn on a broad range of theories. Postmodern feminism is informed by 'postmodern' theories (Wicke 1992, Nicholson 1992 Wiegman 1999), particularly the critique of the Enlightenment claim that there is a universal truth that is unmediated by culture and values (Farginis 19994, 24). Foucault is a particularly important influence, specifically his theory of discourse and power (Foucault 1976, 1980, 1990). Foucault's work on 'madness', the 'criminal', and the 'homosexual' explores the historical (or genealogical) use of those terms, and how discourse mediates what becomes 'known'. Foucault theorises power as productive and generative, rather than a force individuals possess, and therefore change is always possible through the circulation of ideas in discourse.

These theoretical influences led postmodern feminists to understand identity in a particular way (Naffine 2002, 88). Postmodern feminists challenge the notion of a fixed or essential truth for any identity category, but specifically for gender and sex (Butler 1990). They argue that there is no objective experience of being a woman that can be known independently of cultural or other values (Scott 1988; Naffine 2002, 88; Davies & Mack 2004). 'The very idea of speaking authoritatively as a woman therefore became inherently problematic' (Naffine 2002, 87; see also Drakopoulou 2000a). Instead, they argue that feminist identities are constituted and reconstituted in specific socially and historically situated discourses (Wiegman 1999).

Postmodern feminists critique the essentialism which, it argues, underpins the earlier 'waves' of feminism (Thornton 1986, 8, 2010, 94; Genovese 1996, 168; Janus 2013).[3] Those waves include liberal feminism, difference feminism, and radical feminism (Farginis 1994; Naffine 1990). Although describing feminism in waves simplifies the overlapping and ongoing interactions between these different feminisms (Drakopoulou 2000a; Bulbeck 2006; Janus 2013; Snyder 2008, 178, 192), it is nonetheless a useful framework for analysing the postmodern feminist critique of essentialism.

Liberal feminism, or first-wave feminism, argues that women should have equal 'inclusion in the political structure' (Farginis 1994, 28), and argues for the removal of gender based barriers and constraints. While liberal feminism does not explicitly suggest that there is a unified experience or subject position, it implicitly relies on a universal, undifferentiated experience of 'women' to generate its critical insights and political targets (Harris 1990). Postmodern feminists critique liberal feminism for assuming that gender is the principal basis for inequality and generally failing to distinguish between the experiences of different women based on other identity categories such as class, race, ability, and sexuality (Scott 1988; Nicholson 1992, 59).

There are two branches of second-wave feminism, difference feminism and radical feminism. Difference feminism articulates and then reinserts the values of 'women' into institutional structures (Gilligan 1982; West 1987, 1988). Radical feminism argues that society reinforces a hierarchical relationship between the sexes, a relationship which privileges male power and systemically subordinates women's interests. This 'fixes' the identity of 'women' in a power structure that defines women as 'oppressed' (Mackinnon 1983; Scales 1986). Thornton argues that radical feminism suggests that 'victimhood is an immutable condition' (Thornton 2004, 10). What both branches of second-wave feminism share is the assumption that there is a shared experience of being a 'woman' which derives from either shared biological traits (sex) and/or social practices of gender (Snyder 2008, 184). In doing so, these branches both accept 'singularity as a social category … as the basis for identifying a common struggle' (Wicke 1992, 30).

Postfeminists argue that the assumption of a (unified) gender-based subject underpinning the first and the second-wave of feminism leads to political strategies that are in 'danger of a profound oversimplification of our understanding of social and political life' (Genovese 2013, 54). Postmodern feminism is critical of the various ways each of these theories of feminism draw upon gender, or being a woman, as a common basis for political action.

While the 'postmodern turn' (Fraser & Nicholson 1989), or the third-wave, has prompted legal feminists to explicitly theorise the experiences of differently situated women (Wishnik 1985, 72–73; Kline 1989), new problems have emerged.

Just over 20 years ago, an Australian legal feminist scholar Rosemary Hunter asked: 'How can Australian legal feminists continue to engage with law in non-essentialist ways?' (Hunter 1996, 136). Today, legal feminists remain critical of the postmodern turn and argue that it has contributed to a depoliticisation of feminism (Thornton 2004, 7). Drakopoulou notes that:

> In striving to resolve the tension between the positing of a subject which captures the essence of the oppression women suffer by law, and translating this onto historically specific women, feminists have fundamentally challenged the idea of a universal knowing subject and thereby seriously undermined the validity of the associated politics of legal reform.
>
> (Drakopoulou 2000b, 51)

Naffine, Thornton, and others identify a number of ways that the postmodern turn in feminist theory has been thought to undermine feminist politics (Naffine 2002; Thornton 2004). Pausing to reflect on the two main ways helps to articulate the different and interrelated assumptions about what feminist legal scholars understand to be an effective politics.

First, the critics of postmodern feminism (hereafter referred to as 'the critics') claim that postmodern feminism fragments the political category 'women'. That is, when one argues that identity is contextual and shifting, fewer women are able to share a common view. This in turn leads to a 'weakening of the collective underpinnings of feminism' (Thornton 2004, 7). If political unity is strength in numbers, then by questioning a shared experience, postmodern feminism undermines its political impact. In this way, questioning the unified subject position makes a feminist politics of law reform less effective and vulnerable to being ignored (Thornton 2004, 9).

Second, the critics argue that postmodern feminism generates 'political inertia' (Thornton 2004, 13). There are two main reasons for this. First, postmodern feminism is thought to encourage working in a manner that is too abstract and/or introspective (Thornton 2004, 13). Some legal feminists argue that a feminist focus on abstract theory limits its material or practical benefit (Conaghan 2000, 354). Postfeminism is thought to deter scholars from engaging in a feminist politics of law reform because it renders feminism unable to address practical issues that affect women, such as ongoing violence (Nussbaum 1999). Second, as there is no position outside of constituted power relations, the critics argue that this leads to moral relativism. This is because there is also no longer any objective measure through which to evaluate whether a change is 'feminist' or not, or why feminist political goals are worthier than others (Barron 2000, 278). As a consequence, feminism loses its political 'foundations' (Snyder 2008, 186). The critics conclude that since there is no hope that one will be successful in changing the system, postmodern feminism paralyses feminist political action (Barron 2000, 278). In these different ways, the critics argue that postmodern feminism creates obstacles for legal feminists wishing to engage in concrete political action including law reform.

While the challenge to essentialism has been an important theoretical contribution by postmodern feminism, the critics, particularly in the legal academy, have raised some important concerns about what going beyond the gendered subject might mean for the future of a feminist politics of law reform. Thinking through these concerns is the focus of the remainder of this chapter.

The myth of political unity and a new hope

This section aims to critically challenge the assumption that a shared collective identity leads to an effective politics of law reform. It does this by drawing on Derrick Bell's theory of 'interest convergence' (Bell 1980), and his critical re-reading of the US decision in *Brown v Board of Education of Topeka* 347 U.S. 483 (1954) *('Brown')*. While neither a postmodern theory nor a feminist theory, the theory of interest convergence clearly challenges the assumption that a unified voice is required for legal change. This section demonstrates the usefulness of this theory in a feminist context by using it to analyse the introduction of the Child Support Scheme in Australia. While the argument that lasting legal change is not possible even when there is a sense of a unified political identity might be considered a pessimistic one, I argue that it enables a re-orientation of a feminist politics.

Derrick Bell develops a theory of interest convergence to explain the failure of the US decision of *Brown* to live up to its transformative promise (Bell 1980). *Brown* is widely known as the decision that created racial equality in America through dismantling racial segregation in American schools. He seeks to explain why, despite the Court's landmark decision, the quality of the education that African American children receive today continues to be of much poorer quality than for white children.

Bell's theory of interest convergence suggests that while racial equality is a moral and political imperative in society, it is not the only one (Bell 1980, 523). Despite applauding the outcome of the legal decision in *Brown*, Bell argues that racial equality in schools was not the main reason for the legal decision. Bell argues that racial equality in education was achieved because it converged with the interests of the racially dominant group in the USA, that is, white Americans. 'The interest of blacks in achieving racial equality will be accommodated only when it converges with the interests of whites' (Bell 1980, 523). Bell identifies the dominant interests behind the decision in *Brown* as; countering international Soviet criticism during the cold war (Bell 1980, 524), international responsibility towards the treatment of African American World War II veterans (Bell 1980, 524), a path towards economic modernisation in the Southern states of the USA (Bell 1980, 525), and a need to bolster the authority of the Supreme Court and other federal structures (Bell 1980, 529). Although initially only a theory, Mary Dudziak later uncovered empirical evidence to support Bell's arguments (Dudziak 1988).

Bell develops interest convergence to explain how despite the landmark status now attributed to *Brown*, African American children remain disadvantaged in schools compared to white American children (Bell 1980, 531). He contends that changes in the law that appear to benefit marginalised groups only succeed when they coincide with, or confirm, the interests of the majority. The theory of interest convergence has been subsequently applied in Australia to analyse the failure of landmark cases such as *Mabo* to bring any real change in conditions of racial equality to indigenous Australians (Allen 2007).

While Bell himself does not use interest convergence theory to highlight the problem of essentialism, this chapter argues that Bell's argument demonstrates that conditions of political unity do not necessarily secure law reform. At the time of *Brown*, there was arguably a clear, unified racial identity politics pushing for civil rights in the USA. Yet Bell's theory suggests that a coherent political identity is not a sufficient condition for an effective politics of legal reform.

Bell's theory of interest convergence provides new insights into the impasse in feminist politics created by the theoretical collapse of the category 'woman'. Interest convergence is useful in critically challenging the assumption that unity in the category 'women' is required for an effective feminist politics of law reform. To illustrate its potential in a feminist context, interest convergence can be used to explain why the introduction of the Child Support Scheme in Australia was not as deeply transformative for gender equality as had been hoped. Further, interest convergence suggests that the Scheme was only introduced when the interests of feminists aligned with the economic interests of an emerging neo-liberal state, rather than through any unified political stance arising from the political activities organised in the interests of 'women'.

In the 1980s, Australian legal feminism arguably made inroads into addressing gendered economic inequality (Graycar 1990, 154). Many women's organisations lobbied heavily to highlight the difficult financial situation women often found themselves in, particularly after divorce (Graycar 1990, 153). With divorce numbers rising following the introduction of the Family Law Act 1975 (Cth), there were serious concerns that many women were living in poverty. Scholarship suggested that following divorce, while re-partnered men and re-partnered women were roughly on par financially, single women found it more difficult to recover financially than single men (MacDonald 1986). Moreover, single men were re-partnering at a much higher rate, and when they did, they were much better off financially than single women (Smyth & Weston 2000). Research identified that the economic disparity was gendered due to the fact that women were shouldering a higher proportion of childcare and were experiencing labour market and wage discrimination (Weston & Smyth 2000; Cerise et al. 2009). In addition, the legal system was compounding the issue. There were low numbers of maintenance orders made in courts that might have addressed this structural inequality (Parker 1991, 26; Weston & Smyth 2000, 11). Further, even when maintenance orders were made, only 30% were paid (National Maintenance Inquiry 1984; Graycar 2008, 83).

One important reform introduced to address the gendered economic disadvantage following separation was the Child Support Act 1988 (Cth).[4] This Act was to become part of the Child Support Scheme ('the Scheme'), which created a legal obligation of all parents to child support, and an administrative mechanism to collect it. Interest convergence theory would suggest that the Australian Parliament introduced these changes only when women's interests aligned with the wider interests. A closer analysis of the introduction of the Scheme supports this theory.

Although women's lobby groups had worked hard for the Scheme, women's economic security was neither of the two explicit policy objectives mentioned in the parliamentary debates. One explicit objective of the reform was to alleviate the poverty of children living with sole parents (Howe 1987; Young et al. 2016, 740). Since 80% of sole parents were women (Summerfield et al. 2010), this practically went some way to addressing the financial disadvantage women faced upon separation. However, the gendered reality of sole parenting remained unacknowledged. The parliamentary debates do not refer to the fact that sole parents were predominantly women (Cerise et al. 2009, 14). The language used mentions only 'non-custodial' and 'custodial' parents (Howe 1987).

The other explicitly stated objective of the Child Support Scheme was to reduce state welfare payments (Howe 1987). This objective 'reflected and dovetailed with the mainstream political agenda of modernisation and reform' (Thornton 2010, 93). Child support was framed in Australia as an individual arrangement between two parents, rather than as a payment by the non-carer parent (mostly the father) to the carer–parent (mostly the mother) for the labour costs involved in caring for the children (Parker 1991). This ensured that the financial and economic needs of the carer-parent would be satisfied by the non-carer parent, before the carer-parent could turn to state support. In other words, the objective of the Scheme was to shift the economic burden of financial care of children from the state onto the private individual (Graycar 2008, 90). Feminist legal scholars critiqued the implementation of this Scheme which perpetuated women's economic dependence on men (Graycar 2008), and ignored issues of gender-based economic disadvantage and patterns of care.

Beyond these two explicit objectives, there are arguably further interests that the Scheme supported, which aligned with wider interests of dominant society. The legal feminist strategy of engaging with legislative reform enhances the role of state as protector. In Australia in the 1980s, legal feminists were very active in negotiating with the state to introduce a wide range of legislative reforms (Ryan 1990; Eisenstein 1990). In the criminal law context, feminist legal scholars have argued that a reliance on legislative reform also creates

> a wounded subjectivity which requires protection from the state 'leads almost inevitably to increased calls for state regulation, with little or no critical attention paid to the role of law and state power in producing and reproducing the very conditions that make rape not only possible but ubiquitous'.
> (Pendleton & Serisier 2009, 84 quoting Wendy Brown).

The reliance by feminist groups on legislative reform bolsters the state's legitimate role as a benevolent protector of women. Australian legal feminists were actively engaged with lobbying the state rather than pursuing action through litigation and the courts, which was the preferred strategy in other jurisdictions (Chappell 2000).

Bell's interest convergence theory can be used to re-evaluate not only the reasons for the lack of radical transformation achieved by the Scheme, but its political drivers. The theory suggests that, while a unified feminist collective lobbied for the Scheme, legislation was not passed until the interests of gender equality could be aligned with the interests of the dominant group. The dominant interests in introducing the Scheme analysed were reducing child poverty, protecting state economic interests, and affirming that the government was a benevolent protector of women.

If interest convergence suggests that political action by unified groups is, at most, likely to realise only temporary change, does this signal the end of a feminist politics altogether? Legal feminist scholars are rightly wary of political paralysis, and it would seem that interest convergence might have a similarly pessimistic end. However, Bell himself addresses political pessimism in the struggle for racial equality, calling for 'racial realism' (Bell 1992). Bell observes that even in the face of unlikely change, his theory of interest convergence does not mean that political struggles end. He writes, 'The fight in itself has meaning and should give us hope for the future' (Ibid, 378–379). I interpret his racial realism as an ethical prompt to activists to articulate why they are taking action. It prompts activists to let go of any desire to be recognised as the makers or instigators of change or reform. Instead, political engagement is about the ethical commitment to the values (such as equality) that underpin the struggle, rather than about the chances of a successful outcome or progress.

What might a postmodern feminist ethics of politics look like? It would, for instance, likely include a commitment to the values of diversity and difference in identity politics (Snyder 2008). It would likely also recognise the importance of the fluid construction of identity, including gender. Moreover, even while postmodern feminists have challenged a biological, fixed, and essentialised truth of the category 'woman', the category still has discursive currency. A critical analysis of gendered experiences can therefore continue to be made without sliding into either moral relativism or political nihilism, and therefore an ethical basis for an engagement remains.

A post-essential politics?

Butler raises an important question for postmodern feminism when she asks, 'What new shape of politics emerges when identity as a common ground no longer constrains the discourse of feminist politics?' (Butler 1990, xi). In attempting to answer the challenge of essentialism, feminist scholars have explored a number of different approaches (Naffine 2002, 89), including strategic essentialism (Spivak 1990; Behrendt 1993). Butler herself has explored parodic performance (Butler 1990). Drakopoulou and Genovese have made 'ethical' arguments to justify contemporary legal feminist projects (Drakopoulou 2000a; Genovese 2013). Naffine turns to reconceptualising the legal subject, and the legal person (Naffine 2002, 95). All of these attempts are valuable contributions to feminist legal thinking and politics in the wake of postmodern feminism, in an era beyond the unified gendered subject.

This section attempts to add to this body of feminist work and suggests that Mouffe's theory of agonism (Mouffe 1992, 1993, 1999, 2000) could sketch the foundations of a post-essential politics. Although developed nearly two decades ago, her theory does not seem to have been taken up by postmodern legal feminists. I argue that Mouffe's theory of political action is useful in a postmodern feminist context because the theory does not rely on unified (essentialised) identity categories (Mouffe 1993, 76–77). The section then suggests that agonism may be made operational through a strategy of coalition.

The starting point for Mouffe's theory of politics is her understanding of modern democracy as a social process that demands the acceptance of value pluralism. Mouffe attempts to theorise a concept of a modern democracy that is informed by postmodern theories of power and truth (Mouffe 1993, 10). Mouffe argues that the concept of democracy in modern communities is underpinned by a radical uncertainty, due to the 'composite, heterogeneous, open, and ultimately indeterminate character of the democratic condition' (Mouffe 1993, 17). Within a democratic community, individuals belong to many communities of identity simultaneously (Mouffe 1993, 86). Any one community is therefore one 'without a definite shape or a definite identity and in continuous re-enactment' (Mouffe 1992, 233). The diversity of individuals who constitute and reconstitute the democratic community through their political actions means that the workings and outcomes of democracy are always radical, never guaranteed or stabilised. A modern, radical democracy must therefore facilitate identity pluralism by negotiating and renegotiating its own values and boundaries, and the values and boundaries of the different communities, and the different actors within and beyond it.

The different identities and interests that make up modern democratic society create contestation and disagreement. In the first instance, these different identities will create antagonistic forces.

> When we understand that identity is relational and that the condition of existence of every identity is the affirmation of difference, the determination of an 'other' that is going to play the role of the 'constitutive' outside, it is possible to see how antagonisms arise.
>
> (Mouffe 1993, 2)

Consequently, antagonism arises as a natural part of the modern, radical, and democratic community.

She then argues that identity (and value) pluralism in democracy needs to be recognised in a meaningful way in political theory. This is not achieved by either liberal or communitarian theories of democracy, because these theories use either individual rights or the common good to recognise diversity. Both liberal and communitarian theories create a shared rational ground or common bond among its members to form a unified political association, an 'us' and 'them' (Mouffe 1992, 234; 1999, 755; 2000, 132). Unless the pluralism of values within a democratic community is meaningfully recognised, 'antagonistic forces will never disappear and politics is characterized by conflict and division' (Mouffe 1992, 235). Individuals who then engage in contestation and disagreement see the 'other' as a threat to a shared political identity, and an enemy to be destroyed (Mouffe 1992, 234). Mouffe argues that seeing others as enemies undermines democratic pluralism, which in turn, eventually leads to the elimination of contestation and the creation of an anti-politics.

In moving away from the idea of rational consensus that creates an 'us', she contends that we might instead see those who contest politics as 'adversaries' rather than 'enemies' (Mouffe 1999, 755, 2000, 134). If so, we would then understand the political as 'the creative evolution and the continuously creative nature of our engagements; the process is one of becoming, rather than finishing. It gives us a permanent and always contingent politics, affirming the importance of ongoing engagement' (Schlosberg 2006, 152). Welcoming conflict and disagreement from adversaries means engaging with those who are excluded from the political community, and acknowledging engagement with them as a part of the construction and reconstruction of a democratic society that meaningfully recognises value (and identity) pluralism.

Mouffe specifically addresses the relevance of her theory for a feminist politics. She acknowledges that since political engagements construct identities, there will always be conflict and disagreement within the community about who is included and who is not. To appreciate the full range of disagreements, she notes that it is important that the identities of social agents are not unified, fixed, or essentialised. 'It is indispensable to develop a theory of the subject that is constructed at the point of intersection of a multiplicity of subject positions between which there exists no a priori or necessary relation' (Mouffe 1993, 12). She suggests that we might still recognise a political identification with an interest or notion such as a 'feminist interest', because these notions are socially useful. However, she would argue that, for any particular political group their identity is only a 'partial fixation of identities through the creation of nodal points' (Mouffe 1993, 78). The nodal points are articulated only where they are relevant, rather than grounded in a specific identity category (Mouffe 1993, 82).

> The absence of a female essential identity and of a pre-given unity, however, does not preclude the construction of multiple forms of unity and common action. As the result of the construction of nodal points, partial fixations can take place and precarious forms of identification can be established around the category 'women' which provide the basis for feminist identity and a feminist struggle.
>
> (Mouffe 1993, 87)

This political theory provides the foundation for postmodern feminists to act in ways that acknowledge non-essentialised identity categories and multiple allegiances. The goal of politics is therefore not to eliminate conflict or antagonism (Mouffe 2000, 134), because the antagonism in the constitution and reconstitution of groups is the basis of radical democracy. Rather, politics should meaningfully recognise the diversity within those groups, and understand that contestation is valuable. Politics in a radical democracy should see conflict not as antagonism, but as agonism. Mouffe quotes Žižek and states that a politics of agonism is a politics with, 'an ethics that strives to create a new form of bond, a bond that recognises us as divided subjects' (Mouffe 2000, 139). Mouffe's theory of agonism is a useful way of thinking about politics that can acknowledge plurality and diversity, while not requiring any unified (and therefore essentialised) identity category. Mouffe's theory is potentially a theory of a post-essential politics for a postmodern feminist world.

What might activism under this 'post-essential politics' look like? Theorists working at the intersection of race and feminism have explored this, and have suggested coalition as a potential strategy. For instance, Harris argues that every kind of identity must simultaneously call into question 'the stability of that identity' (Harris 1999, 322). The group or community that gathers under that identity category must be a 'community without unity' (Harris 1999, 322). She suggests that a theory of 'coalition' might be a possible strategy to achieve this, although she does not elaborate much more on this. Matsuda also writes that 'we cannot, at this point in history, engage fruitfully in jurisprudence without engaging in coalition' (Matsuda 1991, 1188).

Does the term 'coalition' create opportunities for identity categories to remain fluid and contingent, recognising a shifting diversity of subjects? That is, is coalition a strategy that can enable Mouffe's post-essential politics? The word coalition derives from the Latin term *coalitus*, which means 'growing together'. The word appears to acknowledge a fluid future goal, not a shared departure point or experience base. In fact, the departure point and experience base are irrelevant. This might be the first step then to enable the feminist legal project to move beyond 'the tension between the longing for a stable, authentic and politically efficacious collective identity and the rejection of any particular given identity for its exclusiveness, reductionism and rigidity' (Harris 1999, 314). Definitions of coalition usually emphasise the temporary and transitional nature of its form, so coalition does suggest a politics where relationships and identities need to be continually negotiated and renegotiated.

It is difficult to identify a contemporary example of a coalition strategy, which has supported feminist law reform. The recent condemnation of Harvey Weinstein and the #MeToo movement might, at first, seem to be an example. Many individuals engaged in an act of disclosure, which not only revealed the extent of sexual harassment in the entertainment industry, but laid bare its pervasiveness in everyday life. It may even provide support for the reform of sexual harassment, sexual assault, and violence laws, although in Australia at least, this is still to occur.

However, I would argue that not every political act is a coalition, and that the theory of agonism can help postmodern feminists distinguish between those that are and those that are not. The #MeToo movement might not be a coalition that enacts a post-essential politics because it does not allow for a diversity of identities, and a fluidity of identity boundaries. This is because the #MeToo movement relies on validating (in the sense of echoing) the experiences of well-educated, able-bodied, heteronormative women. Although different women may have engaged in the movement, the hashtag #MeToo has not yet allowed the full diversity of experiences of sexual harassment to emerge. Instead, it arguably serves to validate a certain (and quite limited) understanding of sexual harassment as primarily about outrageous '(hetero)sexed' desire (Thornton 2002). It is timely therefore, for postmodern feminists to explore theories such as agonism to think through the possibilities of post-essential politics, including the potential strategy of coalition and identifying its projects.

Conclusion

While many legal feminists agree that the postmodern turn has led to a clearer theorisation of the needs of differently situated women, they are wary of the implications arising from postfeminism. They argue that a postmodern feminism critique of essentialism has made the category 'woman' disappear, and the possibility of a feminist politics of law reform along with it.

This chapter challenges the assumption that an effective politics requires a unified sense of identity, as is sometimes suggested. Using interest convergence theory, it argues that even where political unity seems to exist, it is not sufficient to achieve law reform. This argument urges legal feminists to let go of the desire for solidarity and unity, and instead ground their action in an ethical commitment to change.

It argues that Mouffe's theory of agonistic politics is consistent with postmodern feminism and helps to think through what a post-essential politics might entail. Mouffe's theory explains that political action in a radical democracy rejects essentialised identity categories. This theory, I suggest, lays a suitable foundation for a post-essential politics, and coalition is a possible strategy for its implementation.

If there is a conflation between choice or neo-feminism and postmodern feminism under the term 'postfeminism', then this needs clarification before conclusions are drawn about its political implications for legal feminism. Teasing out the different meanings of the term creates an opportunity to explore concerns about the political implications of postmodern feminism. This chapter argues that on closer examination, at least some of these fears are unfounded. For while choice feminism may lead to the depoliticisation of feminist law reform, postmodern feminism can also reinvigorate it.

Notes

1 Postmodern is a catch-all phrase. It means many things and includes many different theorists and theories, including post-structuralism, psychoanalysis, and deconstruction. For the purpose of this chapter, these distinctions are not necessary as they all in different ways are anti-essentialist theories of the meaning of identity, and so I

group them all under postmodernism. There is some debate about whether, and how, Derrrida's theory of deconstruction fits into postmodern theories. While it does share elements of postmodernism, deconstruction is a theoretical method that is often misunderstood as only inverting binary terms and hierarchies. Due to the complexity of the theory, and the fact that it is not often used in legal feminism to refute (or recover) essentialism, this chapter will not include a discussion of Derrida. See a fuller discussion in Sheehan 2000.

2 Expression coined by Hunter 1996, 156.

3 Feminists from different theoretical backgrounds have challenged the essentialised nature of women's experiences as presented by the feminist movement, for example Indigenous women and women of colour. Similarly, the LGBTIQ + community have also been very clear that the feminist movement, and their politics about the law, has not always reflected their interests. See Harris 1990, Behrendt 1993, Watson 2007, Moreton Robinson 2013, Jagose 1996.

4 This legislation was later renamed and separated into two Acts, the Child Support (Assessment) Act 1989 (Cth) and the Child Support (Registration and Collection) Act 1988 (Cth).

References

Allen, Dominique. 2007. "Periodic Peaks of Progress: Applying Bell's Interest Convergence Theory to the Mabo Decision." *University of Tasmania Law Review* 26, no. 1: 63–89.

Barron, Anne. 2000. "Feminism, Aestheticism and the Limits of Law." *Feminist Legal Studies* 8: 275–317.

Behrendt, Larissa. 1993. "Aboriginal Women and the White Lies of the Feminist Movement: Implications for Aboriginal Women in Rights Discourse." *The Australian Feminist Law Journal* 27: 27–44.

Bell, Derrick. 1980. "*Brown v Board of Education* and the Interest-Convergence Dilemma." *Harvard Law Review* 93: 518–533.

———. 1992. "Racial Realism." *Connecticut Law Review* 23, no. 2: 363–379.

Budgeon, Shelley. 2015. "Individualized Femininity and Feminist Politics of Choice." *European Journal of Women's Studies* 22, no. 3: 303–318.

Butler, Judith. 1990. *Gender Trouble*. London: Routledge.

Bulbeck, Chilla. 2006. "Explaining the Generation Debate: Envy, History or Feminism's Victories?" *Lilith* 15: 35–47.

Cerise, Somali, Karen O'Connell, Elena Rosenman, and Priya Sarat Chandran. 2009. *Accumulating Poverty? Women's Experiences of Inequality over the Lifecycle*. Sydney: Australian Human Rights Commission.

Chappell, Louise. 2000. "Interacting with the State: Feminist Strategies and Political Opportunities." *International Feminist Journal of Politics* 2, no. 2: 244–275.

Conaghan, Joanne. 2000. "Reassessing the Feminist Theoretical Project in Law." *Journal of Law and Society* 27 no. 3: 351–385.

Davies, Margaret, and Kathy Mack. 2004. "Legal Feminism - Now and Then?" *The Australian Feminist Law Journal* 20: 1–6.

Drakopoulou, Maria. 2000a. "The Ethic of Care, Female Subjectivity and Feminist Legal Scholarship." *Feminist Legal Studies* 8: 199–226.

———. 2000b. "Women's Resolutions of Lawes Reconsidered: Epistemic Shifts and the Emergence of the Feminist Legal Discourse." *Law and Critique* 11: 47–71.

Dudziak, Mary. 1988. "Desegregation as a Cold War Imperative." *Stanford Law Review* 41, no. 1: 61–120.
Duncanson, Ian, and Nan Seuffert. 2005. "Mapping Connections: Postcolonial Feminist and Legal Theory." *The Australian Feminist Law Journal* 22: 1–22.
Eisenstein, Hester. 1990. "Inside Agitators: Australian Femocracts and the State." In *Playing the state: Australian Feminist Interventions* edited by Sophie Watson, 87–103. London: Verso.
Foucault, Michel. 1976. *The Archaeology of Knowledge*. New York: Harper & Row.
———. 1980. *Power/Knowledge: Selected Interviews and Other Writings, 1972–1977*. New York: Pantheon.
———. 1990. *The History of Sexuality Volume 1: An Introduction*. Translated by Robert Hurley. London & New York: Penguin Books.
Fraser, Nancy, and Linda Nicholson. 1989. "Social Criticism without Philosophy. An Encounter between Feminism and Postmodernism." *Social Text* 1: 83–104.
Genovese, Anne. 1996. "Unravelling Identities." *Feminist Review* 52: 135–153.
———. 2013. "Inheriting and Inhabiting the Pleasures and Duties of Our Own Existence: *The Second Sex* and Feminist Jurisprudence." *The Australian Feminist Law Journal* 38: 41–57.
Gilligan, Carol. 1982. *In a Different Voice*. London: Harvard University Press.
Graycar, Regina. 1990. "Feminism and Law Reform: Matrimonial Property Law and Models of Equality." In *Playing the State: Australian Feminist Interventions*, edited by Sophie Watson, 153–168. London, New York: Verso.
———. 2008. "Family law and Social Security in Australia: The Child Support Connection." *Australian Journal of Family Law* 3: 70–92.
Harris, Angela. 1990. "Race and Essentialism in Feminist Legal Theory." *Stanford Law Review* 42, no. 3: 581–616.
———. 1999. "Building Theory/Building Community." *Social and Legal Studies* 8, no. 3: 313–325.
Howe, House of Representatives. 1987. *Parliamentary Debates*, (Commonwealth of Australia, 24 March 1987) 1368.
Hunter, Rosemary. 1996. "Deconstructing the Subject of Feminism: The Essentialism Debate in Feminist Theory and Practice." *The Australian Feminist Law Journal* 6: 135–162.
Jagose, Annamarie. 1996. *Queer Theory*. Carlton: Melbourne University Press.
Janus, Kathleen. 2013. "Finding Common Feminist Ground: The Role of the Next Generation in Shaping Feminist Legal Theory." *Duke Journal of Gender Law & Policy* 20: 255–285.
Kline, Marlee. 1989. "Race, Racism, and Feminist Legal Theory." *Harvard Women's Law Journal* 12: 115–150.
MacDonald, Peter, ed. 1986. *Settling Up: Property and Income Distribution on Divorce in Australia*. Sydney: Prentice-Hall.
Mackinnon, Catherine. 1983. *Feminism Unmodified*. London: Harvard University Press.
Matsuda, Mari. 1991. "Beside My Sister: Facing the Enemy. Legal Theory Out of Coalition." *Stanford Law Review* 43, no. 6: 1183–1192.
McRobbie, Angela. 2004. "Post-feminism and Popular Culture." *Feminist Media Studies* 4, no. 3: 255–264.
Moreton-Robinson, Aileen. 2013. "Towards an Australian Indigenous Women's Standpoint Theory." *Australian Feminist Studies* 28, no. 2: 331–347.

Mouffe, Chantal. 1992. "Democratic Citizenship and the Political Community." In *Dimensions of Radical Democracy: Pluralism, Citizenship and Community*, edited by Chantal Mouffe, 225–239. London: Verso.

———. 1993. *The Return of the Political*. London New York: Verso.

———. 1999. "Deliberative Democracy or Agonistic Pluralism?" *Social Research* 66, no. 3: 745–758.

———. 2000. *The Democratic Paradox*. London: Verso.

Naffine, Ngaire. 1990. *Law and the Sexes: Explorations in Feminist Jurisprudence*. Sydney: Allen and Unwin.

———. 2002. "In Praise of Legal Feminism." *Legal Studies* 22, no. 1: 71–101.

National Maintenance Inquiry. 1984. *A Maintenance Agency for Australia*. Canberra: AGPS.

Nicholson, Linda. 1992. "Feminism and the Politics of Postmodernism." *Boundary 2* 19, no 2: 53–69.

Nussbaum, Martha. 1999. "The Professor of Parody." *The New Republic* 220.16: 37–45.

Parker, Stephen. 1991. "Child Support in Australia: Children's Rights or Public Interest." *International Journal of Law and Family* 5: 24–57.

Pendleton, Mark, and Tanya Serisier. 2009. "Beyond the Desire for Law." *The Australian Feminist Law Journal* 31: 77–98.

Ryan, Lyndall. 1990. "Feminism and the Federal Bureaucracy 1972–1983." In *Playing the State*, edited by Sophie Watson, 71–84. Sydney: Allen & Unwin.

Scales, Ann. 1986. "The Emergence of Feminist Jurisprudence: An Essay." *Yale Law Journal* 95: 1373–1374.

Schlosberg, David. 2006. "The Pluralist Imagination." In *Oxford Handbook of Political Theory*, edited by John S. Dryzek, Bonnie Honig, and Anne Philips. Oxford: Oxford University Press.

Scott, Joan. 1988. "Deconstructing Equality- Versus- Difference: Or, The Uses of Post-structuralist Theory For Feminism." *Feminist Studies* 14, no. 1: 32–50.

Sheehan, Katherine. 2000. "Caring for Deconstruction." *Yale Journal of Law and Feminism* 12: 85–142.

Smyth, Bruce, and Ruth Weston. 2000. *Financial Living Standards After Divorce. A Recent Snapshot*. Research Paper No 23 December. Canberra: Australian Institute of Family Studies.

Snyder, Claire. 2008. "What is third-wave Feminism? A New Directions Essay." *Signs: Journal of Women in Culture and Society* 34, no. 1: 175–196.

Spivak, Gayatri. 1984. "Criticism, Feminism and the Institution." *Thesis Eleven* 10, no. 11: 175–188.

———. 1990. *The Post-Colonial Critic: Interviews, Strategies, Dialogues*. New York: Routledge.

Summerfield, Tracey, Lisa Young, Jade Harman, and Paul Flatau. 2010. "Child Support and Welfare to Work Reforms: The Economic Consequences for Single-Parent Families." *Family Matters* 84: 68–78.

Thornton, Margaret. 1986. "Feminist Jurisprudence: Illusion or Reality?" *Australian Journal of Law and Society* 3: 5–29.

———. 2002. "Sexual Harassment: Losing Sight of Sex Discrimination." *Melbourne University Law Review* 26, no. 2: 422–433.

———. 2004. "Neoliberal Melancholia: The Case of Feminist Legal Scholarship." *The Australian Feminist Law Journal* 20: 7–22.

———. 2010. "Post-Feminism' in the Legal Academy?" *Feminist Review* 95: 92–98.

Watson, Irene. 2007. "Aboriginal Women's Law and Lives: How Might we Keep Growing the Law?" *The Australian Feminist Law Journal* 26: 95–107.

Wiegman, Robyn. 1999. "Feminism, Institutionalism, and the Idiom of Failure." *A Journal of Feminist Cultural Studies* 11, no. 3: 107–136.

West, Robyn. 1987. "The Difference in Women's Hedonic Lives: A Phenomenological Critique of Feminist Legal Theory." *Wisconsin Women's Law Journal* 3: 81–145.

———. 1988. "Jurisprudence and Gender." *The University of Chicago Law Review* 55, no. 1: 1–72.

Weston, Ruth, and Bruce Smyth. 2000. "Financial Living Standards after Divorce: A Recent Snapshot." *Family Matters* 55: 11–15.

Wicke, Jennifer. 1992. "Postmodern Identities and the Politics of the (Legal) Subject." *boundary 2* 19, no. 2: 10–33.

Wishnik, Heather Ruth. 1985. "To Question Everything: The Inquiries of Feminist Jurisprudence." *Berkeley Women's Law Journal* 1: 64–77.

Workplace Gender Equality Agency. "What is the Gender Pay Gap." Australian Government. www.wgea.gov.au/addressing-pay-equity/what-gender-pay-gap.

Young, Lisa, Adiva Sifris, Robyn Carroll, and Geoffrey Monahan. 2016. *Family Law in Australia*. 9th edition, Chatswood: LexisNexis Butterworths.

Cases

Brown v Board of Education of Topeka, 347 U.S. 483 (1954)

Legislation

Child Support Act 1988 (Cth)

Family Law Act 1975 (Cth)

Part III

Law

7 The problem with research

Jennifer M. Nielsen

Introduction: (post)feminism

Western critical legal scholarship has steadily exposed the dissolute functions of the common law tradition, and transgressed its 'deference' to closed logic and doctrinal assumptions of 'neutrality' and 'objectivity'. Feminist legal scholarship has contributed significantly to this project by using new and varied voices to challenge the primacy of the text and by seeking vantage points that expose the gendered normative strategies by which doctrinal law constructs and maintains the dominant social, economic, and political order (Davies 2017, 224–297).

However, while the vantage points achieved within critical scholarship might free us from the assumptions of 'neutrality' and 'objectivity', Distinguished Professor Aileen Moreton-Robinson (1998) reminds us that research is never 'innocent' because the knowledge it produces always holds a 'key to power and meaning', which can be used to communicate, but can also be used to control (284). Professor Margaret Davies (2017) captures it this way:

> [K]nowledge has been seen as power: to have knowledge is to have access to a form of power. Those who know can use their knowledge to their own ends. More recent thought on this matter, often inspired by the works of Michel Foucault, suggests that the inverse is also the case: that the conditions of what counts as 'knowledge' are in fact determined by relations of power. The structures and institutions which control society determine what is 'true' and what is not.
>
> (237)

Feminist legal scholarship does not, of course, pursue a uniform agenda or use a single analytical lens. It is 'context specific' and varied due to the 'truly different ways of experiencing, interacting with and theorising the world' (Davies 2017, 270). Different strands of feminism have been forged by waves of criticism from outside and within, eroding essentialised visions of 'being woman' and the boundaries of liberal rights claims, and propelling new thinking on the complexities involved in 'why women experience inequality on the basis of gender, what the characteristics and dimensions of gendered thinking are, and what to do about it' (Davies 2017, 233). One of these waves is postfeminism.

Recognising feminism's evolutionary nature, Professor Ann Brooks describes postfeminism as a 'political shift in feminism's conceptual and theoretical agenda' (1997, 4), a conceptual frame of reference that 'expresses the intersection of feminism with postmodernism, poststructuralism and post-colonialism' that is 'capable of challenging modernist, patriarchal and imperialist frameworks' (1):

> Postfeminism ... facilitates a broad-based, pluralistic conception of the application of feminism, and addresses the demands of marginalised, diasporic and colonised cultures for a non-hegemonic feminism capable of giving voice to local, indigenous and post-colonial feminisms.
>
> (4)

It is, she says, a 'confident body of theory and politics, representing pluralism and difference and reflecting on its position in relation to other philosophical and political movements similarly demanding change' (1).

Is this wave of feminism reflected in the work of Australian feminist legal theorists? Should it be – can it help us shake up the feminist project? To at least this last question, my answer is yes on account of the possibilities signalled in Brooks' account of postfeminist method and concerns.[1] And writing as a non-Indigenous woman, most particularly I am taken by its potential to de-centre (Watson 2014) Western perspectives within our methods so that we can work with pluralistic conceptions and engage with local, Indigenous, and postcolonial voices. No surprises then that these are concerns with which I have attempted to engage by being mindful of and guided by the critical dialogues led by First Nations women about the capacity of Western feminist thinking to pursue/advance First Nations' concerns. And in light of that critical dialogue, I am taken by the postfeminist potential signalled by Professor Teresa de Laurentis:

> A feminist theory begins when the feminist critique of ideologies becomes conscious of itself and turns to question its own body of writing and critical interpretations, its basic assumptions of terms and the practices which they enable and from which they emerge. This is not merely an expansion or a reconfiguration of boundaries, but a qualitative shift in political and historical consciousness. This shift implies, in my opinion, a dis-placement and a self-displacement: leaving or giving up a place that is safe, that is 'home' (physically, emotionally, linguistically and epistemologically) for another place that is unknown and risky, that is not only emotionally but conceptually other, a place of discourse from which speaking and thinking are at best tentative, uncertain and unguaranteed. But the leaving is not a choice: one could not live there in the first place.
>
> (1988, 138–139, quoted in Brooks 1997, 211)

At first blush, my work tends to demonstrate postfeminist qualities, taking a postmodern and poststructuralist position that regards 'the concept of "truth" [as] always plural and situated' so that 'the very basis of epistemology has to be questioned' (Brooks 1997, 34). With qualifications, which are explained later, it also pursues some postcolonial concerns, through its intent to deconstruct and reposition my thinking, through an iterative process inspired by decolonial thinking. Therefore, using reflections on my engagements within the research process, this chapter explores the opportunities postfeminist methods might open to decentre Western perspectives and engage pluralistic conceptions, and make us capable of more meaningful, respectful, and productive dialogues with diverse local and Indigenous voices and knowledges.

To give context, first this chapter sets out some observations on the critique led by First Nation theorists on Western legal scholarship generally, particularly feminist legal scholarship. Drawing from that critique, I then set out three key insights I gained through my engagement with First Nations knowledge and philosophy: first, history is important; second, race is about white people too; and third, that whiteness is not just about colour. I then look to the opportunities and the challenges raised for non-Indigenous feminists by the First Nations' critique that might helpfully be pursued through a postfeminist intent and approach. Ultimately, I propose that postfeminist methods do offer opportunities to de-centre Western perspectives in our scholarship and to broaden the voices with whom we dialogue and the knowledges with which we engage.

First Nations critiques

First Nations theorists[2] have led sophisticated critiques of Western research methodologies and their potential to colonise Indigenous culture, beliefs, property, minds, bodies, and being (Watson 1998; Tuhiwai Smith 1999; Moreton-Robinson 2000a). These critiques oppose what Professor Irene Watson (1998) calls the 'right knowing' intrinsic in Western methodologies (30), including belief in the division between body, mind, and spirit, and in a hierarchical order of being that divides humans from non-human animals and from the physical environment, and beliefs that are detrimental because they enable 'individuals' to sit separately from 'their community, their physical surroundings and other peoples' realities' (Tunks 2001, 8). As Professor Ian Anderson (1993) explains, because of this 'separation' many researchers 'know Aborigines from picture books' rather than having 'spent time working with Aboriginal communities in an attempt to build constructive relationships' (24). First Nations theorists challenge the Western tendency to regard this separation as necessary to intellectual leadership and academic freedom, because that separation contradicts and damages 'fealty to and interdependence with the collective whole' (Bishop 1994, 181).

By contrast, Indigenous research methodologies support relatedness and interdependence with the collective whole, and are determined by an agenda built from specific First Nations epistemologies, spiritualties, and laws. These methodologies may also involve conversations of decolonisation that Watson explains as a process of dissolving and thinking outside white colonial 'perceived and imposed regimes of thought', which are necessary to resist assimilation and 'survive and remain a Nunga' by knowing in the 'way of the grandmothers' and to see 'the mother beneath my feet' from 'the horizon [of] an indigenous place and space' (1998, 28, 31).

First Nations theorists also point out that our involvement in the academy will implicate us in a 'power structure' that may subordinate or override the interests and priorities of First Nations peoples, refuse them any claim to know, and maintain colonising forces upon their lives and communities (Milroy 1996, 58; Watson 1998, 2005, 2014; Tuhiwai Smith 1999). And whether we fail to appreciate that or simply choose to ignore it, involvement in this power structure remains highly desired within the academy because privileges follow 'authority' and 'expertise' (Bishop 1994, 181).

However, as Professor Russell Bishop (1994) has pointed out, the less obvious consequence of an 'expert stance' is that we distance ourselves 'from the group [which they justify in] elitist terms such as the need for freedom of expression, for academic freedom, individual initiative and for unfettered intellectual leadership' (181). In contrast to cultures where a 'collectivist ethos is paramount', researchers and other specialists are constantly reminded of their interconnectedness and interdependence with the 'collective whole', the Western academy's tendency to pursue the 'expert' stance risks losing the 'interdependence of the researcher with the researched' (Bishop 1994, 181). And what may be less immediately apparent is that by maintaining an 'independent' stance from the collective whole, we continue to produce a less than complete understanding of 'ourselves' as non-Indigenous communities, and in turn, reinforce our distance from *our* spirits and *ourselves.*

Feminism has not been immune from critique by First Nations theorists. The dialogues led by First Nations women (alongside those led by women of colour (e.g. Crenshaw 1990)) have critiqued an essentialised white feminist vision of 'being woman', arguing that what shapes a woman's experience does not depend solely on her gender, but nor is it shaped solely by her race (e.g. Moreton-Robinson 1992; Behrendt 1993). Instead, they explain how a woman's experience will be shaped by her gender *and* her race, *and* all of the facets that intersect and are woven together to make her who she is, and by the combined effect of how these intersecting characteristics are valued by a society at particular times and places (Duclos 1990; Little Nyoongah 1996; Nielsen 2004).

First Nations theorists have also been concerned by the limitations imposed by liberal feminism's framework of rights. Indeed, Watson observes this framework as not only limiting, but as one capable only of maintaining violence:

> Whose concepts of equality will apply? … Or are the aspirations of white women even desired by Aboriginal women? … What can be expected from the notion of equal protection when we see violence and rape of white women and children occurring in mainstream communities?
>
> (2007a, 96)

And they call for a (re)turn to the laws of the grandmothers as a 'continuing strategy for providing a safe and healthy environment for women and children.

In the same way our laws did when they were sovereign to this land' (Watson 2007a, 96). Paraphrasing Professor Moira Gatens (1996, 25), through making themselves 'visible', First Nations theorists collectively 'throw into question the legitimacy of claims and assumptions in philosophy that have been taken as axiomatic'. Thereby they demonstrate what non-Indigenous feminist (and other) philosophies exclude and why that exclusion is 'crucial' to very existence of those philosophies (Gatens 1996, 25). They call out acts of 'epistemic violence' (Moreton-Robinson 2011b; see also, Fricker 2007 and Santos 2014), call for a 'shift' from the 'contemporary racialised, colonised views' to restore an 'Aboriginal humanity' (Watson 2014, 517), and ask uncomfortable questions, such as will 'white women of the universal return stolen lands and resign their shares of corporations that plunder Aboriginal peoples' natural resources?' (Watson 2007a, 106).

How can non-Indigenous feminists meet these concerns? For instance, should we incorporate, adapt, and/or adopt Indigenous research methodologies, or does this assume too much? Because the epistemology that shapes and is followed in our research is never value-neutral but always ontological – dependent upon who (and when) we are and how we know about the social world (Purdy 1997, 43–44, 48). As explained by Professor Patricia Monture-Angus (2000), our location in the research process is where we work from to 'define the problem' to be researched (162). Accordingly, speaking of race without gender, or gender without race in our analyses can entrench rather than unpack the way in which white patriarchy and colonialism entrench and maintain gender, race, and class (and other forms of) inequality (Moreton-Robinson 1992, 9).

Unsettling the common law terrain

In my attempts to work through these concerns, because my worldview is grounded so differently, I have had to acknowledge that I may *never* see any horizon from an Indigenous space or place. But what I have attempted to do is to engage reflexively with Indigenous knowledges and philosophy to open space for that epistemology to meet and disrupt my own (Moreton-Robinson 2000, xvi, xxv). Many of the tools and assumptions of feminism have been vital to pursuing this goal: standpoint, reflexivity, and the challenge to 'truth' and the authority 'to know'. This theoretical engagement has, in turn, made me more conscious of my standpoint within the research process 'and the limitations consequent upon this', and thus more conscious of how I am ontologically connected to what I know (Purdy 1997, 43–44, 48).

In particular, this engagement offered me three insights, which have had a lasting and profound effect on the methods and methodology I use in my work and, significantly, how I 'define the problems' to be researched. They were forged within my postgraduate project on discrimination law – because from the beginning it seemed that my lived experience of discrimination as a white woman was qualitatively different to that shared with me by Indigenous friends, both men and women (Nielsen 2008a; 2008b; see Davies 2017, 233). Though it felt incongruous that I could adopt Indigenous ways of knowing, I was challenged to learn from that different body of knowledge in order to understand the deficiencies in the common law legal order – deficiencies that were hidden from my view. And this engagement was critical to the development of my methodology as it enabled me to understand my standpoint within the research process – and its limitations. The insights I gained proved vital in shifting me in my standpoint towards a greater capacity to engage in knowledge beyond my own.

History is important

First, 'history is important'. This insight accords with Professor Edward Said's (1994, 1) observation that appeals to the past are a common strategy in analyses of the present and future, involving questions about what the past was and, more significantly, whether it is really past or continuing though in a different form. It is significant to us as feminist legal scholars, as our analyses often return to the gendered foundations of law. In theoretical terms, questioning history is typically a postcolonial concern so as to, broadly speaking, interrogate how colonialism continues as a 'condition' suffered by those 'affected in one way or another by a past or present colonialism or imperialism' (Davies 2017, 278, 326).

The tenets of postcolonialism (see e.g. Williams and Chrisman 1993) bear some consistency with First Nations theories: they do not project colonialism as something that has ended, they question whether the past is really past, and the critique of 'epistemological foundationalism' accords with Moreton-Robinson's (2000, xxii) position that 'all knowledge is situated and therefore partial'. However, First Nations theorists also question history differently, challenging colonial ideologies of what the past was, but more specifically, questioning 'colonialism, and its various myths, [including] terra nullius' to see if they are 'really dead' (Watson 1996, 4). These are not simply postcolonial concerns.

Indeed, the work of First Nations theorists demonstrates some very different concerns. They contest any postcolonial 'right knowing' that their Indigenous identity as 'colonised peoples' is ambivalent or has in any way been hybridised. As Anderson (1995) explains, though the 'experience' of colonialism is to fragment, dismember, and create ambiguities within identities, these ambiguities 'do not characterise our existence' as they 'are fissures of tension within bounded identities which are integral to growth and transformation' (38). He says that resisting colonialism 'is to reconnect or to make whole', as it offers the 'potential to conceive of [ourselves] as Aboriginal bodies within an Aboriginal time and landscape' (Anderson 1995, 38) and holds a dignity not experienced within the [postcolonial] hybrid's identity that is reduced to inhabiting 'the shifting and ambiguous realm between the white and the black' (33). This resistant identity is 'an embodied response to the world' that communicates 'our experience' rather than mirroring the 'stereotypes that oppress us' (Anderson 1995, 32) and is a 'symbolic marker for a complex array of experiences, memories, and emotional histories which become situated within our transforming bodies' (Anderson

1995, 36–37). As Watson (1998) puts it, 'we adapt; but that doesn't diminish us or dislodge us from our tradition' (512).

They also foreground colonialism's violence and economic exploitation within their analyses, speaking of it as a 'process of domination, subjugation and genocide' – the *muldarbi*, the 'demon spirit' (Watson 1998, 28) and the *duggaibah,* 'place of whiteness' (Moreton-Robinson 2000, 240). They do not lock colonial violence and its impact into a temporal vacuum but view it as a continued *presence* in the 'different forms of dominance and power' that threatens to devour the entire natural world (Watson 1998, 29, 32–35), fracturing what Davies describes as the 'linear, progressive narrative of history that occupies the citadel of liberal doctrine' (2017, 324). They also foreground the false authority of 'patriarchal white sovereignty' (Moreton-Robinson 2011a) and the founding principle it embedded at invasion – *terra nullius* – and deny that the markers used in white accounts to divide the 'racist past from the nonracist present' (Paisley 1998, 248) (federation, equal (or not) wages, referenda, self-determination, talk of treaties, and *makarratas*, land rights or any other forms of land title) have interrupted colonialism's presence. These conversations speak from the site of First Nations' sovereignty, and its Indigenous ways of knowing and being in the world (Watson 2014). This produces very different vantage points from which to look at our history. These vantage points also ground a different understanding about how the present 'came to be' and thus where our future may be taking us (Huggins 1990, 168).

Reflecting back, I realise that by shifting to these vantage points, I began to understand *why* history is important – because the past, present, and future do not exist in isolation. Whether or not I was seeing this truly from the place of the grandmothers, I was no longer looking at things from the comfort of a space that is 'post' the colonial. By engaging with questions about history and the foundations of how we know 'things', I was able to find a fundamentally different beginning to my doctoral work. Through acknowledging the *presence* of colonialism, I could open questions about the *present* colonial claims of white authority, which made the 'problem of race discrimination' look very different to what I had originally seen (Monture-Angus 2000, 162).

Race and racism are about white people too

I most often use 'race' as the focus of my research, which was initially because the Indigenous people who participated in my postgraduate research cited their racialised experience as Aboriginal peoples as primary to their experience of marginalisation. And in pursuing a critique of how law shaped that experience, the second insight I learned was that the 'naturalness' of the racial order veils the fact that it has been determined by and for the dominant white group (Thornton 1990, 12). That is, while 'race' appears to be about 'othered', less powerful groups, race and racism are white issues too (Moreton-Robinson 2004a).

'Racial' analyses offer a basis to challenge the idea that there are natural racial identities, because identities are socially constructed and shaped by, and in turn shape, other features socially attributed to identity, such as class, religion, gender, and sexuality (Haney López 1996, xiii). Yet, beyond the influence of social relationships, the concept of race is said to be an 'empty category' because we have never actually seen races (Purdy 1997, 28) but instead see combinations of characteristics to which we have attributed meanings through our 'ideas *about* race' (Hollinsworth 1998, 46 (emphasis added)). But our ideas about race are not empty, because whether 'race' exists or not, people experience it in ways that are both real and deadly (Pettman 1992, 3). Moreover, acts of racism are not always a matter of 'conscious and deliberate policy', nor simply a result of the 'prejudice embedded in individual psyches' (Cowlishaw 1988, 245), because our negative ideas about race are mobilised to structure unequal power relationships and are embedded into institutional practices and systems (Hollinsworth 1998, 46–47).

As a white researcher, I found critical race theory (CRT) – much of which still emerges primarily from the United States – an immediately useful framework to pursue a critique of the racialising effects of Australian law (Delgado 1995). By exposing the raced subjectivity of liberalism's 'objective' and 'rational' method, the Race Crits expose how law creates, rather than merely reflects, the dominant social order by making that order appear natural, neutral, and 'universally applicable' – that is, it exposes the unstated raced character of how law works (Delgado 1995, xiv). Through being so 'ingrained' in the common law's terrain, the effects of racism are rendered 'ordinary and natural' to those of the dominant culture (Delgado 1995, xiv).

CRT disabused me of my liberal vision of anti-discrimination law and opened my mind to the idea that the legal recognition of civil rights could be of more value to whites than to 'minority' groups (Matsuda et al 1993, 6; Harris 1994, 750; Delgado 1995, xiv-xv) – which had never occurred to me before. And CRT's call to context, particularity, perspectivism, and moral and political discourse to place 'racial oppression at the center of the analysis' and to privilege the racial subject (Delgado 1995, xiv) remains extremely instructive because it constantly provokes me to reflect on how and whose voices should be given primacy in my work.

But of itself, CRT's frame did not offer me as a white researcher a basis to interrogate my own racialised position, or to move beyond it, leaving me at an impasse – as a white person, how could *I* sensibly contribute to an analysis of race? That impasse was finally broken when my friend, Marcelle Burns, a Kamilaroi woman, told me she had been part of a Talking Circle when a white woman asked the Aunties, 'As a white person, what can I do?' The advice the Aunties gave was, 'You can look after your own mob' (Marcelle Burns, Pers. Comm., June 2003) – and what they meant was, 'don't look at me, look at you' (Sharon Venne in dialogue with Irene Watson: Watson 2007b, 119).

The then emerging field of critical whiteness studies offered me a way to do that, particularly as applied in Moreton-Robinson's work. Her critique (in part) analyses 'race' and racism as social constructs by which privilege is claimed as much as it is denied (Moreton-Robinson 2004, 139). That is, we whites have a 'race', too, and our whiteness holds a meaning that is supported – rather than negated – by racialised practices. And what I was encouraged to do was to reverse and resist the dominance of whiteness and white values by turning my focus on the 'racialisers' rather than the 'racialised' (Moreton-Robinson 2004, 139) – that is, to analyse my own mob, not 'other' mobs.

This insight was profound because it caused a significant shift in my location in the project, from which I could no longer see race and racism in the workplace as an '*Aboriginal* problem'. It moved me beyond simplistic questioning about how Indigenous peoples use the laws and why this may be difficult, to a very different question – whose interests is the law designed to serve?

Whiteness is not just about colour

The third insight is that whiteness is not just about colour. So what is 'whiteness'? Professor Woody Doane says that race is not just a 'socially constructed concept'; this is because, he says, racialisation does not occur in a 'vacuum but under a specific set of social and material circumstances' that produce an 'ideology' of race 'that is grounded in and explains social practice' (Doane 2003, 9). Therefore whiteness

> must be understood as a position in a specific set of social relationships – a '*racialized social system*' – and as a *historically contingent* social identity. While 'white' has been used in a descriptive sense in a variety of settings, ... the hardening of group boundaries and the racialization of whiteness are modern phenomena linked to European conquest and colonialism and the spread of global capitalism.
>
> (Doane 2003, 9)

Thus, while initially, white may be said to refer to the colour of one's skin, white identity follows the social meanings attributed to 'race' by processes of 'affiliation and external ascription' (Doane 2003, 9). However, the social meanings and ideology produced by whiteness signals for whites 'the production and reproduction of dominance rather than subordination, normativity rather than marginality, and privilege rather than disadvantage' (Frankenberg 1993, 236–237). Consequently, whether one is white depends on the diverse elements of identity, and material, social and legal context – that is, who, where, and when one is: in Byron Bay in the afternoon or at two o'clock in the morning, in 1918 or 2018, applying to rent a house, seeking entrance to the Beach Hotel, or talking with police (Haney López 1996, xiii–xiv).

And fundamentally whiteness functions as an ideology permeated by white 'understandings and institutional practices' (Doane 2003, 8, 13; Hartigan Jr 2003, 96; Moreton-Robinson 2004b, 75–78), and the 'invisible norm' against which other races have been and are 'judged in the construction of identity, representation, subjectivity, nationalism and the law' – what the racialised 'other' is not (Doane 2003, 7, 8, 13; Moreton-Robinson 2004b, 75–78). It projects the markers of racial identity that 'legitimise', protect, and enforce the borders of entitlement to privilege – what it means to be truly human (Moreton-Robinson 2004b, 75–78).

Whiteness is also a form of propertied privilege (Harris, 1995). Yet, the enduring 'normativity and "invisibility"' of our white condition can render the concept of 'white race privilege' incomprehensible to us, leaving us white people blissfully to inhabit a world where our culture remains unnamed and our shared 'sameness' reinforces our dominant ideological position (Moreton-Robinson 1999, 28, 29–30). It may also make us 'more likely to resist attempts to redefine the white "center"' (Doane 2003, 8, 13). By asserting that race is *not* about 'white people' and/or that in truth, we are 'colour-blind', we can even choose when race matters and when it does not.

Whiteness theory offered me cogent theoretical insights that put me in a 'better' place to listen more effectively to First Nations theorists, but still did not offer a 'perfect' theoretical stance. In part this is because First Nations theorists require more to be gained through whiteness theory than the possibility of analysing the tension between whites and 'minority' peoples. These theorists position themselves in critiques of race quite differently, through being First Nations peoples, which is unique position that does not necessarily accord with the perspectives of 'minority' peoples (Behrendt 1993, 28). Indeed, they expect the complexity of the 'migrant' position in relation to the colonial past to also be analysed – as Professor Ann Curthoys has described it, 'othered' migrants may share with Indigenous peoples the 'common experience of racial hostility and being defined outside the nation, [but] at the same time occupy significantly different places on the colonial–post-colonial spectrum' (Curthoys 2000, 21, 33; see also Behrendt 1993, 28; Moreton-Robinson 2004, viii). Though whiteness theory can strip away whiteness' claim to 'racial neutrality' (Davies 2017, 281), unless the analysis of whiteness also addresses the complexity of the colonial past (that is, by remembering that history is important), whiteness will be left as a simple problem of 'colour' absent of the influence and source of its privilege.

Which returns us to colonialism, because as Watson's work emphasises, it is not simply a 'context' within which Indigenous peoples are located, but instead is an extreme and prevailing force upon Indigenous lives (see Watson 1998). So for First Nations theorists, the presence of colonialism's claim of white sovereign authority over Indigenous land and being *never* escapes their attention.[3] Thus, First Nations theorists challenge mainstream law's very foundation – they are not intent on securing civil rights and equality within the logic of white sovereignty, but instead, these conversations challenge that sovereignty and seek to secure their own (Watson 1997, 39).

This makes it clear *what* whiteness expresses – the *muldarbi* (Watson 1998, 28), the *duggaibah* (Moreton-Robinson 2000b, 240), and what Anderson calls 'a colonial cultural condition' (Anderson 1995, 31, 35) that propagates a white claim of right to occupy space and assume entitlement to the privileges attendant upon occupation. In my postgraduate fieldwork it became evident as the unstated assumption in discussions with interview participants that characterised

Indigenous people almost as 'invaders' in the workplace. Accordingly, I began to understand mainstream workplaces as sites of the colonial presence within which whiteness functioned not only to define who *looks* like they fit in, but more fundamentally to normalise occupation by defining who *belongs* – who can rightfully be there and rightfully be in control (see Moreton-Robinson 2004a, 136; Watson 2005, 15). That is, while whiteness is about colour, it not *just* about colour – and a focus on this 'cultural condition' helped me to define the problem of discrimination in the workplace very differently – not in the behaviour of Indigenous peoples, but – in the 'acts of cumulative privileging quietly loaded up on whites' (Fine et al. 1997, 57).[4]

The possibilities in a (post)feminist framework

Now I would like to come back to de Laurentis and her observations on feminist theory reproduced above. What I hear in de Laurentis' words is a call for the feminist project to question our basic assumptions. She urges us to seek a qualitative shift in political and historical consciousness that challenges the foundations of truth and knowledge so that we can see and know differently. I hear her encouraging us consciously to leave the comfort and safety of our epistemological 'home' to pursue the unknown and risky, and to dis-place ourselves. And to her, our leaving is not a choice.

As I said, I am taken by de Laurentis' account because it reflects a powerful and inviting form of feminist critique that truly 'aims for a transformation of social relationships' (Davies 2017, 229). And I am taken by the frame she draws because it suggests a theoretical movement that is capable of reflexivity[5] and adaptation as our ways of knowing become more complicated and rich. This is because, like Davies, I see the feminist project as one which (2017, 230, 238)

> poses a challenge … to the fundamental structure of law itself … to the substantive law, to the ordering concepts of law …, to the liberal ideology of law, as well as to decontextualized habits of reasoning. … [And one of its political tasks is to] ensure that … the non-situated, non-subjective, paradigm of knowledge is challenged.

Therefore, reflecting back on the insights gained in my work, here I would like to explore de Laurentis' postfeminist frame to consider the opportunities we can pursue to de-centre Western perspectives, engage pluralistic conceptions, and become capable of engaging 'other' knowledges within meaningful, respectful and productive dialogues.

Knowing differently

I have learned through my work that there are 'multiple truths', and though notorious, this realisation retains cogency: as Davies puts it, the postmodern challenge to 'truth' does not 'mean that truth can be anything at all, but it does mean that the conditions under which knowledge is produced need to be carefully understood' (Davies 2017, 226). My learning that history was important was a significant part of challenging my 'truth', and of questioning the basic assumptions I had been taught to know. However, I learned to do more than reflect back in time, as the shift I achieved in 'political and historical consciousness' was prompted by critical enquiry into the 'conditions under which knowledge is produced' – and the realisation that the way I had been taught to know was not the only one, that there are multiple truths because there are multiple ways to know.

But as feminist legal scholars, are we seeking the qualitative shift that de Laurentis invites us to pursue? We often use our critiques to chip away at the 'truths' of the common law using women's knowledge to eradicate its demand for sameness and to demand respect for difference. But in doing so, how do we negotiate the spectrum of women's multiple truths? What guides our endeavours? Do we know how to listen? Whose truths can we know? And are we able to hear? If we maintain a 'linear, [and] mechanistic understanding of history and human relations' (Tuhiwai Smith 1999), we will continue to generate a very different understanding of phenomena than the knowing of 'marginalised' peoples. Professor Watson reveals this in her analysis of the exchange she documented between Counsel ('Q') assisting the South Australian Royal Commission into Hindmarsh Island Bridge and Nunga man, George Trevorrow ('A'):[6]

Q Let me put a suggestion to you: what you are talking about is a disturbance to the environment. Is that right.

A No more than that. To what those *Ngaitji* are to the people. They are not just animals and fish and snakes and things to us. They are real. They are more like people. Spiritual.

Q So it is really nothing to do with women's business, is it.

A It is combined with those things.

Q … You were saying that the island is significant because it is a place of women's business, and that a bridge linking the mainland to this place of women's business would be a desecration. That's what you're saying is it.

A Yes there is no way.

Q And you don't know, do you, by necessity, about what the women's business is, do you.

A (Witness shakes his head.)

Q So you cannot tell us, can you, in what way the bridge would affect the spirituality of the island, which is women's business, can you.

A No I have no way in the world of explaining that to you. I never come here to talk about the women's business on that site.

Q You are not in a position to talk about it, are you.

A Because I can't, I'm a man.

Q That's right. So your objection to the bridge really comes down to an environmental objection, isn't it.

This exchange illustrates how colonial thinking continues to displace the sovereignty of First Nations men's *and* women's laws (Watson 2007a, 98). Counsel could not grasp that the details of Nunga women's business and law may not be known to a Nunga man but could remain the source of his objection to the building of the bridge; instead, to understand Mr Trevorrow's evidence (and, no doubt, to destroy it), Counsel recast Mr Trevorrow's testimony as founded in the Western-defined concept of an 'environmental objection', rather than as an objection based in women's law (Watson 1997, 50–54).

Watson's critique offers another caution about 'white systemic ignorance which enables racism to influence knowledge production' (Watson 2014, 515); that is, that common law thinking is propelled by a racialised ideology by which First Nations law and knowledge is downgraded as somehow lesser, as 'not' law and 'not' knowledge. So there is cause to reflect on how within our feminist methods, we too may (consciously or otherwise) redefine Indigenous concepts to suit non-Indigenous purposes. The importance of this may be more evident by returning to Professor Gayatri Chakravorty Spivak's concern that the subaltern cannot speak[7]: the subaltern can and has always been speaking (though for too long, outside the academy), so the problem is not so much who *can* speak but more about *to whom we listen* (Moreton-Robinson 1999, 32). Because listening is a very different act to 'allowing' someone else to speak[8] – particularly if we wish to work reflexively and to question our own body of writing and critique.

As made evident in Watson's critique of the Royal Commission into Hindmarsh Island Bridge (1997), these questions not only provoke us to engage with other worldviews and knowledges, they also provoke us to be live to narratives in what we hear and read. Are we unconsciously privileging knowledges that are forged to view only Euro-centred horizons? Do we transplant theory in the same way that our forebears sought to transplant law? Are we tacitly supporting the legal academy's regime of authoritative knowing – its epistemic violence – that keeps its terrain empty, *terra nullius*, of First Nations knowing, law and philosophy?[9] Or taking that knowledge and applying it as our own? (Dr Sharon Venne in dialogue with Irene Watson: Watson 2007b, 118). And when we speak to 'call out' the common law's innate patriarchal voice, are we also calling out its implicit colonial 'truths' that skew how we can know and talk about law, such as 'settlement', 'acts of state', and lawfulness?

There is real cause to reflect upon the cultural setting of our scholarship and its implicit values – if not only because of the power it offers that we are constantly being urged to accept (our 'rightful' place as the 'experts' in the terrain of legal knowledge). A useful example, though old, is offered by Christopher Stone's suggestion that it was 'unthinkable' that nature should have 'rights' (Davies 2017, 470, 478) – now, we realise that it was 'unthinkable' only because it was bounded by Western legal philosophy, rather than by First Nations law and philosophy within which the suggestion is not only 'thinkable' but in fact foundational.[10] Thus, our work requires more than recognising perspective (Davies 2017, 234) or even a 'turn to culture' (Brooks 1997, 7). Because the claims pursued by First Nations theorists are not couched in terms of rights, citizenship or equality but are, instead, founded in a de-centring, a (re)turn to Indigenous sovereignty and law (Watson 2014). So it follows that we must recognise that the body of thought shared with us by First Nations women theorists cannot be reduced to subjectivity, narrative, and/or perspective but instead is a living and embodied set of knowledges, philosophies, and laws that see the horizon from the place of the grandmothers.

Knowing where we stand

De Laurentis urges us to 'dis-place' ourselves and to pursue the unknown and risky. Here I will turn to the question of race. I've found it can be very unpopular to talk about race. The mere mention – particularly through whiteness theory – is typically decried as a form of reinscribing racialisation rather than challenging it. And as indicated by feminist intersectional scholarship, an analysis of race can unintentionally mask the effect of gender (see Brooks 1997, 18). However, ignoring it is also risky because one could overlook the raced dimensions that explain why a woman is *the* woman connected to place and experience at a particular time (Moreton-Robinson 1992, 5; Behrendt 1997), potentially abandoning her to 'other systems of oppression' (Davies 2017, 273). I am not arguing specifically here for a transformation of all scholarship, but instead encouraging reflexivity about what we may unconsciously 'normalise' when we do not think about race.

So here I am inviting reflection on our standpoint in the research process and how race influences what we do – consciously *and* unconsciously. Do we even notice the racism in the systems and practices around us, that we are implicated in and that we – consciously or not – support and participate in on an everyday level? Are we part of the 'white noise' that affects place and space – expressing tensions, excuses, and rationales to resist calls for action, calls for change (Watson, Burns, and Nielsen 2015) – and the many powerful forms of casual racism in what we say and what we avoid? Christos Tsiolkas observes this vividly in his reflection that 'we' (those of us purportedly not affected by race) don't have to 'think through the legacy of colonial history' as it is 'too complex, too difficult, too complicated', with the upshot that 'we can revoke personal responsibility' and remain assured that what we do is 'not tainted by hatred, ignorance and resentment but is sober and considered' (Tsiolkas 2006, 13).

In my view, the potential of whiteness theory to pursue these concerns in our analyses is particularly misunderstood. I agree it is not perfect theory – but it does offer sharp and probing analytical possibilities. If deployed respectfully and meaningfully with other epistemologies and ontologies, it is extremely good at lifting the racial veil to reveal privilege and ideology. It also well suited to guiding the type of 'unknown and risky', the 'emotionally' and 'conceptually other' critique about which de Laurentis speaks (1988, 138–139, quoted in Brooks 1997, 211).

Whiteness theory should provoke us to engage differently with the knowledge of those who have gained 'epistemic privilege' through experiencing marginalisation, as their knowledge offers powerful insights into how disadvantage and marginalisation are produced (Davies 2017, 239). Though I agree that there is cause to resist forcing 'the messiness of identity into a formulaic grid' and avoid founding 'quintessential intersectional' subjects (Davies 2017, 268), I do not agree that these voices reiterate essentialism or that they are of less value through being 'only … very localised and specific' (Davies 2017: 18). Indeed, the work of First Nations theorists invites a very different reading of epistemic privilege because, in contrast to opening concerns about the 'authenticity' or purity of forms of identity, they open questions about the *authority* to speak. For First Nations peoples, their authority is their land and their law, which is a consequence of their relationship to country – that is, their authority is a consequence of who they are, and it is local and specific:

> The localised nature of Indigenous knowledge makes it imperative that, when considering the re-centring of Indigenous ways of being, capacity building need to occur at the local level. … For our knowledge systems to have life they require maintenance at the ground level and in particular on the territories of First Nations peoples, by First Nations peoples of those lands.
>
> (Watson 2014, 511–512)

And these local and specific places offer powerful insights (read: a potentially discomforting gaze) into what needs to be done to challenge and transform privilege. And that unknown and risky space is about 'my mob' – that's about us.

And here, my reading of whiteness theory also helps to explain the one point with which I disagree with de Laurentis: in my view, our leaving *is* a choice – that is, we can choose what we will and won't leave behind. Because as noted before, one of the most powerful things about whiteness is that it enables those of us with it to say when (our) race matters and when it does not.

So my reason for being conscious of standpoint is to make space from which I can engage reflexively on the partiality of my knowledge – what I know and how, what I can know, and what I can't, and how to look beyond my own horizon to learn what I don't know.[11] Which is also why I continue to make race and whiteness important within my work – not to maintain socialised concepts of race, but instead to create a vantage point from which to turn language and thinking back on myself. To me this is necessary because to develop the ability to think beyond race we must first learn how to unthink it – that is, *not thinking* about race is a qualitatively different strategy to *unthinking* it. And to begin the process of unthinking race we must learn about our own racialised identities and build the capacity to work self-consciously through the implications of race and why we continue to cling to it (even if we only do so unconsciously). Only then can we let go – because only then will we develop understanding of why that is important and what we need to leave behind.

And it seems to me that from that location, we might also begin properly to question and reimagine the 'lawfull-ness' of our connection to this place and if/how we might follow those who are peacefully going back to their law (Watson 2014). We might also be able to imagine if/when we engage and challenge our white privilege, what our communities could become.

Where are we going?

Watson explains that Aboriginal women's emancipation

> calls for the decolonization of the natural, political and legal landscape. For it is assumed that we want to become the same, rather than considering there may be another way to participate other than wanting to participate 'equally' in the machinery of oppression. The emancipation of Aboriginal women will come when we have dismantled patriarchy but also the colonial institutions patriarchy has assembled along the course of its own history. Enjoined in that struggle is to hold our position as Aboriginal peoples against the pressures of extinguishment.
>
> (Watson 2007a, 105–106)

What she has also said is that the possibility of our coexistence is 'hampered by a colonialist indifference to Indigenous philosophy' (Watson 2014, 517–518).

What we, non-Indigenous women, share with First Nations women is the need to dismantle the fundamental patriarchal structure of law and of political and social institutions. But the way I can be liberated from my position as a white female coloniser is very different to the struggle waged by an Indigenous woman who is the 'object' of colonisation. So we must never lose sight of the 'fact that there are different "sites of oppression" and different "sites of struggle"' (Brooks 1997, 17). The dialogue of difference is helpful here as it enables us not only to understand the plurality of experience and oppression (see Brooks 1997, 24), but can also help us comprehend and interrogate the interplay of our oppression *and our privilege.*[12]

I think what I have talked about throughout this chapter are (post)feminist concerns because knowing differently creates different relationships and different types of relatedness. Can they also propel us to decolonise ourselves? By engaging with the different body of First Nations philosophy and knowledge can we open better questions to guide our interrogations into the nature of feminist legal scholarship and raise questions about our cultural context (Bishop 1994, 175; Smith 1997, 25): What do we take for granted? What are the purposes of feminist scholarship? What strands of feminist scholarship must we renounce? What questions can *we* ask? And *to whom do we owe responsibility*?

Decolonial turns could offer us different insights into our laws as well as ways to reconceptualise them. And by learning from 'right ways of knowing' that support our collective survival,[13] we might be able to comprehend our interrelationships, and thus what needs to be done. They might guide us to learn how to track feminist paths to decolonisation – not as a separate journey, or even one that is parallel, but as part of many journeys that struggle towards a future which 'had not existed before' (Watson 2007c, 26).

Notes

1 I acknowledge that, like feminism more generally, postfeminism does not refer to a unified theory and practice. Accordingly, for the purposes of this work, I have engaged specifically with the account of postfeminism given by Brooks.

2 I use the term 'First Nations' to refer to the diverse groups of Indigenous peoples including those located in Australia. I have chosen the term 'theorists' to acknowledge that the First Nations peoples who hold knowledge and who lead thinking and scholarship in their communities work inside and outside the formal academy. I acknowledge that the knowledges held and the conversations led by these theorists are diverse and localised.

3 See e.g. the works of Watson and Moreton-Robinson.

4 Naming the cultural terrain of whiteness 'is a vital aspect of questioning and delimiting its authority' (Frankenberg 1993, 634).

5 'To my mind, what is called for in this context from Western legal scholars is 'self-reflectiveness about the philosophical landscape which has facilitated this dominance' (Davies 2017, 323).

6 The extract is reproduced from Watson (1997, 51–52).

7 Spivak, Gayatri Chakravorty. 1988. "Can the Subaltern Speak?" In *Marxism and the Interpretation of Culture*, edited by Cary Nelson and Lawrence Grossberg. 271. Urbana: University of Illinois Press. See also Moreton-Robinson (2011b).

8 And does not involve the 'patriarchal gesture of disenfranchising' First Nations peoples by 'taking over their right to speak' (Davies 2017, 233–234).

9 'We (white Westerners) are quite accustomed to speak unreflectively about the law, as though it is perfectly obvious what we mean. The Western concept of law – essentially legal positivism – admits only one law, and it is the dominant institutionalised state-based version. This linguistic act of exclusion obliterates other laws' (Davies, 2017, 314)

10 See Watson's discussion of Mary Graham's work in Watson (2014, 509–511). The 'South-South' critiques may also offer useful insights by provoking deeper thinking. For example, Santos (2016) argues that the 'concept of the rights of nature is a legal and cultural hybrid because the concepts of rights comes from the west. …This is a form of cognitive extraction having some affinities with the material extraction of natural resources, which is currently the main form of capital accumulation in many parts of the world' (25). I am mindful that Santos' critique has relevance to my own work.

11 'Practical change occurs within a climate of serious reflection' (Davies 2017, 235, 238).

12 Yeatman contends, 'the emergence of the category of difference has permitted feminist theory to investigate the materiality of the discursively interpellated female subject, and thereby to open the significance of difference in embodiment for the politics of difference' (1994, 15, as quoted in Brooks 1997, 25).

13 'Harding maintains that it is not 'experience' itself, but thinking from a contradictory position, that produces feminist knowledge and urges us to become active agents of historical understanding' (Brooks 1997, 19–20).

References

Anderson, Ian, 1993. "Black Suffering, White Wash". *Arena* June–July: 23–25.

———. 1995. "Reclaiming Tru-ger-nan-ner: De-Colonising the Symbol". In *Speaking Positions: Aboriginality, Gender and Ethnicity in Australian Cultural Studies*, edited by P. Van Toom and D. English, 35. Melbourne: Dept. of Humanities, Victoria University of Technology.

Behrendt, Larissa. 1993. "Aboriginal Women and the White Lies of the Feminist Movement: Implications for Aboriginal Women in Rights Discourse". *Australian Feminist Law Journal* 1: 27–44.

———. 1997. "Meeting at the Crossroads: Intersectionality, Affirmative Action and the Legacies of the Aborigines Protection Board". *Australian Journal of Human Rights* 4, no 1: 98–119.

Bishop, Russell. 1994. "Initiating Empowering Research?" *New Zealand Journal of Educational Studies* 29, no 1: 175–188.

Brooks, Ann. 1997. *Postfeminisms: Feminism, Cultural theory and Cultural Forms.* New York: Routledge.

Cowlishaw, Gillian. 1988. *Black, White or Brindle: Race in Rural Australia.* Cambridge: Cambridge University Press.

Crenshaw, Kimberlé. 1990. "A Black Feminist Critique of Antidiscrimination Law and Politics". In *The Politics of Law: A progressive Critique*, edited by David Kairys, 195. New York: Pantheon Books.

Curthoys, Ann. 2000. "An Uneasy Conversation: The Multicultural and the Indigenous". In *Race, Colour and Identity in Australia and New Zealand*, edited by John Docker and Gerard Fischer, 21. Sydney: UNSW Press.

Davies, Margaret. 2017. *Asking the Law Question.* 4th ed. Sydney: Thomson Reuters.

Delgado, Richard, ed. 1995. *Critical Race Theory: The Cutting Edge.* Philadelphia, PA: Temple University Press.

Doane, Woody. 2003. "Rethinking Whiteness Studies". In *White Out: The Continuing Significance of Racism*, edited by Ashley 'Woody' Doane and Eduardo Bonilla-Silva, 3. New York: Routledge.

Duclos, Nitya. 1990. "Lessons of Difference: Feminist Theory on Cultural Diversity". *Buffalo Law Review* 23, no 2: 325–381.

Fine, Michelle, et al., eds. 1997. *Off White: Readings on Race, Power and Society.* New York: Routledge

Frankenberg, Ruth. 1993. *White Women, Race Matters: The Social Construction of Whiteness.* Minnesota: University of Minnesota Press.

Fricker, Miranda. 2007. *Epistemic Injustice: Power and the Ethics of Knowing.* Oxford: Oxford University Press.

Gatens, Moira. 1996. *Imaginary Bodies: Ethics, Power and Corporeality.* London: Routledge.

Haney López, Ian. 1996. *White by Law: The Legal Construction of Race.* New York and London: New York University Press.

Harris, Angela. 1994. "Foreword: The Jurisprudence of Reconstruction". *California Law Review* 82: 741–785.

Harris, Cheryl. 1995. "Whiteness as Property". In *Critical Race Theory: The Key Writings that Formed the Movement,* edited by Kimberlé Crenshaw, Neil Gotanda, Gary Peller and Kendall Thomas, 276. New York: The New Press.

Hartigan Jr, John. 2003. "Who Are These White People?: 'Rednecks', 'Hillbillies', And 'White Trash' as Marked Racial Subjects". In *White Out: The Continuing Significance of Racism*, edited by Ashley 'Woody' Doane and Eduardo Bonilla-Silva, 95. New York and London: Routledge.

Hollinsworth, David. 1998. *Race and Racism in Australia.* 2nd ed. Katoomba: Social Science Press.

Huggins, Jackie. 1990. "Response". In *Through White Eyes,* edited by Susan Janson and Stuart MacIntyre, 168. Sydney: Allen & Unwin.

Little Nyoongah, Janine. 1996. "The Race for Race: Feminist Scholarship and the Positionality Impasse". *Hecate* 22, no 2: 130–139.

Matsuda, Mari, Charles Lawrence III, Richard Delgado, and Kimberlé Crenshaw. 1993. *Words that wound: Critical Race Theory, Assaultive Speech and the First Amendment.* Boulder, CO: Westview Press.

Milroy, Stephanie. 1996. "Maori Women and Domestic Violence: The Methodology of Research and the Maori Perspective". *Waikato Law Review* 4: 58–76.

Monture-Angus, Patricia. 2000. *Journeying Forward – Dreaming Aboriginal Peoples' Independence.* Annandale: Pluto Press Australia.

Moreton-Robinson, Aileen. 1992. "Masking Gender and Exalting Race: Indigenous Women and Commonwealth Employment Policies". *Australian Feminist Studies* 15: 5–10.

———. 1998. "When the Object Speaks, A Postcolonial Encounter: Anthropological Representations and Aboriginal Women's Self-presentations". *Discourse* 19, no. 3: 275–298.

———. 1999. "Unmasking Whiteness: A *Goori Jondal's* Look at Some *Duggai* Business". In *Unmasking Whiteness: Race Relations and Reconciliation*, edited by Belinda McKay, 28. Brisbane: The Queensland Studies Centre.

———. 2000a. *Talkin' up to the White Woman – Indigenous Women and Feminism.* Brisbane: University of Queensland Press.

———. 2000b. "*Duggaibah*, or 'Place of Whiteness': Australian Feminists and Race". In *Race, Colour and Identity in Australia and New Zealand*, edited by John Docker and Gerhard Fischer, 240. Sydney: UNSW Press.

———. 2004a. "Whiteness Matters: Australian Studies and Indigenous Studies". In *Thinking Australian Studies: Teaching Courses across Cultures*, edited by David Carter, Kate Darian-Smith and Gus Worby, 136. Australia: University of Queensland Press.

———. 2004b. "Whiteness, Epistemology and Indigenous Representation". In *Whitening Race*, edited by Aileen Moreton-Robinson, 75. Canberra: Aboriginal Studies Press.

———. 2011a. "Virtuous Racial States: The Possessive Logic of Patriarchal White Sovereignty and the United Nations Declaration on the Rights of Indigenous Peoples". *Griffith Law Review* 20, no. 3: 641–658.

———. 2011b. "The White Man's Burden: Patriarchal White Epistemic Violence and Aboriginal Women's Knowledges within the Academy". *Australian Feminist Studies* 26, no 70: 413–431.

Nielsen, Jennifer. 2002. "Dealing with the Dilemmas: Integrity, Knowledge and Research". *Southern Cross University Law* Review 6: 151–176.

———. 2004. "How Law makes Aboriginal Women 'disappear'". *Indigenous Law Bulletin* 6, no 1: 23–25.

———. 2007. "'There's Always an Easy out': How 'Innocence' and 'Probability' Whitewash Race Discrimination". *ACRAWSA e-journal* 3, no 1. https://acrawsa.org.au/wp-content/uploads/2017/12/CRAWS-Vol-3-No-1-2007.pdf.

———. 2008a. *An Intractable Problem: The Endurance of Whiteness in the Mainstream Workplace.* Unpublished PhD Thesis, University of Melbourne.

———. 2008b. "Whiteness and Anti-Discrimination law–It's in the design". *ACRAWSA e-journal* 3, no 2; Republished in 2014. *Critical Race and Whiteness Studies* 10, no 2. https://acrawsa.org.au/wp-content/uploads/2017/12/CRAWS-Vol-4-No-2-2008.pdf.

———. 2013. "Whiteness at Work". *Australian Journal of Labour Law* 26, no 3:300–325.

Paisley, Fiona. 1998. "Federalising the Aborigines? Constitutional Reform in the Late 1920s". *Australian Historical Studies*, 111: 248–266.

Pettman, Jan. 1992. *Living in the Margins: Racism, Sexism and Feminism in Australia.* Sydney: Allen & Unwin.

Purdy, Jeannine. 1997. *Common Law and Colonised Peoples: Studies in Trinidad and Western Australia.* Dartmouth, England: Ashgate.

Said, Edward. 1994. *Culture and Imperialism.* London: Vintage.

Santos, Boaventura de Sousa. 2014. *Epistemologies of the South: Justice against Epistemicide*. Boulder, CO: Paradigm Publishers.

———. 2016. “Epistemologies of the South and the Future”. *From the European South* 1: 17–29.

Smith, Arthur. 1997. “Indigenous Research Ethics: Policy, Protocol and Practice”. *The Australian Journal of Indigenous Education* 25, no 1: 23–29.

Spivak, Gayatri Chakravorty. 1988. “Can the Subaltern Speak?” In *Marxism and the Interpretation of Culture*, edited by Cary Nelson and Lawrence Grossberg, 271. Urbana: University of Illinois Press.

Thornton, Margaret. 1990. *The Liberal Promise*. South Melbourne: Oxford University Press.

Tsiolkas, Christos. 2006. “Cry Havoc and Unleash the Dogs of War”. *Storyline* 14, Autumn: 12–14.

Tuhiwai Smith, Linda. 1999. *Decolonizing Methodologies: Research and Indigenous Peoples*. Dunedin: University of Otago Press.

Tunks, Andrea. 2001. “He Wero ki te Ture: Maori Legal Research Methodology”. Paper presented to the ALTA Conference, University of the South Pacific, Vanuatu.

Watson, Irene 1996. “Nungas in the Nineties”. In *Majah* edited by Greta Bird, Gary Martin, and Jennifer Nielsen, 4. Sydney: The Federation Press.

———. 1997. “Indigenous Peoples’ Law-Ways: Survival against the Colonial State”. *Australian Feminist Law Journal* 8: 39–58.

———. 1998. “Power of the Muldarbi, the Road to Its Demise”. *Australian Feminist Law Journal* 11: 28–45.

———. 2005. “Illusionists and Hunters: Being Aboriginal in this Occupied Space”. *Australian Feminist Law Journal* 22: 15–28.

———. 2007a. “Aboriginal Women’s Laws and Lives: How Might We Keep Growing the Law?” *Australian Feminist Law Journal* 26: 95–107.

———. 2007b. “Decolonisation and Aboriginal Peoples: Past and Future Strategies”. (Interview with Sharon Venne) *Australian Feminist Law Journal* 26: 111–121.

———. 2007c. “Aboriginal Sovereignties”. In *Our Patch*, edited by Suvendrini Perera, 23. Perth: Network Books.

———. 2014 “Re-Centring First Nations Knowledge and Places in a Terra Nullius Space”. *AlterNative* 10, no 5: 508–520.

Watson, Irene, Marcelle Burns, and Jennifer Nielsen. 2015. “How Might we Better Engage Indigenous Knowledge in the Academy and Move towards Putting the Colonial Imaginary of the Savage to Rest?”, Plenary Panel, *Inside Outside*, LSAANZ Conference, Flinders University, Adelaide.

Williams, Patrick, and Laura Chrisman, eds. 1993. *Colonial Discourse and Post-colonial Theory: A Reader*. New York: Harvester Wheatsheaf.

8 Breaking free from the orbit of legal centralism

Religious minority women in a postcolonial context

Joyce Das

Introduction

Historically excluded from the mainstream knowledge creation processes, feminists have raised the epistemological question of women's experiences and the subjugated nature of their knowledge. Feminist epistemology critiques 'objective' knowledge, which is situated outside the knower, reflecting an independent external world to be tested and validated and universal in nature (Harding 1987). Feminist theorists argue that this traditional epistemology has delegitimised women as knowers. Feminist researchers consider women's experiences as an important indicator of the reality that women face. Feminism's epistemological engagement with legitimising women's subjugated knowledge has also had an impact on legal feminism. This engagement has brought legal feminists to focus on the question of women's experiences of law.

Feminist legal theories have contributed significantly to the feminist agenda that have resulted in women gaining more formal rights. However, while legal feminists have contributed significantly to the scholarship of gender and law, they have mostly interacted with laws that are associated with the state. In other words, they have primarily confined themselves to the legal centralist paradigm by leaving non-state laws out of their inquiries. This insight begs the question in the postfeminist present: Can women's full experiences of law be captured by feminists' engagement with the state's legal framework?

To answer this question, I turn to the concept of postfeminism. The concept of postfeminism is often defined as the feminist thinking that came after second-wave feminism (Griffin 2017). Third-wave feminists use the concept of postfeminism in order to describe a time when the ideological and epistemological positions of the second-wave no longer hold (Griffin 2017). The idea that the positions of second-wave feminism no longer hold is, however, highly contested among feminist theorists. Such an understanding of postfeminism

> ... signals that the breadth of feminist issues is more extensive than in previous times and as such is not against (or after) feminism but about a feminism which reconsiders and makes a clear shift in its categories and questions.
> (Lewis 2014, 1849)

In this chapter, the notion of postfeminism is understood as an 'epistemological break within feminism', where '"Post"… implies transformation and change within feminism' (Gill and Scharff 2011, 3). The transformative potential of postfeminism might ground a new focus for legal feminists to consider wider sources of law.

Based on my ethnographic research on Christians, a religious minority community in postcolonial Bangladesh, I argue in this chapter that women's full experiences of law cannot be captured just by engaging with the state's legal system. This chapter argues that while interacting with state law, most legal feminists have overlooked other sources of law that are vital to understanding women's experiences. In order to capture women's full experiences and interactions with law, we need to expand the horizon of law. Instead of seeing the state as the sole source of law, we need to consider other social sources of laws.

Similar to other South Asian countries, Bangladesh has different personal laws for different religious groups (Muslims, Hindus, and Christians). Personal laws govern areas of social life such as marriage, divorce, inheritance, and custody. This creates a situation of legal pluralism based on religious identity.[1] These religion-specific personal laws originated from British colonisation. Many personal laws are highly gender-discriminatory, particularly for minority communities, and they have not been amended for more than a century. For example, Bangladesh still has laws for its Christian populations such as the Christian Marriage Act 1872, and the Divorce Act 1869, which have been enforced since colonial times without being amended. While the content of these laws does not necessarily reflect religious texts or current practices, personal laws have religious significance because they govern the practices of respective religious groups around key aspects of life.

Historically in South Asia, minorities have actively promoted their collective autonomy by asserting their culture, traditions, religion, or language. These attributes became their primary group identity markers (Rajan 2003). The postcolonial South Asian states, including Bangladesh, India, and Pakistan, are confronted with diverse societal groups that seek autonomy over the governance of families through their customary laws. As a result, the state and religious or cultural groups engage in an ongoing process of negotiation over state personal laws and the extent to which these groups enjoy autonomy in the governance of their respective families.

In this chapter, I will first show how different waves of legal feminism operate within the state legal system and rely on the legal centralist paradigm. I will then engage with the critiques of legal centralism by other feminist scholars. In my final section, I will focus on the case of minority Christians in Bangladesh and show how a feminist analysis of the first, second, and third waves fails to capture women's full experiences of laws. In this chapter, I call for postfeminism to break with these earlier waves and broaden the horizon of laws by making the analytical shift to include other social sources of law.

Feminism and the legal centralist paradigm

Since the 1970s, feminist legal theories have contributed significantly towards promoting the feminist agenda by engaging with the question of women's experiences of law. However, I argue that each of these three waves of feminist legal theories is situated within the legal centralist paradigm, where the state is viewed as the primary locus of law. Scholars have problematised the assumption that women's experiences can be captured within a legal centralist paradigm. While researching women's experiences of law in postcolonial Africa, Manji (1999) argues that feminist theoretical work that privileges state law is only capable of capturing partial accounts of women's experiences of law. While feminists have been engaged in 'an anti-sexist project, which involves challenging and deconstructing phallocentric discourses' (Grosz 2013, 190), Manji (1999, 436) argues that 'the phallocentric theoretical system of legal centralism – and its privileging of the state law – has been left untouched'. Through this process, feminism has conformed to legal monism by endorsing the idea that the state is the only source of law.

The first-wave of feminist legal scholars founded their feminist agenda on an equality model (Fineman 2005, 15). They challenged discriminatory laws and critiqued laws that prevented women from having the same opportunities as men (Jethmalani 1986; Mehta 1987; Venkataramiah 1987). Feminists, inspired by liberal feminism, asserted that law had exacerbated women's oppression by discriminatory treatment. They attacked gender differences codified in law and the stereotypes that justified them (Kapur and Cossman 1996). These first-wave legal feminists tended to rely entirely on the legal centralist paradigm. In their arguments, they deconstructed the male-biased treatment of law without challenging the state as the only source of law. Instead, they advocated for gender equality within the framework of positivist laws.

Critiquing the equality model, the second-wave of legal feminists argued that even law, which appears 'neutral', can create gender inequality. They developed theories based on the concept of gender 'difference' (MacKinnon 1979). Yet these feminists did not challenge the centralist view of law. Bounded by the perimeter of state law, they argued that formal equal treatment by law can merely eliminate the ideological and structural inequalities that women face. Some of these scholars emphasised that since women are 'naturally weaker' than men, they should be 'protected' by law (read state law) (Deshpande 1984; Anthony 1985; Kapur and Cossman 1996). According to the proponents of this 'difference' model, because women are situated in an inferior position in society compared to their male counterparts, they require 'special' concerns (MacKinnon 1979). Along a similar path, Fineman (2005) critically analysed the first-wave feminist theory and argued for differential treatment for men and women based on their respective social circumstances. Such an approach not only accepted the traditional and patriarchal discourses that portrayed the role of law to be about protecting women, but also confirmed their confinement to the centralist paradigm of law.

Under the 'difference' model, existing law was critiqued as male-biased. Some scholars went as far as identifying law as male (Gilligan 1993). For example, Stubbs (1991, 267), in her research on battered woman syndrome in Australia, shows how the state legal system is 'poorly equipped to deal with the experiences of women ... where male standards of reasonableness or other legal tests apply'. A decade earlier, in the American context, Russell (1982, 44–48) found that many rape victims or victims of sexual assault by acquaintances often respond to the question, 'Have you ever been raped?' with expressions such as, 'Well ... not exactly'. According to Russell (1982), the pause between 'well' and 'not exactly' indicates the gaps between the legal interpretation of rape, how women actually experience it in their lives, and the ways information or data on such phenomenon are constructed and collected. More recently, Baker and Oberman (2016) explored the complex relationship between women's sexual autonomy, women's celebration of their own sexual objectification in contemporary culture, and the persistently high rates of non-consensual sex. They showed how a legal presumption against consent would neither reduce the rate of non-consensual sex nor raise the rate of reported rapes. Through this argument, Baker and Oberman (2016) indicate that a gap exists between the legal interpretation of non-consensual sex and the way women experience it. Although many second-wave legal feminists critiqued the law and its failure to recognise women's lived experience, they focused primarily on the state-made law.

This traditional view of the legal paradigm does not challenge the patriarchy, its assumptions, or its categories adequately. Hence, according to Wishik (1985, 68), such a paradigm keeps women's experiences 'hidden'. Recently, a similar concern was raised by Williams (2013, 81), 'Asking how women are different from men focuses attention on women's characteristics rather than on the ways in which institutions ... privilege certain people ... at the expense of others'. Instead, it simply considers women's exclusion as 'an error' (Wishik 1985, 68) and provides the 'solution' as 'add-women-and-stir' (Boxer 1982, 682). Moreover, within the difference model, feminists focused on how women's perspectives and experiences differ from those of men, in which again 'men have remained the unstated standard of analysis' (Rhode 1989, 618). There is no doubt that by challenging law (specifically state law), these scholars have contributed significantly to the feminist agenda. However, they address the problem only partially because they do not acknowledge law beyond the state and its institutions.

In the Global South, feminists have engaged in state law reform. This is reflected in their engagement with the Convention on the Elimination of All Forms of Discrimination against Women (CEDAW) 1979 and the UN's Security Council Resolution 1325 (S/RES/1325). In Bangladesh, the Domestic Violence (Prevention and Protection) Act 2010 (Act no. LVIII of 2010) is another example of feminist engagement in reforming state law (Chowdhury 2011). Feminists' advocacy for a uniform civil code also indicates their reliance on and trust in state law, which they see as one of the most effective ways to achieve gender equality (Parashar 1992).

Manji (1999) identifies two main reasons why feminists rely on state law reform. First, during the 1990s, an increasing number of non-governmental organisations (NGOs) working on gender issues have been in operation in developing countries. According to Manji, these NGOs function as 'foreign-funded watchdogs on behalf of the international community' (Manji 1999, 440). As a result, a state-centred ideology was promulgated in developing countries through the international development sector. Second, in developing countries, legal practitioners and other professionals working on women's issues are members of the 'postcolonial bourgeoisie', or in other words, 'state bureaucratic elites' (Manji 1999, 440). Therefore, the NGOs' close association with states means that 'endeavours to ameliorate the position of women remain within the magnetic field of the state law and within the dominant paradigm of legal centralism' (Manji 1999, 440). In this way, the analysis of the relationships between women and law remains stuck in the gravitational pull of state law.

Legal feminists contributed significantly to feminist projects by questioning how women's voices, experiences, and concerns are reflected in state-based law (Schneider 1986; Minow 1989). But soon they encountered the question of which women's voices feminists should consider. The attention of third-wave feminists then focused on the 'differences' between women. Parashar (1996) argues that although intersectionality has taken an important position in feminist legal theory by drawing attention to the intersection of gender and race, the focus of intersectional third-wave feminism is still centred on North America. If women's experiences are recognised as a valid source of knowledge, then feminism must incorporate the experience of non-Western women as well (Parashar 1996). The advocates of intersectionality argue in favour of the plurality of women's subjective positions and multiple experiences without acknowledging the plurality of law in their respective legal worlds. Under the legal centralist paradigm, law is associated with the state and, in the process, other sources of law are not acknowledged. Hence, this paradigm can provide only a partial picture of how women experience law.

Recognising such shortcomings, some scholars argue for decentring and broadening the horizons of law. For example, Kapur (1996, 2) challenged the traditional boundaries of law and showed that it is necessary 'to decentre law', which means 'to make law but one area of inquiry into the multiple ways in which women are subordinated and oppressed'. By decentring law, Kapur (1996) attempts to challenge the positivist claim of law as an objective, neutral, and singular truth. Both Kapur (1996) and Parashar (1996) call for feminism to broaden its boundaries by moving law from the centre of analysis to the periphery. These theorists do not challenge the positivist view of law that is embedded in the legal centralism paradigm. Instead, they attempt to reduce the weight that has been traditionally assigned to law and incorporate contexts.

In order to broaden the sphere of law, Davies' (2008) notion of horizontal law is useful. Davies (2008, 282) outlines two modalities of law in her flat law theory – vertical and horizontal – where the vertical is exclusively associated with the nation-state and the horizontal is situated within the 'relationships of actual proximity or contiguity'. While Davies (2008) believes that it is still important for feminism to engage with the vertical law (particularly to promote women's new rights, gender mainstreaming in institutions, and anti-discrimination initiatives at a formal level), she argues that feminists need to go beyond this framework. Davies writes, '[M]y intention is to build upon 'alternative' practices of law, 'alternative' knowledge about law, 'alternative' localities in which law exists, and 'alternative' legal subjectivities' (Davies 2008, 287). In my view, as long as we use the term 'alternative', as Davies does, we are again falling into the trap of acknowledging the state law as the 'standard' reference point that is primary and the 'other' as an 'alternative' from the mainstream. In this chapter, I argue that if we remove the term 'alternative', then Davies' horizontal law theory becomes a cornerstone of legal feminism.

Similar to Davies' concept of flat law, legal pluralism is also seen by some scholars as a path to exit the orbit of the legal centralist paradigm. Manji similarly argues that feminists should engage with legal pluralism (Manji 1999). In modern society, law is 'plural rather than monolithic, that it is private as well as the public in character and that the national (public, official) legal system is often a secondary rather than primary locus of regulation' (Galanter 1981, 20). Based on this, Manji argues that it is particularly true for women whose legal world does not entirely depend on the state legal system, but instead depends on other systems (Manji 1999). Therefore, by using the legal pluralism framework, we would be able to obtain a more accurate picture of how law interplays with gender within a society.

Since the 1970s, different waves of legal feminism have dealt with gender and law differently. However, their common thread is their preoccupation with state law. Yet, women's experiences of law are much more than their experience of state law. This is where postfeminism has the potential to challenge the state law narrative because it flags an analytical shift which might highlight women's experience of law. The following section shows this by presenting a case of a religious minority woman from the Christian community in Bangladesh.

Minority women's experiences of laws: Rupali's story

In 2014, I met Rupali Halder[2] while doing my fieldwork in Bangladesh. Rupali's experience demonstrates how women from a religious minority community experience the plurality of law. Rupali is an educated Bengali woman in her late 20s from the minority Christian community in the north-western part of Bangladesh and now works in the private sector in Dhaka. When she was 18 years old, Rupali had a relationship with a Catholic man. Although her family initially did not approve of her relationship, later they decided that the couple should marry. In 2006, at the age of 19, Rupali married the man in her local Baptist church. However, her husband's church did not accept their marriage as it did not conform to the Catholic rites. Later, to gain the acceptance of her husband's church community, Rupali converted to Catholicism and the couple had a second wedding in the Catholic Church. However, within a few months, they began to have severe marital problems because of her husband's violence against her and his alcohol and drug problems. Rupali's in-laws and other relatives asked her to be patient. A few years later, she moved out and returned to live with her mother. The Catholic Church became involved in the matter and called the couple in for counselling. Rupali and her husband had several sessions with the Church priests, but each time the Church conveyed to them that there is no provision for divorce in the Catholic Church. Therefore, the Church wanted them to consider ways to live within this marriage peacefully.

After living separately for about two years, both Rupali and her husband decided to divorce. Rupali's lawyer explained that divorce would be difficult for her because of the Christian divorce law of the country. He told her that for Christians, a divorce is not possible without a complaint of adultery. Moreover, the lawyer explained that adultery alone would not be enough for Rupali to initiate divorce, as according to the personal law, she also would have to bring additional grounds such as cruelty. The claim of physical abuse would also have to be supported by evidence. Rupali quickly realised that it would be almost impossible for her to obtain a dignified divorce. But later, from another lawyer, she discovered that there was an alternative process of 'mutual divorce' for Christians, which involved the signing of an affidavit to declare that the couple was divorced from then on. She also heard that many Christians had recently taken this path in order to avoid the difficulties of legal proceedings in courts and social scandal. Many who had taken this alternative path of divorce were even remarrying. Rupali had doubts about this process and knew that there must be some loopholes in this type of divorce. However, at that particular moment, getting a divorce by affidavit appeared to be the best option for Rupali without going through the trouble of the court proceedings and to minimise any social scandal. Finally, Rupali and her husband proceeded and signed an affidavit in 2011 to declare that they were divorced and they could remarry if they wished.

Rupali's interaction with laws as a religious minority woman, compared to her counterparts in the majority groups, accentuates the complexity of her situation. In South Asia, the issue of minorities sits at the heart of its political problems. The Partition of India in 1947, which was carried out based on religious 'minority' and 'majority' populations (Khan 2007, 3), completely reframed the issue of minorities in this region. Therefore, the postcolonial states – Bangladesh (then East Pakistan), India, and Pakistan (then West Pakistan) – inherited minority 'problems' at the moment these nation states were founded. In Bangladesh, minorities became the subject of violence by majority groups. Killing minorities and looting their properties and possessions are everyday events even today (Rafi 2005).

Where minorities encounter discrimination and violence from the majority groups, Rupali's situation stands at a critical point in a postcolonial context where her religious minority identity intersects with her gender and multiple legal systems. In order to receive a divorce, she needed to prove not only her husband's adultery, but also at least one of the eight conditions, which included cruelty, incest, bigamy, sodomy, and bestiality. By contrast, it was enough for her husband to divorce her by bringing a single charge of adultery against her.[3] Rupali's story exposes us to a range of other issues beyond the boundaries of personal laws. As a Catholic woman, her marriage was indissoluble and was considered a sacrament according to the Code of Canon Law. Moreover, the alternative form of divorce by affidavit, which she and her husband mutually agreed on, was not a legal divorce, although both parties regarded it as having the same consequences as a legal divorce. Her society imposed patriarchal ideologies on her and told her to endure her husband's abuse. The Church could not approve a divorce, and neither did the personal laws for Christians. As a result, Rupali finally chose an alternative process, bypassing both the state and church law to give her what she wanted.

Rupali represents about 16 million[4] women in Bangladesh belonging to religious minority groups that not only encounter a lack of decent remedies for marital and other familial issues afforded by law, but are also often subject to related discrimination and abuse. The Constitution of Bangladesh guarantees equality as a fundamental right (Articles 27 and 28) and specifically prohibits discrimination on the grounds of religious affiliation and gender (Article 28). However, this equality is only theoretical, as different religious family laws continue to discriminate against women (Parashar 1992). These women often experience child marriage, adultery, domestic violence, substance abuse, restriction of freedom of movement and profession, no formal separation or divorce, no effective help from the churches or other religious institutions, and may even be prevented from meeting with their children (Pereira 2011).

Legal feminism in the Global South: using intersectionalism in the argument for law reform

Rupali Halder, the protagonist of my story, stands in a position where her experience of law goes beyond the state's legal framework. Rupali took an alternative path to exit her marriage. She bypassed the state personal laws as well as Church law. Rupali's alternative divorce was not a 'legal' remedy in the eyes of either the state or the Church. Although Rupali was aware of the difficulties and disadvantages of the process she followed, it did not stop her from taking the alternative path. She said:

> I had reached a point, where I just needed some sort of document, which somehow falls within the legal framework, and that states my marital status as 'divorced'. I just needed to come out of that relationship and this option seemed the best among what I had.

For Rupali, the perceptions of the state and the Church were less important than her own need to get away from her husband. This shows that women's day-to-day experiences of how law is gendered may be incomprehensible if the analytical framework is not broadened from the state law by including other social sources of law.

Women's positions in a religious minority community in a postcolonial context such as South Asia demonstrate the complexity of legal pluralism. Legal pluralism in this region took the current shape because of encounters with colonial legal systems between the 18th and the 20th century. Pre-colonial India was ruled first by the Hindu kings and then by the Mughals, who were Muslims. There had already been pre-existing legal systems and institutions when the British arrived (Panday and Hossain 2011).

While legislating state laws, the colonial rulers incorporated the local law and hence the legal system became a mixed system – partly indigenous and partly foreign. They legislated the Anglo-Hindu and Anglo-Muslim laws by hiring interlocutors to interpret pre-colonial local Hindu and Muslim practices and customs (Mitra and Fischer 2002; Mallampalli 2010). These Anglo-Hindu and Anglo-Muslim laws gave pre-colonial practices a modern legal status. Although these laws were labelled as 'customary' or 'religious' laws, they did not necessarily match existing customs or social norms, nor religious texts. Moreover, these laws were formulated in English, a language that the majority of 'natives' did not speak. There is no doubt that many of these laws remained 'distant from the local law … [and] its effective reach limited to urban areas where the institutionalised presence of the state legal system was strongest' (Tamanaha 2008, 384).

At the centre of these minority issues, there is a conflict between the state's control over its citizens and the minority community's autonomy. The situation of legal pluralism converges with minority issues in multi-religious, multi-ethnic, and culturally plural postcolonial countries, in which states and religious groups compete and struggle over governing and regulating the family (Manchanda 2009). In postcolonial settings in Bangladesh, India, and Pakistan, religion-based minority communities are viewed as separate and isolated from the mainstream and averse to change. This is because many minority communities believe that isolation will protect their interests and identity (Rajan 2003). Isolation has a significant impact on the lives of minority women. In her work on women, law, and citizenship in postcolonial India, Rajan (2003) argues that women are neither excluded nor marginalised. Instead, women of religious minorities take centre stage in identity politics. She further notes that unlike men, these women are not seen as 'constituting' the communities; but are described as 'belonging' to them and become 'symbolic figures' for communities (Rajan 2003, 163–164). In this way and as I have shown elsewhere (Das 2016), women become an instrument of creating and protecting community identities.

Postcolonial states continue their efforts towards nation-building projects (Heuer 2005; Loos 2006). Such nation-building efforts require balancing economic development, social cohesion, and political stability, as well as creating a national consciousness that is often achieved through legislation, adjudication, and the enforcement of laws (Solanki 2011). With this aim, the states, therefore, seek to modernise key institutions, such as families and marriage, and shape ethnic, religious, sexual, and gender identities through law. Proponents of state-centric regulation of families argue that the state should be the locus of governance for families and that religious or cultural differences should only be recognised in the private sphere.

For example, Rawls (1996) argues that diverse conflicting doctrines should be located within a single political conception in order to serve justice in the public domain of culturally or religiously plural societies. In other words, state-centric regulation should not recognise differences in the public realm; difference should only be a matter for the private realm. Similarly, Sangari (1995) asks if gender justice should be sought within the framework of separate personal laws when it is desired by both state and community. Many feminists have relied on a similar argument to advocate for a uniform family code (Pereira 2002; Parashar and Dhanda 2008).

Among various religious and cultural groups, minorities show a marked sense of solidarity towards preserving their culture, traditions, religion, and language (Mishra and Singh 2002). Religious and cultural groups identify their respective customary laws as markers of their group identities and hence through the process, promote self-autonomy (Woods 2004). The state, on the other hand, accommodates peoples' aspirations for 'self-rule' and allows them autonomy for self-government. Such accommodation of self-rule is used as a tool to allow minority groups 'to exercise direct control over affairs' directly of interest to them, while allowing the majority 'to exercise those powers that govern common interests' (Manchanda 2009, 20). As a result, the state and religious or cultural groups engage in an ongoing process of negotiation over personal laws and the extent to which these groups enjoy autonomy in the governance of their respective families. As Rajan argues,

> Personal law, since it is envisaged as a means of securing community identity and respecting religious difference ... any proposed reform or removal of personal laws becomes a fraught issue and is perceived as a threat to community identity and/or traditional patriarchal arrangements. (Rajan 2003, 148)

The threat perceived by minority communities around the issue of the reform of personal law also creates resistance.

Group rights through personal law pose major challenges for realising women's rights. The conflict between religious or cultural group rights and women's rights is played out in the everyday lives of many women – through the denial of their rights of inheritance, divorce, maintenance, and child custody. These denials appear to be a direct violation of Article 16 of the UN Convention on the Elimination of All Forms of Discrimination against Women (CEDAW) that provides women with equal rights within a marital relationship, and to which many South Asian countries, including Bangladesh, are signatories.

Feminists, therefore, resist the idea of such religious minority group autonomy, particularly on family matters. They argue that groups tend to form their values and norms based on patriarchal ideologies that do not provide women with their full human rights. This mismatch between group autonomy and women's rights cause many feminists to criticise states' choices to adopt multiple laws to recognise cultural and religious pluralism over ensuring women's rights in their families (Kukathas 1992; Parashar 1992; Cook 1994; Moghadam 1994; Okin 1997; Mahajan 2005).

But the questions arise: Where to from here? How can legal feminists engage with other non-state laws and bring the social sources of law into their analysis? Can postfeminism help in responding to these questions? Here, I suggest the idea of legal pluralism can assist legal feminist research. During the 1970s, at a time when feminism attracted significant attention from scholars, the concept of legal pluralism also emerged as a separate, highly contested, analytical concept in the fields of sociology and anthropology. The concept of legal pluralism emerged from a critique of legal centralism. Although legal pluralism scholarship has developed since the 1970s, not many interactions can be found between legal feminists and legal pluralists.

In the postfeminist present, can 'legal pluralism' be the magic bullet to help feminism exit the orbit of legal centralism? I argue that the epistemological transformation facilitated by postfeminism has the potential to make legal pluralism flourish. A body of literature identifies postfeminism as feminism within the poststructuralist theory (Gillis and Munford 2004; Lewis 2014; Robinson 2011). Mann calls postfeminism 'the postmodern offspring of feminism' (1994, 239). According to Brooks, it is the '... intersection of feminism with a number of other anti-foundationalist movements including postmodernism, poststructuralism and post-colonialism' (Brooks 1997, 1). Later Gamble defines postfeminism as 'pluralistic epistemology dedicated to disrupting universalising patterns of thoughts' (2001, 50). But above all, postfeminism is capable of bringing about a transformation within feminism by challenging its traditional epistemological standpoint (Gill and Scharff 2011).

Conclusion: where to?

Minority women's lives are not regulated only by the state's legal system. Hence, their experience of laws cannot be captured with the feminists' exclusive engagement with the state's legal framework. In this chapter, I have shown this through the eyes of a religious minority woman in Bangladesh. Engaging with the legal centralist paradigm, legal feminists of the first three waves have only been able to capture a partial picture of women's experience of laws. In order to capture women's full experiences of law, feminists should exit the periphery of state law and enter into a broader arena of law that includes non-state laws. In order to break free from the orbit of legal centralism, feminists should focus on laws in people's everyday lives. This focus better accommodates the intersectionality and diversity of their experiences. A transformative break within feminism is offered by postfeminism because it creates an epistemological shift. It creates an inter-disciplinary dialogue between legal feminism and legal pluralism.

Notes

1 Generally, legal pluralism is defined as a situation where multiple legal systems co-exist within a broader legal context. The essential elements that commonly exist in order to create a situation of legal pluralism are multiple legal systems that contain law

or other normative orders, a broader context where these legal systems cohabit, and all these laws and normative orders being active or interplaying at the same time.
2 I have used a pseudonym.
3 According to Section 10, the Divorce Act 1869.
4 The total population of Bangladesh is 158.96 million (Bangladesh Bureau of Statistics 2015). Muslim: 90%, Hindu: 9%, Buddhist: 0.6%, Christian: 0.3%, Others: 0.1% (Bangladesh Bureau of Statistics 2015).

References

Anthony, M. J. 1985. *Women's Rights*. New Delhi: Dialogue Publications.

Baker, Katharine K., and Michelle Oberman. 2016. "Women's Sexual Agency and the Law of Rape in the 21st Century." In *Special Issue: Feminist Legal Theory*, edited by Austin Sarat, Maxine Eichner and Clare Huntington, 63–111. Bingley: Emerald Group Publishing Limited.

Bangladesh Bureau of Statistics. 2015. *Statistical Pocket Book Bangladesh 2015*. Dhaka: Bangladesh Bureau of Statistics.

Boxer, Marilyn J. 1982. "For and about women: The theory and practice of women's studies in the United States." *Signs* 7, no. 3: 661–695.

Brooks, Abigail. 1997. *Postfeminisms: Feminism, Cultural Theory and Cultural Forms*. London: Routledge.

Chowdhury, Elora Halim. 2011. *Transnationalism Reversed: Women Organizing against Gendered Violence in Bangladesh*. New York: SUNY Press.

Cook, Rebecca. 1994. *Human Rights of Women: National and International Perspectives*. Philadelphia: University of Pennsylvania Press.

Das, Joyce. 2016. "Good laws, bad outcomes: Land rights and inheritance practices for Christian women in Bangladesh." *The Journal of Legal Pluralism and Unofficial Law* 48, no. 2: 159–185. doi: 10.1080/07329113.2016.1197512.

Davies, Margaret. 2008. "Feminism and the flat law theory." *Feminist Legal Studies* 16, no. 3: 281–304.

Deshpande, V. S. 1984. *Women and the New Law*. Chandigarh: Punjab University Publications.

Fineman, Martha Albertson. 2005. "Feminist legal theory." *Journal of Gender, Social Policy & the Law* 13, no. 1: 13–23.

Galanter, Marc. 1981. "Justice in many rooms: Courts, private ordering and indigenous law." *Journal of Legal Pluralism and Unofficial Law* 19: 1–47.

Gamble, Sarah. 2001. *The Routledge Companion to Feminism and Postfeminism*. London: Routledge.

Gill, Rosalind, and Christina Scharff. 2011. *New femininities: Postfeminism, Neoliberalism, and Subjectivity*. New York, Houndmills, Basingstoke, Hampshire: Palgrave Macmillan.

Gilligan, Carol. 1993. *In a Different Voice: Psychological Theory and Women's Development*. Cambridge, MA: Harvard University Press.

Gillis, Stacy, and Rebecca Munford. 2004. "Genealogies and generations: The politics and praxis of third wave feminism." *Women's History Review* 13, no. 2: 165–182.

Griffin, Gabriele. 2017. *A Dictionary of Gender Studies*. Oxford University Press.

Grosz, Elizabeth. 2013. "What is feminist theory?" In *Feminist challenges: Social and political theory*, edited by Carole Pateman and Elizabeth Grosz, 190–205. London: Allen & Unwin.

Harding, Sandra G. 1987. *Feminism and Methodology: Social Science Issues.* Milton Keynes, Buckinghamshire: Indiana University Press.

Heuer, Jennifer Ngaire. 2005. *The Family and the Nation: Gender and Citizenship in Revolutionary France, 1789–1830.* Ithaca, NY: Cornell University Press.

Jethmalani, Rani. 1986. "India: Law and Women." In *Empowerment and the Law*, edited by Margaret Schuler, 60. Washington DC: OEF International.

Kapur, Ratna. 1996. "Feminist Terrains in Legal Domains: An Introduction." In *Feminist Terrains in Legal Domains: Interdisciplinary Essays on Women and Law in India*, edited by Ratna Kapur, 1. New Delhi: Kali for Women.

Kapur, Ratna, and Brenda Cossman. 1996. *Subversive Sites: Feminist Engagements with Law in India.* New Delhi: Sage.

Khan, Yasmin. 2007. *The Great Partition: The Making of India and Pakistan.* New Haven, CT: Yale University Press.

Kukathas, Chandran. 1992. "Are there any cultural rights?" *Political Theory* 20, no. 1: 105–139.

Lewis, P. 2014. "Postfeminism, femininities and organization studies: Exploring a new agenda." *Organization Studies* 35, no. 12: 1845–1866.

Loos, Tamara Lynn. 2006. *Subject Siam: Family, Law, and Colonial Modernity in Thailand.* Ithaca, NY: Cornell University Press.

MacKinnon, C. A. 1979. *Sexual Harassment of Working Women: A Case of Sex Discrimination.* New Haven, CT: Yale University Press.

Mahajan, Gurpreet. 2005. "Can Intra-group Equality Co-exist with Cultural Diversity? Re-examining Multucultural Frameworks of Accommodation." In *Minorities within Minorities: Equality, Rights and Diversity*, edited by Avigail Eisenberg and Jeff Spinner-Halev, 90–112. Cambridge: Cambridge University Press.

Mallampalli, Chandra. 2010. "Escaping the grip of personal law in colonial India: Proving custom, negotiating Hinduness." *Law and History Review* 28, no. 04: 1043–1065.

Manchanda, Rita. 2009. *The No Nonsense Guide to Minority Rights in South Asia.* Los Angeles, CA: Sage.

Manji, Ambreena S. 1999. "Imagining women's' legal world': Towards a feminist theory of legal pluralism in Africa." *Social & Legal Studies* 8, no. 4: 435–455.

Mann, Patricia S. 1994. "On the postfeminist frontier." *Socialist Review* 24, no. 1–2: 255–264.

Mehta, Rama. 1987. *Socio-legal Status of Women in India.* New Delhi: Mittal Publications.

Minow, Martha. 1989. "Beyond universality." *University of Chicago Legal Forum* 1989, no. 1: 115–138.

Mishra, Navin, and Sudhir Kumar Singh. 2002. *Status of Minorities in South Asia.* Delhi: Authorspress.

Mitra, Subrata K., and Alexander Fischer. 2002. "Sacred laws and the secular state: An analytical narrative of the controversy over personal laws in India." *India Review* 1, no. 3: 99–130.

Moghadam, Valentine M. 1994. *Identity Politics and Women: Cultural Reassertions and Feminisms in International Perspective.* Boulder, CO: Westview Press.

Okin, Susan M. 1997. "Is multiculturalism bad for women?" *Boston Review* 22, no. 5: 25–28.

Panday, Pranab Kumar, and Awal Hossain Mollah. 2011. "The judicial system of Bangladesh: An overview from historical viewpoint." *International Journal of Law and Management* 53, no. 1: 6–31.

Parashar, Archana. 1992. *Women and Family Law Reform in India: Uniform Civil Code and Gender Equality.* Newbury Park, CA: Sage.

———. 1996. "Essentialism or Pluralism: The Future of Legal Feminism." In *Feminist Terrains in Legal Domains: Interdisciplinary Essays on Eomen and Law in India*, edited by Ratna Kapur. New Delhi: Kali for Women.

Parashar, Archana, and Amita Dhanda. 2008. *Redefining Family Law in India: Essays in Honour of B. Sivaramayya*. New Delhi: Routledge.

Pereira, Faustina. 2002. *The Fractured Scales: The Search for a Uniform Personal Code*. Calcutta: Stree Publishers.

———. 2011. *Civil Laws Governing Christians in Bangladesh: A Proposal for Reform*. Dhaka: The South Asian Institute of Advanced Legal and Human Rights Studies (SAILS).

Rafi, Mohammad. 2005. *Can We Get Along?: An Account of Communal Relationship in Bangladesh*. Dhaka: Panjeree Publications.

Rajan, Rajeswari Sunder. 2003. *The Scandal of the State: Women, Law, Citizenship in Postcolonial India*. New Delhi: Permanent Black.

Rawls, John. 1996. *Political Liberalism*. New York: Columbia University Press.

Rhode, Deborah L. 1989. "Feminist critical theories." *Stanford Law Review* 42: 617–638.

Robinson, Penelope. 2011. "Mobilizing postfeminism: Young Australian women discuss Sex and the City and Desperate Housewives." *Continuum: Journal of Media and Cultural Studies* 25, no. 1: 111–124.

Russell, Diana EH. 1982. *Rape in Marriage*. New York: Macmillan.

Sangari, Kumkum. 1995. "Politics of diversity: Religious communities and multiple patriarchies." *Economic and Political Weekly* 30, no. 51: 3287–3310.

Schneider, Elizabeth M. 1986. "The dialectic of rights and politics: Perspectives from the women's movement." *New York University Law Review* 61: 589–652.

Solanki, Gopika. 2011. *Adjudication in Religious Family Laws: Cultural Accommodation, Legal Pluralism, and Gender Equality in India*. New York: Cambridge University Press.

Stubbs, Julie. 1991. "Battered woman syndrome: An advance for women or further evidence of the legal system's inability to comprehend women's experience?" *Current Issues in Criminal Justice* 3, no. 2: 267–270.

Tamanaha, Brian Z. 2008. "Understanding legal pluralism: Past to present, local to global." *Sydney Law Review* 30, no. 3: 375–411.

Venkataramiah, Engalaguppe S. 1987. "Women and the Law." In *Problems and concerns of Indian women*, edited by B. K. Pal. New Delhi: ABC Publishing House.

Williams, Susan H. 2013. "Feminist legal epistemology." *Berkeley Journal of Gender, Law & Justice* 8, no. 1: 63–105.

Wishik, Heather Ruth. 1985. "To question everything: The inquiries of feminist jurisprudence." *Berkeley Women's Law Journal* 1, no. 1: 64–77.

Woods, Patricia. 2004. "Gender and Reproduction and Maintenance of Group Boundaries: Why the "secular" State Matters to Religious Authorities in Israel." In *Boundaries and Belonging: States and Societies in the Struggle to Shape Identities and Local Practices*, edited by Joel Migdal. Cambridge: Cambridge University Press.

9 Beyond identity

In theory

Margaret Davies

The post-20th century and the era of post-theories

The 20th century was an era in which a number of ideological '-isms' reached peak intensity – liberalism, modernism, Marxism, capitalism, to name a few. Even colonialism, beginning many centuries earlier, did not reach full expansiveness until most of Africa was subjugated in the early 20th century. However, the 20th century was also the era in which these movements, whether theoretical, political, or both, began to show their flaws and to break down. In the second half of the century this resulted in the enthusiastic deployment of a terminology in which things became problematised, placed into the past, and yet understood to have a powerful continuing influence: thus, we have the invention of the 'post' prefix attached to all manner of theoretical and institutional forms.[1]

Is the 21st century to be the era of post-isms? Put another way, do we presently live in the post-20th century? Or have we passed peak 'post' and are we therefore heading for another, future-oriented, time? In this chapter I outline the terrain of some key 'post' theories in order to situate the ideas of postfeminism and posthumanism in the theoretical contexts of recent decades. In doing this my intention is not to examine forensically the specific meanings and connections of all of these 'post' ideas. Rather, my aim is to point to the development of an attitude or ethos in theory that is essentially transitional, but temporally and normatively complex. I argue that, at present, postfeminism is probably not a helpful concept, but that there is certainly much potential in the idea of a posthuman feminism. My ultimate aim is to ask how these changing theoretical conditions affect the foundations of a feminist legality, specifically in the notion of gendered subjectivity and identity.

Post theories and the present

Introductory materials about postmodernism and postcolonialism often begin with an explanatory gesture about the nature of 'post' theories. This gesture takes a variety of forms but normally indicates, first, that the 'post' prefix involves a situation in which a system, ideology, theory, or politics (such as colonialism or modernism) has been repudiated or surpassed but, second, nonetheless has a continuing effect in the present. For example, postcoloniality is said to exist historically after colonialism has ended in a particular location. Nonetheless, colonialism continues in cultural forms, in consciousness, in institutions, and in law (Quayson 2000, 2). Postcolonialism therefore points to the development of hybrid identities or institutions (Bhabha 1985; Kapur 1999) by contrast to the divided nature of colonial society (Fanon 1965). Similarly, postmodernism is said to be temporally and theoretically after modernism and rejects modernism, but modernism remains politically, philosophically, and culturally significant – if only as the ideology that is being rejected (see, e.g. Lyotard 1984, 79–81). Old things do not end, but leave a residue – or even their form and structure – in new situations. Similar points could be made (and endlessly debated) about posthumanism, post-Marxism, postliberalism, poststructuralism, postcapitalism, and post-anarchism. The system that we have moved beyond – or that we are in the process of moving beyond – remains influential and is often quite ingrained in the cultural or theoretical consciousness. In many cases, there may also be a normative intent behind the deployment of this 'post' structure in the suggestion that the system referred to is redundant and that we *must* move past it (despite its continuing influence).

The first significant theoretical 'posts' were postmodernism and poststructuralism. In keeping with the logic of post-isms, postmodernism never entirely supplanted modernism but provided a set of critical questions and tools to break apart the modernist emphasis on singular identity, grand theory, and historical progress (Lyotard 1984). It was sometimes said to involve a 'radical break' with modernism (Jameson 1984, 53), a break that was perhaps more persuasive in relation to art and architecture than it was for philosophy. Postmodernism and poststructuralism were sometimes accused of over-emphasising discursive, cultural, and constructionist factors at the expense of materiality (Fraser 1997; Norrie 2000) and, although discourse and culture was a preoccupation of many commentators who adopted a postmodern or poststructuralist orientation, it was by no means uniform and the neglect of materiality was not a necessary consequence of these theoretical orientations (Butler 1993, 1997).

The 'post' in 'postcolonialism' is more complex, since, rather than attitude or the theoretical 'moves' characteristic of more abstract theory (Culler 1997, 7–8), it is typically applied to geo-political situations with very contested relationships to past and present. Despite official narratives of independence that would place colonialism in the past, some colonised nations including Australia have barely moved beyond their colonial history and mentality and continue the practices of division and violence that characterise colonialism (cf Fanon 1965; Watson 2009, 46, 58 n20). Independence of who and from what are unavoidable questions here: in the absence of adequate acknowledgement of the compromised legality that is a result of our colonial foundations, a nation such as Australia can hardly be characterised as anything other than colonial (Giannacopoulos 2017). At the same time, the colonising nations of Europe (and elsewhere) have failed to fully reconcile their official self-image as mature players in a world of equal rights and dignity with their own histories as colonisers.

'Posts' might have a particular temporal structure (ceasing, continuing, looking beyond) in common but it is also important to differentiate them. For a start, we need to consider the normative and ethical differences of the systems being surpassed. Colonialism was associated with slavery, with white and Christian supremacy, and with many other forms of exploitation and oppression. Despite being embraced enthusiastically by rent-seeking European nations of the post-feudal era, colonialism and imperialism are no longer openly defended, but are rather recognised as having been destructive of peoples, cultures, and their prior ecological affluence. 'Post' colonialism therefore carries an implication of progress and relative freedom, even if its central agenda is an analysis of the ongoing nature of coloniality. Modernism, liberalism, and capitalism have been implicated in these same narratives of European superiority and control, but are still in the present promoted in some circles in more constructive ways as progressive and development-enhancing. Many of us living in the Western world are the beneficiaries in a material sense of liberalism, capitalism, and modernism, as well as of colonialism, even if our thinking and worldviews have also been impoverished by dualistic, individualistic, and non-relational epistemologies (Plumwood 1993). In relation to such '-isms', the prefix 'post' signifies critique, which is both political and epistemological as well as resistive. At the same time, it suggests that we remain captive to the thing we desire to surpass.

What is postfeminism?

By contrast to colonialism, modernism, and liberalism, several others '-isms' – notably Marxism, anarchism, and feminism – began in social action and critique or, at least, in more recent social change movements than those of liberalism and modernism.[2] Post-anarchism and post-Marxism build upon their respective '-isms': rather than representing a radical break or attempted repudiation, they involve a plain recognition of a need to modify a theory or perspective without totally rejecting their intellectual origins or political impulses. Of these post-things, the idea of postfeminism is possibly the most contestable because it suggests that 'feminism' – a real and continuing political movement – can in some sense be placed into the past. There are clear intellectual and political grounds for moving beyond modernism, liberalism, structuralism, capitalism, Marxism, and traditional anarchism, even though there may also be grounds for strategic adoption and compromise with some of their principles in specific contexts.[3] There are clear grounds for rejecting completely the ideologies and practices of colonialism though many of us remain complicit in the history and ongoing dispossessions of colonialism.

Can the same ethical points be made about feminism? Is there any plausible argument that its utility has expired, that it needs to be rethought, or that it is fundamentally problematic? Other '-isms' are exploitative (colonialism), ideologically limited (liberalism, capitalism), and politically compromised (Marxism). On what basis could feminism be questioned in any of these ways when it remains completely necessary to the project of equality?

The answer to this question depends, of course, on what is understood by 'feminism' and by 'post' feminism. As discussed in other chapters of this book, several possible definitions of postfeminism can be found in the literature. There is the unfounded and factually incorrect proposition that feminism is a thing of the past because our social and political situations have evolved to a state of equality where feminism is no longer necessary. This could only be true on the most formal of liberal criteria. Second, in the 1990s the term 'postfeminism' denoted a movement beyond feminism, on the grounds that it was too narrow, too victim-oriented, and/or of no relevance to generations of women who did not live through the 1970s. As described by Susan Faludi, postfeminism was associated with the media-fuelled neo-conservative 'backlash' of the late 1980s and 1990s (Faludi 1991, 11). However, like the other 'post' theories described above this postfeminism was not simplistically anti-feminist. As Sarah Gamble comments, 'for Faludi, postfeminism *is* the backlash, and its triumph lies in its ability to define itself as an ironic, pseudo-intellectual critique on the feminist movement, rather than an overtly hostile response to it' (Gamble 2006, 38). In reality the 'feminism' that was critiqued by the so-called postfeminism of the 1990s was a media-constructed caricature of the (diverse and non-unified) women's movements of the 1970s and 1980s (see discussion in Gamble 2006, 38–39).

More realistically and not at all ironically, postfeminism might situate feminism in the past not because gender equality has been achieved but because the feminist 'moment' in theory and activism has in practice been politically overtaken by the backlash and a reassertion of masculine power. Such 'postfeminism' would be a recognition of factual change, evidenced in an apparent waning of feminism from the early 1990s until a few years ago. In this context the term might also point to a possible return of feminism, as indeed we are witnessing right now (a post-post-feminism, or a return of pre-post-feminism perhaps?)

Maybe, finally, postfeminism is simply a diversification of second wave feminism, a combining of postmodern anti-foundationalism and feminism, and a recognition that identity, including gender identity, is complex and non-binary and that therefore any gender-based movement needs to move beyond the female identity that is the basis of feminist consciousness (see generally Brooks, 1997). However, assuming that feminism is not limited to a fixed view of gender as binary, is there any reason that a post-identity gender consciousness is not (also) feminist? In this last sense, 'postfeminism' might be simply a revitalised feminism – a tautology in a sense, since feminism has always been about change and the future, and has never been a singular or monolithic theory (despite, it is true, the existence of some efforts to control its meanings).

Feminism remains necessary and has proven its dynamism and adaptability. For this reason, any defensible idea of postfeminism (at least for the moment) collapses into feminism. It points either to a decline in feminism that can always return (and in fact has returned), or a diverse and non-binary feminism that has always been implicit if not fully visible in feminism.

There is much more that could be said about these mid- to late 20th-century 'post' theories, however I do not wish to complicate matters unduly. The key point that emerges from the brief outline above is that while the prefix 'post' illustrates some alignment of ideas, there are nonetheless significant political and normative differences underlying them. More broadly, theory does appear to have been passing through several decades of obsession with ideas that are 'post' something. It is useful to step back from this historical point for the purposes of observing it as a movement and a method of processing large political and ideological systems.

Posthumanism

As I have suggested, the idea of postfeminism is different to many of the other post-things that surround us intellectually. Essentially, its meanings are less agreed upon, less theoretically useful, and much less politically defensible. Another post-theory that is different – though differently different – is post-humanism. 'Human' is a species and an ontological condition, while its '-ism' is a politics, a cultural environment, and a critical stance. Humanism is largely presumed by contemporary Western ideology and underpins certain other critical stances such as liberalism and feminism. Posthumanism can be understood as both 'posthuman-ism' and 'post-humanism'. In other words, it critiques both the separated ontological and biological status of the human as well as the human-centred world view promoted by the scholarly and cultural traditions of humanism (see generally Hayles 1999; Braidotti 2013). In general, posthumanism leads us away, if that is possible, from things defined around the human or entirely centred on the condition of being human, towards notions of identity, subjectivity, and agency that exist beyond the human in some way. Such engagements beyond the human focus upon our connectedness with technology and 'nature' rather than our individual separateness. Posthumanism therefore brings forth our contingency, connectedness, and vulnerability rather than our universality, separateness, and strength (Grear 2017).

The idea of the posthuman has been theorised in two seemingly quite distinct ways. First, posthuman agents have been understood as detached from human embodiment, emphasising information, cyborg entities, and the intelligence of computers and machines (Haraway 1991; Hayles 1999). This first form of posthumanism might be considered to move theory beyond an entirely human subject, but is also a kind of hyper-humanism or an intensification of the human – artificial intelligence, while certainly testing the boundaries of the human, is nonetheless also *of* the human. It is still a product of human design even if some autonomous decision-making is now possible. Even if, as in many science fiction scenarios, such intelligence somehow breaks free of the human, it will always have its origins in the human. Having said that, artificial intelligence certainly does shift the locus of subjectivity and agency to a *more than human* relationality. In consequence, the easy distinction between a knowing subject and her object of cognition is fundamentally altered: 'distributed cognition' removes the locus of understanding from the individual human to networked and relating entities (Hayles 1999, 288). Knowledge emerges from systems rather than simply from human minds (Hayles 1999, 288–299, discussing Hutchins 1995). Katherine Hayles (1999) emphasises that such posthumanism is not *anti*-humanism because there is exchange between humans and artificial intelligences: nonetheless, 'a dynamic partnership between humans and intelligent machines replaces the liberal humanist subject's manifest destiny to dominate and control nature' (288).

Second, in new materialist thought, posthumanism refers to relationships of substance, where the mind and the self are not contained in an individual body, but are socialised and realised in material interactions with the physical world. Posthumanism in this sense places the human body–mind organism in its extended physicality and ecological relations of reliance and exchange. By contrast to the first, this second form of the posthuman transcends human exceptionalism from the start because it necessarily engages a world of matter continuous with but also only partly controlled by the human sphere. Fundamental distinctions of Western thought, in particular those of nature–culture, body–mind, and matter–meaning, are instantly placed into question by an ecocentric and materialist posthumanism (Barad 2003; Latimer and Miele 2013). Although it is a movement within Western theory, this form of posthumanism aligns with, and often draws inspiration from, aspects of First Nations philosophies. The ethical implications are profound as the human is no longer the measure and source of meaning: not only do we not begin with the individuated human being, but we no longer begin with humanity. Rather, the foundation for ethics is the entangled human–nonhuman condition or, as Stacy Alaimo has termed it 'transcorporeality' (Alaimo 2010).

Both forms of posthumanity remove consciousness and cognition from an individual self, and allow us to see the self as epiphenomenal, an effect or symptom of the innumerable and complex interactions between body, environment, and other subjectivities. This raises some critical questions for feminism and the understanding of law within this new theoretical terrain. In particular, are there ways of understanding the legal world that start from the interactions between subjects and material objects, and the intra-actions (Barad 2007), which bring them into being in the first place? What are the possibilities for developing a theoretical approach to law in which concepts are attuned to the dynamics of making and re-making subjects and objects, abstractions and matter? (Davies 2017) Where would we place 'law' itself in such a conception and what are the modalities in which gender is expressed and challenged?

Past the post: a prefigurative present

Before considering some of these questions, I want to return to the issue with which I started: are Western theorists currently trapped in a post-world (which is post-20th century and post-everything) or are we ready to move into a constructive phase in which we try to imagine a new world? As I will explain further, posthumanism arguably represents a transitional phase between 'post' theories and something else entirely, as it points to a world that is completely different from the one defined by humanist, modernist, and liberal preoccupations. It does this in part by emphasising a shift of critique from the past to the projected future. Critical theory, implicit in many 'post'-approaches, addresses both the socio-political implications and the epistemological foundations of a system of thought (Wacquant 2004; Douzinas 2005). But as I have indicated, the 'post' prefix has generally been used to suggest that past meanings have a continuing effect even after they have been critiqued or surpassed in some way. Hence 'post' positions have a particular utility: they foreground radical critique and the necessary process of fully understanding the conditions of conventional knowledge and politics without proposing blueprints or alternative models.

An objective of critique is social and political change, but exactly what this means or how to achieve it is not always part of the process of critique. A conventional critical approach would involve analysing the contestable foundations of thought and where possible exposing the distributions of power embedded within it. Conceptual change occurring as a result of this approach often emerges from the critique and is not necessarily purposive. Critique denormalises convention and in so doing enables change: it opens the field of knowledge so that debate can be less constrained than it would otherwise be (Butler 2009, 775–776). Critique *is* change, but it primarily takes the form of questioning and destabilisation, rather than providing new grounds or norms, or new systems, beliefs, or values. In many respects, this form of change seems tentative because it appears not to move socio-political consciousness forward in any way. It loosens the foundations of knowledge and of institutions without securing other solid foundations elsewhere. It is nonetheless integral to change because it exposes the contingency of the present and emphasises that things *can* be different.

Alongside the more specifically critical thought embedded in post-theories, social thought offers a slightly different orientation that is explicitly future-oriented and that actively tries to mobilise the space just *beyond* convention and its embedded concepts. Prefigurative theory, as I have termed it elsewhere (Davies 2007, 2017), refers to those writers who adopt 'hopeful methodologies'[4] – methodologies that are hopeful in the sense that they imagine and create at the same time as engage with and describe the world (see for instance Haraway 1988; Cooper 2014, 24–44; Gibson-Graham 2006). Hopeful scholarship deploys a range of methodologies, and essentially exploits the surplus of meanings that are available in a given situation and that are exposed by critique. Meaning is never entirely constrained and therefore conceptualising an alternative is always possible, even though making the alternative a reality might seem remote in many circumstances. Judges have leeways of choice within limits defined by precedent (Stone 1959), a fact which reveals possibilities for feminist judging (Hunter et al. 2010). Activists have leeways of possible action defined by context enabling them to 'be the change', that is, enact or prefigure a better future as part of the present (Swain 2017; Raekstad 2018). Similarly, theorists and empirical scholars have leeways of perception and interpretation within limits defined by experience and situation (Law and Urry 2004). In this way, prefigurative scholarship chooses a present in order to imagine a future (Davies 2007; Cooper 2014).

Davina Cooper's work on what she calls 'everyday utopias' is exemplary in this context. An everyday utopia is an actual space and set of relations in which people perform their lives in a way that imagines a different social world from the mainstream present. Cooper's locations include an alternative school, a women's bath house, speakers' corner at Hyde Park in London, and a bartering economy. Such utopian practices emphasise 'what is doable and viable given the conditions of the present' but at the same time 'capture a sense of hope and potential, in that they anticipate something more' (Cooper 2014, 4). The future orientation of efforts to practice utopia illustrate the emergent nature of change: it is not fully planned or laid out but rather emerges from doing things differently. Moreover and more importantly, as Cooper reveals, everyday utopias are sites of conceptual change that might be captured and enhanced by scholarship: doing and thinking differently are connected practices (Cooper 2014, 11). In Cooper's world view, concepts are not static categories of thought but rather the 'oscillation between imagining and actualisation' (Cooper 2014, 43; cf Cooper 2017). They emerge, in other words, from the ongoing creativity involved in the adaptation of practice to imagination.

Without exploring all of the ways that theorists have mobilised the potential implicit in the present, it seems evident that the new wave of future-oriented scholarly activity may itself be prefiguring a more widespread constructive agenda for theory. In other words, it is possible that Western theory is finally moving past its 'post' phase into a more open space where the thought and practice of newness is possible.[5] Of course, to repeat an old point, newness is never actually possible because everything is made from something else: at the same time newness is inevitable because every instantiation is different from the last. The insistence on incremental change in theory and societal structures is built on this perception. However, as indicated above, critique and post-theories have emphasised the constraints of the past, which are considerable, while prefigurative approaches emphasise the possibilities for the future implicit in the present. This may consist of little more than a change of focus, but it is nonetheless a significant one.

Beyond the logic that demonstrates that newness is always possible, the present also offers conditions for a qualitative shift of foundations in Western thought more radical than any experienced in recent times and possibly as fundamental as the shift to the human-based thinking of the Enlightenment. As we have seen, the posthuman is different from other posts because it is based on a changed understanding of the condition of being human: instead of individual organisms distinct from nature and with conceptually separated bodies and minds, the posthuman is constituted materially in an ecosystem and is always reliant upon and related to other material entities.

It is difficult to evaluate the present as it is still unfolding but, in summary, my sense is that (1) there is still much value in the 'post' prefix insofar as it points to concepts and systems that Western theory remains captive to but needs to move beyond and (2) resources are emerging in theory that enable a creative and hopeful attitude to the future. In the remainder of the chapter I will look at how an approach that combines 'post' and prefigurative attitudes can be used to understand the changing nature of law and the gendered identities and subjects that shape it.

The ecosocial foundations of law and identity

Posthumanism aligns strongly with several themes of feminism, in particular, critiques of the model or idealised rational human being and of the nature–culture distinction. As I have said, I am doubtful of the utility of 'postfeminism' and think that the entire 'post' movement may be a passing theoretical phase. I am nonetheless of the view that the concept of posthuman feminism provides a helpful theoretical focal point for reimagining some of the constructs that feminists have grappled with for many years. Indeed, within the Western context, some of what is now termed 'posthumanism' was itself prefigured by the feminism of the 1970s to the 1990s, for instance in ecofeminism (Merchant 1980; Plumwood 1993) and techno-scientific feminism (Haraway 1991). These feminisms critiqued the distinctions between nature and culture and, in common with other feminisms, also aimed to decentralise the rational (European) man as the benchmark of humanity. They aimed to rethink the foundations of sociality and identity using relational and materialist benchmarks. To return to the questions I have posed, what do these changed foundations mean for law? And what do they mean for identity? What are the implications for feminist legal thinking?

Humans are bodies living in an interconnected world, and we are also imagined beings with boundaries, identities, properties and 'natures'. We are, in other words, entirely part of the physical world even as – in the West – we imagine ourselves as outside and somehow in control of the physical world. It is in this imagined state, one form of which is the Western individualised self, that humans are seen as the archetypal agents capable of creating law as commands or acts of will. As explained above, however, posthumanism points to a view where the human subsists in an extended human–nonhuman domain of natureculture.[6] It is an explicit challenge to a human-centred perspective in theory. It does not eliminate the human agent (as if that were possible) but consists in reorienting theory away from human-centredness and in particular away from a distinctly Western individualised and controlling model of the human (Hayles 1999, 286).

Of course, we all are human and typically conceive of social formations and law as intrinsically human. We cannot discard the human or the human role in law creation, but we can step aside from the worldview where the human is the measure and determinant of all things and to bring into view the connectedness of the human and the nonhuman. It is possible, for instance, to frame law as emergent from material and located relations and actions rather than as an imposition of sovereign, parliamentary, or the reified people's will. Part of this framing was supplied early in the 20th century by legal realism and was richly extended and fleshed out by socio-legal scholarship later in the century. Thinking the Earth, the human, the social, and the legal together is an ethical imperative in the so-called Anthropocene (Gibson et al. 2015; Grear 2015).[7] However, this requires essentially rethinking everything, given how disconnected Western philosophy has been from Earth systems.

In thinking about the nature of law in this context, it is useful to start – as legal philosophers do – by considering its foundations. In the dominant Western tradition, law is understood to be a social product, created by human society through their institutional constructions. There is great diversity across legal theory about the extent to which society is part of the concept of law. In legal positivism, society remains in the background as the preceding condition of a relatively autonomous law. In feminism, critical race theory, and legal realism, society and law cannot be separated in this way because they are simply not different spheres.

The commonality across legal theory, however, lies in the basic constituents of 'society.' As Latour (2005) has argued, the definition of 'the social' in post-Enlightenment thought has been unduly limited to the human domain (6; cf Latimer and Miele 2013). This is as true of legal theory as it is of many other areas. Society has been understood as essentially about relationships between humans within a human sphere and the meanings and institutions that consolidate from these relationships. By contrast to this conceptually limited society, however, there is in fact no entirely or essentially human domain: what we understand as *human* society consists not only of inter-human relations and institutions but of all sorts of relations and connections between humans, human creations, and the so-called natural world. 'Society' consists of associations between human and nonhuman entities as much as it consists of purely human relationships. This extended field of connections is essentially ecological, a wide term that encompasses the many forms of relating that underpin and surround life.[8]

Placing law in this new (for Western thought) understanding of the social means seeing it as produced by relations that extend well beyond human relations. But this does not mean that law is a product of nature or of God as the 'natural law' tradition has held.[9] Rather, a posthuman concept of law would need to understand law as produced in the multiple forms of relating that constitute the social: these are essentially associations between bodies and things, in particular places, that emerge as norms and laws (see generally Davies 2017). Understanding law as emerging from these material interactions, rather than as the form that shapes them, means that legal analysis starts from a much larger and more complex field than the limited field of positive law. Legal consciousness studies (e.g. Ewick and Silbey 1992) and legal geography research (e.g. Delaney 2010; Blomley 2013) have covered part but not all of this field. This material reorientation is only just beginning, and the mechanics of law production in a posthuman world remain to be fully explored.

Thoughts on posthuman legal feminism

What happens to the gendered human and legal subject in this field? A prefigurative and posthuman account of identity would move beyond gender and other categories towards non-binary existence. In the context of posthumanism 'non-binary' refers to gender but also to experiential categories such as that between the mind and the body and nature and culture: these categories are mapped onto gender categories and so challenging the reality of these distinctions is a key part of disrupting systemic formulations of gender (Merchant 1980; Plumwood 1993). As outlined above, the idea of the posthuman disrupts human subjectivity as the pinnacle of existence. This is a significant move for feminism because it has the potential to displace the strong association of the 'subject' with 'rational man'. As we know, Eurocentric philosophy has often taken a masculinist and male-identified abstract subjectivity as the ideal and aspiration for human freedom. The body, object-status, being trapped by circumstance and captive to social relations, are positions that are regarded from this limited but powerful perspective as universal others. As Simone de Beauvoir (2011) put it, 'The category of *Other* is as original as consciousness itself.... No group ever defines itself as One without immediately setting up the Other opposite itself' (26).

There is the one and then there are the others. It has been the task of feminism, anti-colonial, and anti-racist thought *either* to ensure that everyone can occupy the position of the One *or* to instate relationality and situatedness as the central case of subjectivity. In so doing critical theories displace and demythologise abstract subjectivity and the notion that freedom is based on self-determination. The problem, as we have discovered by experience, is that abstract subjectivity all too often remains in place: all the while the abstract subject is imaginable it can barely be disturbed and is almost impossible to disrupt politically. An insistence on inter-subjective and situated selves as universal human nature is still seemingly powerless when it comes to the entitled male and Western subject. It seems impossible to ostracise from subjectivity those who have the social capital to position themselves as autonomous and free of their material situation.

The Earth has the potential to change all of that because – to put it somewhat bluntly – we are all, including those who occupy the position of abstract subjectivity, othered by it in the sense that we cannot control it and more importantly we are entirely dependent upon it. There is no freedom from the flesh or from our ecological conditions. Anthropocentrism – in reality this is androcentrism and Eurocentrism – involves an othering of the natural world as against a human centre and a valuing of the masculinist subject against the feminised and racialised other. But anthropocentrism is no longer much of an option. The promise of posthumanism is at the very least that as subjects we are forced to acknowledge our connectedness – as one theorist has put it that we are 'interbeings', not beings (Adams 2007; discussed by Grear 2011, 41). In other words, posthumanism removes the assumptions in which it is possible to create the category of the separated One in the first place. Material connection comes first, not individuation.

Although in an abstract sense, human beings are understood to be subjects and to have the dignity of free beings, the Western world – where the insistence on subjectivity has been the most intense – has comprehensively failed to operationalise its own rhetoric, turning some into subjects and others into objects. Can an ecologically relational subject disrupt this pattern? Would a posthuman feminism eradicate the 'subject'? The very suggestion seems implausible. Rosi Braidotti (2013) has argued strongly, rather, for the rethinking of subjectivity based on ecological connections:

> I define the critical posthuman subject within an ecophilosophy of multiple belongings, as a relational subject constituted in and by multiplicity, that is to say a subject that works across differences and is also internally differentiated, but still grounded and accountable.
>
> (39)

And later:

> One needs at least *some* subject position: this need not be either unitary or exclusively anthropocentric, but it must be the site for political and ethical accountability, for collective imaginaries and shared aspirations.
>
> (Braidotti 2013, 76)

While I certainly accept the point that ethical and political subjectivity, and consequently legal subjectivity, needs redefining in the way that Braidotti describes, I also have to admit to some scepticism about the ontology of the subject in this ecological frame.[10] Relational subjectivity embeds the fact that subjects emerge from multiple connections within and between living forms, physical places, and inert things. But it does not seem to fully reflect the extent to which we *owe* our entire existence to our ecological situation and are therefore – within the dualistic frame that makes any 'subject' possible – also objects or others: we are othered within both the human and an ecological context in the sense that we are emergent from, acted upon and engaged with. In other words, an anthropocentric perspective regards humans as subjects and everything else as others. As soon as we endeavour to think beyond anthropocentrism and enter into relation with these others, we ourselves become others – the system can't be composed only of subjects with no objects. To quote de Beauvoir (2011) again, 'whether one likes it or not, individuals and groups have no choice but to recognise the reciprocity of their relation' (27).

If we are not, or at least not only, subjects, what are we? Is there a way of more fully capturing that we are objects as well as subjects? Or ought we to move beyond this division, and beyond everything it implies (including the gendered subject)? At the least, we can retain subject and object and regard them as interchangeable, as positions in a dynamic dance of exchange and relationality. Instead of abstract subjects and passive objects posthumanism sees a world composed of 'material subjects and vital objects' emerging from intra-action and existing in interchangeable positions (Davies 2016). As subjects, human beings are materially connected and we are also objects of ecological systems. Subjectivity is no more than an effect of these dynamics and is neither transcendent nor permanent. At the same time, as an effect it is immensely powerful and the lynchpin of political, legal, and economic organisation in Western ontology. It is therefore implausible at the present time to think of an alternative to the subject within this frame and, as Braidotti argues (2013, 76), it is politically and ethically necessary to retain the subject.

Conclusion

Within Western theory, it is difficult to think outside the framework of subject–object or One–Other. It is of course possible to problematise the dualisms and to emphasise that they are the effects of connectedness, though in doing so it is also necessary to remember that using this language at all reinstates the idea of a divided world, rather than a connected one. Equally crucial is the acknowledgement of ontological systems that do not divide humans from nonhuman others: for instance, Aboriginal knowledge, in the words of Mary Graham (2008), 'maintains that there is no division between the observing mind and anything else' and that 'identity is essentially always embedded in land and defined by … relationships to it and to other people' (189, 187). To return to the dilemmas raised by dealing with the present while imagining a different future, it is here that theory remains caught between socio-political necessity and prefigurative possibility. Western thought cannot for the moment escape the notions of the subject and identity and indeed we need these ideas both to understand and to deal with our political situation. But it is critical to acknowledge and draw inspiration from the existence of worldviews not based on these foundations and to deploy imaginative strategies to move beyond the limitations of a divided world.

Post-theories resonate with the past and, although they might be a necessary step in the process of constructing the future (because they help us to dislodge the ongoing effects of past paradigms), they are of limited assistance in *envisaging* a different world. Posthumanism is, as I have argued, a slightly different 'post' from others of the late 20th century. In addition to critique, it promises changed foundations for both theory and action, and demands that attention be turned to a non-binary world past gendered divisions of mind and body, culture and nature, subject and object. Much remains to be done, however, in working through the potential of such an image.

Notes

1 In many cases the 'post' – usually associated with the political Left – has been accompanied by a 'neo' movement, which is more likely to be associated with the political right and represents an intensification or renewal of the original thing in a new form. Hence we have neoliberalism, neofeminism, neocolonialism, and so forth. The exception is neo/post-Marxism, which seem to refer to essentially the same group of theorists. I do not address the many lines of connection and resistance between the 'post' and the 'neo' here.

2 The critique-non-critique distinction is not entirely sound and itself has a temporal dimension: there was a critical element in the origins of modernism, liberalism, capitalism, and even colonialism, but one which is now rather distant. Marxism, originating in a critique of capitalism, became for some a system in itself, obscuring its critical origins. Some might say that the same is true of feminism, but – unlike Marxism – it has never been politically institutionalised.
3 For instance, the fight for marriage equality has been won on the essentially liberal grounds that formal equality in civil and political rights is fundamental.
4 This term has been used in other contexts, but I heard it first in conversation with Davina Cooper.
5 The statement of course must be qualified by the recognition that perhaps newness is not actually possible because everything (including ideas) is made from something else.
6 The term 'natureculture', from Donna Haraway 2003, brings together in one term the two spheres that Western thought has traditionally separated. In combining them in a single term it denotes that they exist in a continuous plane.
7 Although the impact of humans on Earth systems is incontestable, the term 'Anthropocene' – the era defined by changes attributable to humans – remains controversial, for several reasons: it appears to attribute the changes to the whole of humanity rather than part of it; it is possibly premature to designate an epoch that in geological terms is extremely recent; naming an epoch after ourselves represents another case of human hubris. See, for instance, Malm and Hornberg (2014), Grear (2015).
8 It is true that, on this view, the term 'eco-social' is a tautology, because the 'social' already refers to the 'eco-': however it is a useful term because it makes explicit the connection of human and non-human in the social: it is too easy otherwise for 'society' to be understood as limited to a human sphere.
9 The 'nature' of the Western natural law tradition has little to do with the physical environment, but is rather something much less tangible: universal human nature and rationality or the nature of the cosmos.
10 Or, indeed, in any frame. See Kofman (1991), discussing Nietzsche's critique of Descartes' *cogito ergo sum*.

References

Adams, Will. 2007. "The Primacy of Interrelating: Practicing Ecological Psychology with Buber, Levinas, and Merleau-Ponty." *Journal of Phenomenological Psychology* 38: 24–61.

Alaimo, Stacy. 2010. *Bodily Natures: Science, Environment, and the Material Self.* Bloomington: Indiana University Press.

Barad, Karen. 2003. "Posthumanist Performativity: Toward an Understanding of how Matter Comes to Matter." *Signs: Journal of Women in Culture and Society* 28, no. 3: 801–831.

———. 2007. *Meeting the Universe Halfway: Quantum Physics and the Entanglement of Matter and Meaning.* Durham, NC: Duke University Press.

Bhabha, Homi K. 1985. "Signs Taken for Wonders: Questions of Ambivalence and Authority Outside a Tree in Delhi, May 1817." *Critical Inquiry* 12: 144–165.

Blomley, Nicholas. 2013. "Performing Property: Making the World." *Canadian Journal of Law and Jurisprudence* 26: 23–48.

Braidotti, Rosi. 2013. *The Posthuman*. Cambridge: Polity.

Brooks, Ann. 1997. *Postfeminisms: Feminism, Cultural Theory, and Cultural Forms.* London and New York: Routledge.

Butler, Judith. 1993. *Bodies That Matter: On the Discursive Limits of 'Sex'*. New York: Routledge.

———. 1997. "Merely Cultural." *Social Text* 52–53: 255–277.

———. 2009. "Critique, Dissent, Disciplinarity." *Critical Inquiry* 35: 773–795.

Cooper, Davina. 2014. *Everyday Utopias: The Conceptual Life of Promising Spaces.* Durham, NC: Duke University Press.

———. 2017. "Prefiguring the State." *Antipode* 49, no. 2: 335–356.

Culler, Jonathan. 1997. *Literary Theory: A Very Short Introduction.* Oxford: Oxford University Press.

Davies, Margaret. 2007. "Beyond Unity: Feminism, Sexuality, and the Idea of Law." In *Sexuality and the Law: Feminist Engagements,* edited by Vanessa Munro and Carl Stychin, 151–170. London: Cavendish Press.

———. 2016. "Material Subjects and Vital Objects." *Australian Journal of Human Rights* 22, no. 2: 37–60.

———. 2017. *Law Unlimited: Materialism, Pluralism, and Legal Theory.* London: Routledge.

De Beauvoir, Simone. 2011. *The Second Sex.* Translated by Constance Borde and Sheila Malovaney-Chevallier. New York: Vintage Books.

Delaney, David. 2010. *The Spatial, the Legal, and the Pragmatics of World-Making: Nomospheric Investigations.* London: Routledge.

Douzinas, Costas. 2005. "Oubliez Critique." *Law and Critique* 16: 47–69.

Elliott, Anthony. 2016. *Identity Troubles: An Introduction.* London: Routledge.

Ewick, Patricia and Susan Silbey. 1992. "Conformity, Contestation, and Resistance: An Account of Legal Consciousness." *New England Law Review* 26: 731–749.

Faludi, Susan. 1991. *Backlash: The Undeclared War on American Women.* Rivers Pres: New York.

Fanon, Frantz. 1965. *The Wretched of the Earth.* New York: Grove Press.

Fraser, Nancy. 1997. *Justice Interruptus: Critical Reflections on the 'Postsocialist' Condition.* New York: Routledge.

Gamble, Sarah. 2006. "Postfeminism." In *The Routledge Companion to Feminism and Postfeminism,* edited by Sarah Gamble, 36–45. London: Routledge.

Giannacopoulos, Maria. 2017. "Sovereign Debt Crises, Referendums, and the Changing Face of Colonial Power." *Continuum: Journal of Media and Cultural Studies* 31, no. 1: 33–42.

Gibson, Katherine, Deborah Bird and Ruth Fincher, eds. 2015. *Manifesto for Living in the Anthropocene.* New York: Punctum Books.

Gibson-Graham, JK. 2006. *The End of Capitalism (As We Knew It).* Minneapolis: University of Minnesota Press.

Grear, Anna. 2011. "The Vulnerable Living Order: Human Rights and the Environment in a Critical and Philosophical Perspective." *Journal of Human Rights and the Environment* 2: 23–44.

———. 2015. "Deconstructing Anthropos: A Critical Legal Reflection on 'Anthropocentric' Law and Anthropocene 'Humanity'". *Law and Critique* 26: 225–249.

———. 2017. "Foregrounding Vulnerability: Materiality's Porous Affectability as a Methodological Platform." In *Research Methods in Environmental Law: A Handbook,* edited by Andreas Philippopoulos-Mihalopoulos and Victoria Brooks, 3–28. Cheltenham: Edward Elgar Publishing.

Graham, Mary. 2008. "Some Thoughts about the Philosophical Underpinnings of Aboriginal Worldviews." *Australian Humanities Review* 45: 181–94.

Haraway, Donna. 1988. "Situated Knowledges: The Science Question in Feminism and the Privilege of Partial Perspective." *Feminist Studies* 14, no. 3: 575–599.

———. 1991. *Simians, Cyborgs, and Women: The Reinvention of Nature*. New York: Routledge.
———. 2003. *The Companion Species Manifesto: Dogs, People, and Significant Otherness*. Chicago, IL: Prickly Paradigm Press.
Hayles, Katherine N. 1999. *How We Became Posthuman: Virtual Bodies in Cybernetics, Literature, and Informatics*. Chicago, IL: University of Chicago Press.
Hunter, Rosemary, Clare McGlynn and Erika Rackley. 2010. *Feminist Judgments: From Theory to Practice*. Oxford: Hart Publishing.
Hutchins, Edwin. 1995. *Cognition in the Wild*. Boston, MA: MIT Press.
Jameson, Fredric. 1984. "Postmodernism or, The Cultural Logic of Late Capitalism." *New Left Review* I/146: 53–92.
Kapur, Ratna. 1999. ""A Love Song to Our Mongrel Selves": Hybridity, Sexuality, and the Law." *Social and Legal Studies* 12: 353–368.
Kofman, Sarah. 1991. "Descartes Entrapped." In *Who Comes After the Subject?*, edited by Eduardo Cadava, Peter Connor, and Jean-Luc Nancy, 178–197. New York: Routledge.
Latimer, Joanna and Mara Miele. 2013. "Naturecultures? Science, Affect, and the Non-human." *Theory, Culture, and Society* 30, no. 7/8: 5–31.
Latour, Bruno. 2005. *Reassembling the Social: An Introduction to Actor-Network Theory*. Oxford: Oxford University Press.
Law, John and John Urry. 2004. "Enacting the Social." *Economy and Society* 33, no: 3: 390–410.
Lyotard, Jean-François. 1984. *The Postmodern Condition: A Report on Knowledge*. Manchester University Press: Manchester.
Malm, Andreas and Alf Hornberg. 2014. "The Geology of Mankind? A Critique of the Anthropocene Narrative." *The Anthropocene Review* 1, no. 1: 62–69.
Merchant, Carolyn. 1980. *The Death of Nature: Women, Ecology, and the Scientific Revolution*. San Francisco, CA: Harper and Rowe.
Norrie, Alan. 2000. "From Critical to Socio-Legal Studies: Three Dialectics in Search of a Subject." *Social and Legal Studies* 9: 85–113.
Plumwood, Val. 1993. *Feminism and the Mastery of Nature*. London: Routledge.
Quayson, Ato. 2000. *Postcolonialism: Theory, Practice, or Process*. Cambridge: Polity.
Raekstad, Paul. 2018 "Revolutionary Practice and Prefigurative Politics: A Clarification and Defense." *Constellations* 25, no3: 359–372.
Stone, Julius. 1959. 'The Ratio of the *Ratio Decidendi*.' *Modern Law Review* 22: 597–620.
Swain, Dan. 2017. "Not Not but Not Yet: Present and Future in Prefigurative Politics." *Political Studies* 2017 (online): 1–16. doi:10.1177/00323217177233.
Wacquant, Loic. 2004. "Critical Thought as Solvent of Doxa." *Constellations* 11: 97–101.
Watson, Irene. 2009. "In the Northern Territory Intervention – What is Saved or Rescued and at What Cost?" *Cultural Studies Review* 15, no. 2: 45–60.

Index

www.ingramcontent.com/pod-product-compliance
Ingram Content Group UK Ltd.
Pitfield, Milton Keynes, MK11 3LW, UK
UKHW022019180926
475701UK00005B/930
* 9 7 8 0 3 6 7 6 6 3 0 7 0 *